CELINE *Dion*

C E L

IN COLLABORATION WITH
GEORGES-HÉBERT GERMAIN

TRANSLATED FROM THE FRENCH BY
BRUCE BENDERSON

 WILLIAM MORROW

MY STORY, MY DREAM

An Imprint of HarperCollins*Publishers*

FIRST EDITION

Designed by Betty Lew

Printed on acid-free paper

Library of Congress Cataloging-in-Publication Data
Dion, Celine.
Celine Dion : my story, my dream / by Celine Dion.—1st ed.
p.   cm.
ISBN 0-06-019797-8
1. Dion, Celine. 2. Singers—Canada—Biography.
ML.420.D565 A3   2000
782.42164'092—dc21   00-045567
[B]

00 01 02 03 04   RRD   10 9 8 7 6 5 4 3 2 1

For René,

the man of my life

Dear Georges-Hébert,

Over the years, I have had many occasions to talk about myself and the people I love, but I have never done so with as much pleasure and heart as I have with you for this book.

I will always remember our hasty meetings, crazy laughter, and the unforeseen bends in the road, where confidences and secrets were discovered.

You have a remarkable talent for listening, which means that my words and emotions unfolded during the hours we spent together talking. And now they have been rendered by your magic pen into a book in which I recognize myself without reservation.

Thank you, my friend, for being faithful to my thoughts and relating my intentions and feelings just as I expressed them.

It is a great art to use one's talent in the service of a friend. That is what you have done, and I thank you with all my heart.

Affectionately,
Celine

CELINE Dion

PROLOGUE

One beautiful morning last winter, a manatee appeared in the canal right behind our house in Jupiter, Florida. It stayed there for hours, as if it were waiting for something. Or somebody. As soon as I went into the water, it started coming toward me. I spoke to it, petted it, and we swam together for a while.

This was no big feat. A lot of people in southern Florida have fun swimming with manatees. They're nice, large, very affectionate animals that we call sea cows. People say they come from the legend of the Sirens because of the very sweet and unsettling sound they make.

The incident made me realize how much I've changed during these last months. When I was working on my singing career, and was subject to certain precautions, the idea never would have come to me to dive right into cloudy water and go make friends with an unknown animal.

But on that morning I hadn't been working for more than three months, and I was already doing all sorts of things that had been almost unimaginable before, things that even I sometimes found surprising.

While I was swimming with my Siren, a flood of memories crashed through my head, clear, precise images of my childhood, of summer, of happiness.

I was eight, nine, ten years old. I was on a picnic with my brothers and sisters in the Laurentides or in Lanaudière, just north of Montreal. There were farms, a lot of animals, planted fields, woods, a river, horses that my sisters and I rode. I saw all of it again so clearly. I saw myself climbing trees, swimming in the river, walking in the woods. And I was saying to whoever would hear me that one day I'd buy a horse, as soon as I earned my first money as a singer.

And then I forgot all about it, carried away by another dream of being a singer, a dream that left room for nothing else in my life. A few years later, when I got my first pay as a singer, my thoughts were already elsewhere. Instead of a horse, I bought myself a pair of high heels.

Now, twenty years later, it was all springing forth from my memory. That horse I never bought and never thought about again, the light of summer, the freshness and the smell of the Laurentides rivers and lakes, the fragrance of the earth and of cut hay. Again I saw the path that we took to get down to the river, the overturned canoe on the beach, the laughter of my sisters, the thick trees my brothers dove from, the pebbles, the sand, the raspberry bushes that scratched our legs, the crackling of burning branches in the fires we made during evenings on the shore. And all of us singing together late into the night, watching shooting stars and northern lights.

As I got out of the canal after saying goodbye to my Siren, I didn't feel like speaking or being spoken to. I hardly dared move, my head was so filled to the brim with all these memories, and I didn't want to lose a single drop. I wanted to keep these images in me as long as possible, to review them one by one and maybe to remember others.

I don't think it was nostalgia, but rather a kind of curiosity about a very faraway period of my life that I thought I'd forgotten, and in any case, had never thought about so intensely. I felt as if I were seeing and hearing the real living little girl I had been, feeling her very close to me again, so close I could recognize her dreams, her wishes, her plans. And I felt a little like one of those dolls that contain a series of smaller dolls, each inside the other, with that little girl Celine inside of me.

But these images quickly began to lose their color and clarity. Afterward, I thought for days and days about my childhood, and the whole journey I had traveled. Of what I'd been and done or tried to do for twenty years, starting with my first performances and that first pair of high heels.

And I kept asking myself why I wanted and dreamed so much about all of this, all that's happened to me. Why, at twenty, fifteen, at twelve, even at eight, I think, and even at five, I so wanted to succeed, why I dreamed so much of becoming a famous singer who'd be listened to in every corner of the planet.

Not everyone is driven by such ambition. A lot of young boys and girls spend a long time wondering what to do with their lives. Some never find an answer. But I always knew. Not that I claim any credit for knowing. I'm like that tubby Obélix, a character in a famous French comic strip, who fell into a magic potion when he was a baby. As soon as I was born, I fell into singing, show business. And once in it, I felt like a fish in water.

I've loved every bit of the life I've led up to this sabbatical. I lived my most beautiful dreams to the fullest—a rare piece of luck. I've been fulfilled emotionally, professionally, artistically, and I always will be. I love and I'm loved. I sing and that is my happiness. And I thank heaven for it every day of my life.

And then, I consciously decided to leave this life. For a year or two. For the first time in almost twenty years, there was nothing in my datebook, no engagement, no performance coming up, no interview, no recording session, no gala. From now on, I could live my life from day to day.

A year ago, such freedom would have overwhelmed me with anguish.

But so many things had happened in the course of that single year. I was no longer the same person, I knew. I no longer had the same fears, the same apprehensions. And I was confident, happy about my newfound freedom, about the unknown waiting for me.

I believe that to live is to change, to discover what's new and to find surprises in everything, in music, in one's life and loves . . .

For a long time, I couldn't think of all this happiness in my life and my career without feeling a kind of fear or anxiety, without asking myself a thousand and one questions, for which I had no answers.

Will it all last? What do you do, become, where do you go, when you've already realized your fondest dreams? Do you have to stay there and just watch the clouds roll by? Can you find other dreams to fulfill? Other lives to live? Is there life after the dream, after show business? Outside of show business?

And what will I do when my sabbatical is over? What will I have to say, to sing? And will I be able to find the audience I left behind on the night of January 1, 2000? Will I be able to reconnect with them? Will I find that we are still on the same wavelength?

I would always keep on singing. It seemed obvious to me. This sabbatical was only a pause. But I couldn't help thinking that I wouldn't be the same at the end of it.

For more than a year, for any number of reasons, we put off the day, month after month. Each time I realized that I was relieved, even if I didn't dare admit it. I was in the jaws of a strange dilemma. More and more I wanted to stop, to rest, recharge, and be alone with the man of my life. I wanted to take stock of my career, my life, my loves; and at the same time, doing such a thing really frightened me.

I thought of everything I was leaving behind—the stage, the crowds, the incredibly exciting life of touring, nights spent at the studio with the musicians, the life of an artist, and traveling around the world.

At every performance, as soon as the countdown started, there were pangs in my heart, as I experienced that magical contact with the audience, when we really connected and were so close, so together, the current between us flowing so perfectly.

Bringing a crowd to its feet is such an amazing feeling that nothing in the world can replace it. And I felt that I'd miss those electrifying moments terribly. At the end of each show, I always told the audience: "I'm taking you with me. You'll always be in my heart."

So I left with all these people in my heart. All I needed to do was close my eyes to sense their presence, to hear them. . . . Still, a memory, even a happy one, can never replace reality; it's never as moving, as thrilling, or as true. All memories, even the strongest and most cherished, inevitably end by losing their color and clarity.

I have gone through extraordinary live experiences. I have traveled the world; I have met people I will never forget. I have been pampered, loved, and acclaimed.

But there was always stage fright, pressure, bigger and bigger crowds every day, larger and larger stadiums. It's been terrifying. And it's been good, really good.

I had become a real "stress junkie." I needed my dose every day. Every time I stopped, I went into withdrawal, and didn't feel right about myself. Marathoners who are kept from running because of an injury apparently experience nausea, dizzy spells. And they say that no one is more depressed than a cyclist who just finished the Tour de France, even if he won.

Therefore, the prospect of living a stress-free, quiet, cozy life seemed stressful to me. I thought I'd have to struggle to decompress from stress and discipline, to forget my voice, to get free of it. During more than half my life, I've been a slave to my voice, a happy and consenting slave who was afraid of the idea of living in freedom. What would happen in my head and heart when I was deprived of this sweet slavery, this tension, this tremendous sense of exaltation you feel when the crowd goes wild?

To reassure myself, of course, I prepared a very detailed schedule for living. I planned out my sabbatical. I visualized how it would all go, as I had done for my shows.

But I couldn't, especially during the first months, come to a final agreement with myself on the scenario.

One day I would swear to myself that I would not sing a note as long as this sabbatical lasted. Then the next day I would tell myself that I would never be able to resist if somebody offered me a great part in a movie or a beautiful song to record or an appearance in a huge show featuring artists that I admired.

In the end, all my speculations turned out to be wrong.

I had told myself: "No vocal training, old girl, no long silences to rest your voice. It's not needed anymore. Off with discipline, off with training. You're gonna play golf every day. And, to keep your mind busy, you'll take Spanish and drawing lessons."

I even bought colored pencils, pastels, charcoals, watercolors, and fancy drawing paper.

"You're also gonna take piano lessons. And you'll listen to everything that comes out in the musical world, good or not, to remain plugged in to show business."

I began to make a list of albums I wanted to listen to.

"And you'll sleep late, all day if you want to."

I had only begun my sabbatical, and I already knew that things were going to be different. And that they would have nothing to do with what I had imagined.

Contrary to what I'd expected, everything went smoothly, without misery or pain. I slipped into that sabbatical as if into a nice warm bath. And I knew right away that nothing would lure me out, even if I was offered the chance to sing on the moon or on Venus, in front of a crowd of extraterrestrials.

To my great astonishment and to René's great pleasure, I started getting up early . . . and in a good mood. In the past, it had taken several hours for me to wake up completely. When I got up I wouldn't speak to anyone, and I didn't want anyone to speak to me. I really hated mornings. Whenever possible, I spent them asleep. I always ate breakfast alone. And now here I am, on leave, with absolutely nothing to do, on my feet at dawn, listening to birds singing or watching my flowers opening or preparing orange juice or coffee for the whole household.

Three months after the beginning of my sabbatical, I was not listening to any music at all—neither mine nor anyone else's—and I would only glance at fashion magazines once in a while. I had believed I was never going to be able to remain silent anymore, and I was now spending long hours, sometimes even days, without saying a word, just for the pleasure of it, for its peace, its sweetness. And I especially didn't miss stress or stage fright.

I had already postponed my Spanish lessons until the spring, then summer, then autumn, then next winter. I never unwrapped my colored pencils and my pastels. After two or three weeks of total inactivity, I started singing again, constantly, everywhere, in the shower, on the golf course, while driving, in the kitchen. And it gave me a fantastic feeling of happiness, a new, unexpected joy.

I even started training my voice again and doing my singing exercises regularly. I did this so that I wouldn't lose what I'd acquired, but I also did it for the simple pleasure that comes from training. And I spent whole evenings watching television, something I'd never done in my life. With René, I followed from beginning to end the play-offs for the National Hockey League. And I loved it.

I am good at being happy. Happiness comes to me in waves,

always unexpected and unexplainable. I'm not talking about the sweet and shallow feeling that comes with a platinum album or a good review, but about real happiness, the kind that comes and goes without warning.

I have never felt this happiness so close at hand, so overwhelming, as I did that winter of 2000, during the first months of my sabbatical.

I had just lived through the worst moments of my life. And yet, I saw something good, something beautiful and meaningful everywhere, even in the hard times we had gone through . . .

At the beginning, such an idea would have been unthinkable, almost monstrous. But little by little, I began to accept it. Today I know that there is good in all misfortune. And I thank heaven for the misfortune that befell us, because it transformed us.

René, the man of my life, my entire life, was seriously ill. Together we went through a very difficult ordeal and emerged stronger, more united, more in love than ever. However, I know that from now on, anxiety will be a part of our life. A kind of carefreeness has, without a doubt, disappeared forever from our lives. But at the same time, I know that it's possible to experience—even during the worst ordeal, even in pain and fear—great moments of happiness.

Because we love each other.

Our ordeal changed me more than all my professional experiences. Thanks to it, I've learned a lot about myself, about the man I love, about love, even about life. I also learned of his need for me. For the first time, he left himself go and truly confided in me, and cried on my shoulder. And he told me he couldn't live without me.

I've also had the extraordinary chance to discover that there is a life outside of show business. Of course I knew it—in theory—but I've learned it for real, in my heart, through my tears, through hope and waiting.

Actually, when I took my leave from public life, I already saw things differently. People, my profession. And all my other projects, including having a child, had taken a new twist. René's health had become what counted the most for me.

Despite all that we have lived, or maybe because of it—I'll never know which—we've rediscovered a kind of confidence in life, an appetite for living what's offered us, whether we wanted it, decided it, or not.

We had not given up the idea of having a child. The year before, a few days before René had his first chemotherapy treatments, we had gone to a sperm bank. It was obviously not the most romantic experience a couple could dream of. But it gave us the confidence that, whatever happenes, our dearest dream was possible.

But I had ceased to believe that our happiness depended only on this child.

Of course, I promised myself that I would start taking all the necessary measures as soon as possible. My gynecologist, Dr. Ronald Ackerman, had explained to us at length the procedures of in vitro fertilization and intrauterine insemination. And I had decided to go through the first steps after a few months of rest. If, afterward, this child became a part of my life, so much the better. If not, I was gonna live without him or her. That's what I told myself. I especially did not want to lay a guilt trip on this child by putting my happiness in its hands, even before it was born. I didn't want to dream, to write any particular scenario. I wanted to take life as it came, and not as I had dreamed it.

Last winter, we learned to enjoy life as never before. I saw René change a lot as well. He began to take his time watching the sun set, dolphins swimming, or a cloud floating by. He also started getting the most out of the moments he spent with me, with his friends, or alone. Even his laugh changed, his expression. He's more aware of others than he ever was, aware of happiness, especially. He finds crumbs of it everywhere . . . and he sweeps them carefully together. And he himself is amazed.

At the beginning, I would do nothing for days; I'd live without a plan, without makeup, with nothing but shorts and a T-shirt, barefoot. I didn't have to care about my looks or spend energy trying to find something smart to say in order to please the media.

And through all that, I've discovered small pleasures I could never have thought I'd have before. They're a sign, I believe, of a deep change that I don't altogether understand yet, and one that I'm not really trying to understand.

For example, when people gave me flowers, I never knew what to do with them or where to put them. I smelled them quickly, hardly looked at them. Today, I can spend hours making and remaking bouquets, arrangements. I'm learning their names, their odors. I watch them push up from my flower beds, wither, and then bloom again. I read books about them. I ask gardeners and florists questions.

What is more, every day, at suppertime, I fiddle for a long time with the candlelight in each room of the house and the patio and the terraces. I'm learning how to create atmosphere, how to set a table, receive guests . . . me . . . the one who was so often the guest . . . perhaps too often.

And in doing all that, I discover in myself quirks and traits of character that I never noticed or never took the time to see. Some make me happy, others don't.

For example, I've learned that I'm excessively concerned about details that are often very insignificant. Even to the point of getting on my own nerves. Everything has to be perfect all the time. If I notice something wrong—a water stain on a wall, the wrong crease in the draperies, a candle that isn't standing straight up—I don't stop thinking about it, I get obsessed, I get up to wipe the stain, smooth out the crease, straighten the candle. . . . If someone around me isn't doing his work well, I ask him to start again, or if I can't, I go behind him and try to do it better myself.

Other days, I try to free myself of my tendency to correct things. I'm getting there, slowly but surely. I'll never be careless, and I'll never like disorder, but I believe that I could become more relaxed, let a few dead leaves drop onto the patio or in the pool without rushing to pick them up.

All the rigor and meticulousness with which I practiced my singing for nearly twenty years have remained in me. And I've transferred them to what now concerns me the most—René's health, first and before all—but also the thousand and one details of daily life—the upkeep of this house in Jupiter that I so love, the knickknacks, the paintings, the furniture that I've filled it with. I also focus on the house that we're having built in Quebec. I want to see everything, understand everything, participate in every decision, see the plans, the construction site, and the design.

I'll admit that I'm a stickler for detail. I've always been one, even as a little girl. If I had the smallest stain or the least tear in my dress or my pajamas, I wanted my mother or my sisters to change me. I like order and cleanliness. I need it. In my house, just as in my thoughts, I want everything to be impeccable, clear, precise.

That's doubtlessly why our reconciliations last longer than our lovers' quarrels. When we argue, I tend to sulk a little, but afterward I want René to describe in detail what he was feeling. I want to know if he was feeling anger or sorrow, how much, and for how long. And I don't let up as long as the least cloud persists between us, as long as there is the least confusion or friction in our emotions.

I'm the same way with everyone I love and everyone I work with. And with myself. I like to be proud of myself. And I regularly take stock, examine my conscience, whereas in the past I really wasn't that interested in it. Looking back has never been my forte.

I try to take life as it comes. But I don't restrain myself from making plans. There are so many things, things that might seem simple and easy to most people but that I had never known or done because I was in show business. A walk on a busy street; a warm spring evening with old girlfriends; mingling with the crowd without being recognized; or a dinner at home, alone with the man I love; going shopping by myself; having a purse filled with personal belongings, a credit card, keys. And not knowing what tomorrow will bring, what I will do or where I will be in three weeks, in six months.

Likewise, I'm planning in detail the pleasure trip I want to take with René to Europe, to visit the cities that we passed through too quickly, that we didn't take the time to know and love!

I want to visit the world's most beautiful museums and its most famous castles, with guides who will teach me everything about the world's treasures.

I'm making plans, itineraries. I think of the dress I'll wear and what I'll have René wear when we take a walk, some wonderfully mild evening, perhaps in Venice, hand in hand, alone, without a bodyguard or a photographer, incognito. We will travel very slowly, enjoying each other, enjoying life, without demanding anything from it. We will simply be satisfied and happy with whatever it brings us.

Yet once again, life brought us even more than we had imagined. Something incredible happened, something that could very well be the most important event of our life together.

In May, as planned, I met in New York with Dr. Zev Rosenwaks, a renowned fertility specialist. He suggested that we try a new fertility method. The idea is to isolate one spermatozoon, and to inject it in an egg with an extremely small needle. The doctor then proceeds to place the embryo in the uterus.

We already had millions of spermatozoa in a freezer. So now our main concern was for me to produce as many eggs as possible.

"This method calls for a lot of patience and courage," the doctor told me, as if he was about to give me a long speech on the hard times I'd soon be going through.

I immediately stopped him. "My mother already had thirteen children when she became pregnant with me," I told him. "And I know her well enough to tell you for certain that she had all the patience and courage she would need."

I don't pretend to have more courage than other women, but I was in great shape and I had all the time I needed. And what's more, I could give this experiment a try knowing I fulfilled all the requirements. I had everything I needed, mentally and physically.

"I have to tell you that it is impossible to guarantee the success of this method," the doctor said. "The success rate for in vitro fertilization, by whatever method, is still only twenty-five percent."

"As far as I know, Doctor, even the old natural way is never one hundred percent sure."

"Fair enough," he said, "but what I'm offering you is a bit less pleasurable."

That's for sure!

To begin this process, I had to prepare my body by injecting myself every day with an "antiestrogen" that would regulate and control my ovulation.

I returned to New York, where I began to receive massive injections of hormones that would create a "superovulation." Almost every day I had to have blood tests and sonograms so the doctors could adjust my levels. Because of these hormones, my belly swelled up like a little balloon. It was certainly not comfortable, but it really made René and me laugh and dream. Luckily, I didn't have any of the dizziness and hot flashes that many women have during this treatment.

When my ova reached maturity, the doctors took them out of me and placed them in a test tube. Then they were put in contact with the spermatozoa. This happened on May 25. Three days later, three little eggs were back inside me. By this method, I could possibly have had twins or triplets. But that would also be problematic. For more than a month, up to mid-July, I injected myself daily with progesterone, a hormone that insures the continuation of the pregnancy.

All of these procedures had nothing to do with poetry. It was all very technical and cold. Nothing to do with the beautiful act we call love.

But René was always by my side, fascinated, caring, and very tender. We went through all the steps together. It had become our dearest dream. We would talk all the time to each other and to our friend. To the public too. We had never hidden our fertility problems. And we were not going to keep this experiment secret. Nor the results— whatever they would be.

I had to spend a few days without moving so that the small eggs would stay attached. I decided to follow all the rules very carefully. I had told the doctors: "I want to put every chance on my side. Even if it's difficult, even if it's painful. If you want, I can stop moving altogether for nine months."

They were not asking for so much. But they did warn me more than once that I had to be very careful, especially during the first month.

On the morning of June 8, Dr. Ronald Ackerman dropped by my house in Jupiter. He had been coming very often for the past months. But that day I was not expecting him. He had come by the day before, had examined me, and taken a blood sample. He had left saying it would still take two or three days before he knew if I was pregnant or not.

He had just arrived when Alain, my sister Linda's husband, came to tell me that Dr. Rosenwaks was on the phone. I was also talking to him every day. This morning, strangely, he did not ask about my health, nor did he ask to speak to Dr. Ackerman as he always did. He simply asked what I was doing.

"Eating lunch," I answered.

"What?"

"Toast, pâté, tea."

"What about René?"

"I think he's in his office."

"And you?"

"In the kitchen, with Dr. Ackerman."

"Better get René."

"He can talk to you from there."

He was about to come to Florida and I thought he probably wanted to organize a golf game with René or something like that. But he hesitated a few seconds and then he said: "I want to talk to both of you together. I want you to be in the same room."

I called René on the intercom. I had a really hard time trying not to sound nervous and excited. I had finally understood what was happening. I knew that the doctor had really, really big news for us. And Dr. Ackerman could see that I knew. I could see him trying to avoid my eyes. It was obvious that he wanted to laugh.

When René arrived in the kitchen, I was also trying to look very calm. He did not have a clue either. He didn't even know who was on the phone.

Linda had set the phone so everybody could hear Dr. Rosenwaks saying: "Are you there, René?"

"Yes!"

"You there, Ronald?"

"Okay, go."

And when we were all together, Zev and Ronald told us: "Congratulations, lovers!"

I immediately saw my love's eyes fill with tears. He came close to me and took me in his arms.

"You're pregnant, Celine," Zev and Ronald kept saying.

"Congratulations to the both of you," added René.

Even this dream, which I'd practically forbidden myself from having because it seemed so fragile, was now going to be realized. I was going to have a baby with the man I love.

I was in René's arms, and he was laughing through his tears. For quite a while we stood holding each other in the middle of the kitchen.

Both of us knew that we couldn't hide our great joy for very long. The secret was too big and too beautiful to keep just to ourselves.

We spent the rest of the day on the telephone. We called my parents, all my brothers and sisters, René's children, and our friends in Montreal, New York, Paris, Los Angeles, to tell them the good news.

But they couldn't keep the secret either. By evening the offices of our publicists in Montreal and Los Angeles were swamped with reporters, and by the next morning there had to be a press release announcing my pregnancy.

In any case, our happiness had to be known. For twenty years we'd shared a kind of intimacy with the public at large. I wanted them to share our joy just as they'd shared our suffering.

I believe you should never hide your happiness. It lights up and cheers up the world. To keep it only for yourself is to lose it.

That day I felt a great strength and peace coming over us. Definitely, it came from somewhere else. But I knew that René was the one who had summoned that strength and peace to us.

When he fell ill, he had to fight it. He couldn't just give up and let our happiness die. Instead of giving up, he chose to fight with all his strength. He had to because of his love for life, because of his love for me and for his children and his friends.

And now that life that he had so valiantly defended was struggling and growing in me. It would be the proof that you have to believe in happiness, the proof that love exists with as much intensity and as long as you believe in it.

Two weeks later, we saw the heart of our child beating, a small and rapid sound.

"One hundred and forty-two beats a minute. That's very good," said one of the doctors.

Then he made a quick count and announced that I was going to give birth on February 14, 2001.

Later, in August, after three months of pregnancy, we heard its little heart beat. At 162 beats a minute, a strong pulse. We recorded it, and since then have been listening to it every night before going to sleep.

We knew that all of it was still tenuous, that we needed patience, passion, joy, strength, and a lot of luck as well.

But we also knew that whatever happened, life had already triumphed.

1

'll never forget the day I sang in public for the first time. It was at the wedding of my brother Michel, who is also my godfather. I was five years old. I wore a long dress, blue with small white flowers, and white gloves. It must have been during the summer because Michel was married on his birthday, which is August 18.

My brothers and sisters had put together a real show for the newlyweds. They set up an entire stage, complete with lighting and amplifiers. They even did sound checks. We began by singing folk songs together, then each of us did his or her own little number. During the few days before, Maman had me practice several tunes, including "Mamy Blue" (Granny Blue), which I loved and which I was going to sing accompanied by my brother Daniel at the piano.

Until that moment, I'd only sung at our place, with the family. Almost every evening after supper, we formed a chorus and sang songs from the old days, in rounds. Or we did big hits by Jimi Hendrix or Creedence Clearwater Revival that we all loved so much. A

lot of times my father took out his accordion and my mother her violin. Daniel and my sister Ghislaine could play any instrument. And
if there were no drum sets in the house, they tapped on tables, walls,
pots, the refrigerator . . .

While the family did the dishes, somebody stood me up on the
kitchen table—my first stage, a kind of theater in the round like the
ones I prefer today, with the audience on every side. I sang with all
my might, using a fork, spoon, or dishmop as a mike. And I made
them all laugh. I wasn't afraid of anything or anyone. The only problem was that I never wanted to stop singing. Once I got started, it
was difficult to get me off the table.

One evening, as a joke, or just because they'd had enough, as soon
as the dishes were done, my family signaled to each other to slip into
the living room, after turning off the light, leaving me all alone on
the table with my dishmop in my hands.

It didn't really bother me. In the first place, I knew they didn't
intend anything mean by it. None of my brothers or sisters has ever
wanted to hurt me; of this I'm sure. What is more, never in my life,
in the past or present, have I doubted for a fraction of a second my
family's love for me, or the love my brothers and sisters feel for each
other and for my parents. When they walked out on my "kitchen
concert," I knew it was a game, a trick they were playing on me.
They wanted to make us all laugh. So I calmly got off the table and
joined them in the living room, where they made sure I had a really
good time. We've always loved playing tricks in my family. I think
we get it from my father.

When people visited—my brothers' friends or girlfriends or pals
of my sisters—the atmosphere was completely different. For me,
anyway. I would never have climbed on the table or even sung alone.
Unless these outsiders were themselves musicians or singers, which
often happened to be the case. In fact, our house attracted all the young

people in the area who liked to make music. And we often had "guest stars" appear with our band. Those times, I stayed quiet. I just listened. And when I felt confident enough, I added my voice to the others'. But for a long time, my singing was private, purely a family affair.

As a result, I'd never sung for an audience as important or as unfamiliar as the one that was gathered at Michel's wedding. When it was my turn to go onstage, I became paralyzed by stage fright. Everyone was watching me and waiting for me to begin. These people intimidated me: cousins I'd hardly ever seen, friends of my brothers and sisters who probably knew nothing about music and didn't really want to hear me perform.

A friend of Michel, Pierre Tremblay, played the first chords of "Mamy Blue." I was standing next to him, staring at the floor, a very unpleasant ringing in my ears. Pierre winked at me and began his intro again. But I stood there frozen. Then I felt my mother's hand on my back, pushing me gently and firmly. And her voice was saying to me: "Go ahead, my little girl, go ahead, it's your turn."

So I stepped forward and sang.

I don't remember exactly what happened after this, but I do remember not wanting to stop and begging Michel to let me sing other songs. I also sang in all the groups formed by my brothers and sisters.

That day gave me great pleasure, a feeling of having conquered my fear, my stage fright. And I definitely knew for the first time in my life that unforgettable sensation felt by a singer when she realizes that she's captivated a listener, that she's being heard, applauded.

That day I knew I would be singing my whole life. And that I'd discover my happiness in doing so.

was born on March 30, 1968. I was a mistake, an accident, and the cause of a serious quandary for my mother.

The day she learned she was pregnant, she had to relinquish plans she'd been cherishing a long time. I was in no way a part of these plans. My birth was unwanted and unexpected. By coming into the world, I crushed her dreams. I've always loved her so much that if I had known this, I think I would not have been able to let myself be born.

My mother had already brought up thirteen children. For more than twenty years she'd kept house. She did the washing and the housework, the cleaning, the ironing, the meals. And she did it all over and over again, during good times and bad times, 365 days a year. By the time she became pregnant with me, she thought, and she had a right to think, that she had finished her work. My mother believed that at long last she would be able to do something else.

Her two youngest children at that time, Paul and Pauline, who were twins, were entering school the following fall. My mother would have some free time. She could leave the house and see the world. She wanted to get a job and make a little money. Maybe she'd travel with my father to see the sea and the part of Quebec called the Gaspé peninsula again. They had both spent their childhoods there, and they hadn't been back since their marriage.

My mother had gone so far as to see the parish priest to ask him if she could "stop having children," as they said at the time, which meant using contraceptives. At the time the priests of Quebec had a lot of authority. This one began preaching to her. He told her she didn't have the right to defy nature. My mother was furious. So was I when she told me the story. But at the same time, I have to admit that, in a way, I owe my life to that priest.

The twins were celebrating their sixth birthday on the day my mother and I came home from Le Gardeur Hospital, where I had been born four days earlier. Maman left me in the arms of my sisters and brothers and made a chocolate cake for the twins. At our place, children were always entitled on the day of their birthday to a big chocolate or vanilla cake with candles, as well as the presents that my parents had bought them.

So it was a day of celebration, but my mother's heart was heavy. With me, who'd come to mess up her plans, on the scene, she found herself thrown back to square one, once again confined to the small world that she so much wanted to leave. I was forcing her to put off her dream of a new life, a dream she'd thought she was about to realize.

I imagine that despite herself, at the bottom of her heart, she held my being born against me a bit. But I also know that she didn't waste much time feeling sorry for herself. That's simply not her way. My mother is happy to take care of everybody, but she's never had much sympathy for complainers and crybabies.

I don't know how it happened, but, in some way, and despite myself, I succeeded in making my presence felt. I must have found a way to make peace with the mother who hadn't really wanted me at first. Somehow I must have won her over. But I can't take too much credit for it. My mother was always crazy about babies—hers and other people's. And what's more, I seem to have been a good baby. I didn't cry too much and I quickly began sleeping nights. Of course, I had fifteen people at my beck and call.

I spent the first days, weeks, or maybe months of my life in the arms of my mother or father, or one of my thirteen older brothers and sisters. I was the focus of interest for these fifteen people, without a doubt the most attentive and indulgent audience I've ever had. They watched me, pampered me, worshiped me. In the evening they argued about whose bed I'd sleep in.

My sister Ghislaine, who was almost ten, made a surprising discovery at the time. Every time she softly sang my name in a tiny, very high falsetto, I would begin to cry—as if on cue. Quite naturally, she inferred from this that I didn't like my name. My mother had chosen it because, during her pregnancy, the Hugues Aufray song "Celine" was an enormous success in Quebec and France. "Celine" tells the story of the oldest of many children, the mother of whom dies while giving birth to the last child. The eldest has sacrificed her youth to her brothers and sisters. And the years have gone by without her having known love.

Ghislaine sang other names in the same tone of voice, to see how I'd react. And I cried just as much. So clearly it was the pitch or the key of the song that bothered me. The other children began amusing themselves by making me cry until my mother intervened. No more singing in that key. But they weren't kept from playing music and singing in all the other keys.

I had the incredible luck to be born into a home that was filled with music and song from morning until night—sometimes even from evening until morning. The music of others—Janis Joplin, Jimi Hendrix, Felix Leclerc, Jacques Brel, Barbra Streisand, and Ginette Reno—as well as our own music. The music that my parents played—my father with his accordion and my mother with her violin—reels, gigs, the lively dance music called rigadoons. And the music that my brothers and sisters played with their guitars, pianos, percussion instruments . . . Is it any wonder that all of us have remained deeply attached to our childhoods?

We were far from rich. But we loved each other. And we had our music, which in addition to health and love, represents what's most beautiful and precious in this world.

I really believe that where there is music, happiness can't be far behind. As my brother Clement says, music attracts happiness like the wooden decoys that hunters use attract deer or moose.

This explains why family has always been so important to me, why it is directly connected to my happiness and my emotional equilibrium, to my everyday life and my career.

I've always been very close to my parents, to my brothers and sisters, but especially to my mother. Even when I reached the age when almost all girls break away from their mothers, distance themselves, try to emancipate themselves or even openly rebel, I continued to see my mother as a role model. She was my friend, my confidante and pal, as well as that irreplaceable, essential, unique being that a mother is. My mother is the pillar of our family. She wrote my first songs. She was my first manager. If today I've met the man who has made me happy, it's thanks to her . . . and it's in spite of her as well.

My father's temperament is altogether different from my mother's. He's much more private and discreet than my mother, and less authoritarian as well, perhaps less sure of himself in front of others, or at least more withdrawn. His wife is the authority. And I think that's the bargain he has struck. She decides; he goes with the flow. She takes care of the problems; he detests getting embroiled in them. She participates in anything that concerns the family; he flees disputes, conflicts. Too much, perhaps.

My father talks a lot, but most often he does this to entertain, to make people laugh, to make them forget their cares and worries. He's always been a master at turning everything into a joke. He doesn't want to see misery, misfortune, sadness, or suffering at home or at the homes of others. He hates going to hospitals, for example. Even when my mother and my sisters were giving birth, it was practically impossible to get him to visit them. But I believe that in most cases men just don't like these kinds of situations.

My father doesn't connect with others as easily as my mother. Even with his children—or with me, at any rate—he doesn't try to communicate on intimate levels or to know what others are thinking or feeling. He just wants everybody to be happy. He always sees only the good side of things and people. He doesn't see, or he keeps himself from seeing, the ugly side. For instance, I don't ever remember hearing him complain about something or speak badly about anyone at all.

He loves to fish, even when the fish aren't biting. He loves golf, even when he's playing way above par. He likes the peacefulness of these activities, and their beautiful environments.

My father is very good with his hands. He can build an entire house—lay the foundation, do all the carpentry, put in the windows, the electrical wiring, the insulation and plumbing—everything. And he's done it. I've even thought that when something broke or was cracked in our house, he was glad about it. He gets out his tool chest and puts everything back together. He was my brothers' idol and they learned a lot from him. What he likes less is all the finishing and detail work, the "finicky stuff at the end," as he calls it.

Papa is an extraordinary accordion player. When I was small, he was part of an orchestra that played at weddings and holiday celebrations, not only in our little suburban village of Charlemagne but everywhere in the region—in Repentigny, in Lanaudière, in east Montreal. When he rehearsed alone or with his friends, the sound of his accordion thrilled me, so fluid and joyful, so very sweet—just like him. He always had a very distinctive way of playing. Basically, my father revealed a lot more about himself to us through his music than he did by talking to us. When he played, he even looked different. And he was always smiling.

So I used to listen to him and so did the other members of my family. He played standing up, his back against the wall of the kitchen or the living room. And I think all of us were surprised to see that this man, who ordinarily demanded so little attention, suddenly stood out when he played his accordion. He did more than play. He put "soul" into the music. And that was something we all could feel; it "knocked us out." Sometimes, as well, he would improvise, or he mixed musical genres and all sorts of melodies, old tunes he'd taught us and rock riffs that my brothers were listening to at the time. Then he could feel he had hold of us, and he was happy . . . and so were we. And he'd wink at us. My father is the world champion of winkers.

Playing music is also how he seduced my mother. I can guess well enough how he went about it. When my father plays the accordion, he can become dangerously seductive. As a musician, he has this unusual talent of entering directly into people's hearts, of really touching them.

Like him, my mother had been transplanted from the Gaspé peninsula—from sea, forest, and sky—to La Tuque, which is in the most remote part of the Mauricie region of Quebec—with its factories and smoke. That's where they met. She was seventeen, he was twenty-one. He had his accordion, she her violin. They both knew the same repertoire of reels. They played the "Hanging Man Reel" (Le Reel du pendu). He showed her the chords to "Mockingbird" (L'Oiseau moqueur). A year later, they were married. And then came the children, from Denise to the twins, thirteen children in sixteen years—quite a figure. Then me, unexpected, a mistake, a few years later.

When I've tried to recount my childhood, I've asked myself if the memories I've kept of it were really mine or if I re-created them in my mind based on what my oldest siblings have told me. At our house, everybody remembers the day I was born. They've spoken to me about it so much that I can say what the weather was like—cloudy and windy. All my brothers and sisters witnessed my first steps; they all waited for and heard my first words. They also remember the first songs I sang with them, and the car accident that nearly cost me my life when I was two years old. I ended up in the hospital with a fractured skull and a concussion.

I can visualize the scenery perfectly. It was very sunny. One of the first days of spring. The earth and the nearby river smelled good.

My brothers Michel, Jacques, and Daniel were doing spring cleaning in the yard. They had to rake up the old grass, clean the flower beds, and pick up the dead branches. I was playing in my sandbox. Through the hedge—a very thin hedge—that enclosed the yard, I saw a woman pushing a baby carriage—a blue baby carriage.

I thought it was my sister Denise with her baby Christian. Apparently, I was really fixated on Denise and her baby. So I went toward them. I was in the middle of the street when I realized that I'd made a mistake. It wasn't my sister but a neighbor out with her baby.

My brothers, who were in the yard, heard the screech of tires and the cries of the woman. Two seconds later, they were at the scene of the accident, in front of the house. They saw a big black car stopped in the very middle of the rue Notre-Dame, the door open, a man standing beside it, unmoving, and me spread out under the bumper.

Michel threw himself to the ground to get me out of there. Daniel and Jacques tried to hold back my mother, who'd come running out of the house because she thought I'd been seriously hurt, that maybe I was dead, and they didn't want her to see me.

From then on, the versions differ somewhat, as is usually the case with this kind of story.

"You were crying your heart out," my brothers will say.

"She wasn't making a sound," contests my mother. "And that's exactly what worried me the most. She wasn't crying but her eyes were rolled up into her head."

I wasn't bleeding either, but I had black and blue marks and bad bruises on my arms and forehead.

"Papa was there," maintain Daniel and Jacques.

"Impossible," claim Maman and Michel. "He would have been working at that hour [at the time he was a meat inspector at the

Cooperative Federation of Quebec]. The ambulance had already left when he arrived. There was nobody there but policemen finishing their report."

A few years ago, when I began collecting family souvenirs to put together an album for my parents—a gift I have yet to finish—my father took out of his wallet an old piece of pink paper that he'd held on to for more than twenty-five years. It was the police report. Thanks to this document and to the accounts of my brothers, I know the make and color of the car that hit me as well as the name of the man who was driving it—Jacques Picard.

He'd offered my brothers twenty dollars not to call the police. My father understood why a few weeks later, when he saw the gentleman's face on page three of the *Journal de Montréal*. The man belonged to the east Montreal underworld. And he'd been bumped off by other criminals for some alleged crime or other. God take his soul!

That evening, for the first time in my life, I slept all alone, far from my mother, in a children's hospital. Obviously, I don't remember any of it, no more than I do the accident. I was only two years old. But it took years for me to experience being alone again.

When I was small, I never wanted to go to bed. If I slept at the house of one of my married sisters, where my mother sometimes left me for two or three days, I'd always make a big scene. I wanted to stay near her all the time, no matter where she was or what she was doing. I think she basically got used to it. Until I was eighteen or nineteen, we were practically inseparable.

Wherever I am today, I'm still very connected to my family. Two of my sisters, Manon and Linda, live near me on nearly a permanent basis. My brothers Michel and Clement are never very far away. The others I see regularly when I'm in Montreal or when they come to Florida or Las Vegas. And a day doesn't pass that I don't speak to my mother. In addition, she visits me often with my father and my aunt

Jeanne, her eldest sister, in Jupiter, Florida, where René and I have our house.

My relatives went with me on tour for years; my mother, of course, who has endless energy and likes big cities: New York, London, and especially Paris. Through her, I always know what is happening in the family—whether it be with brothers, sisters, sisters-in-law, brothers-in-law, nephews and nieces—who's doing what, where, when, how, who's got a cold, who was promoted at work, who's bought a new car, who thinks she's pregnant, who's fighting with whom and why.

We see each other a lot and we talk a great deal, about what's happening to us now but also especially about the time when we were all together in the little house in Charlemagne. We think of that house as if it were a lost paradise that we all dream of returning to—as if we wish all sixteen of us could be crammed together, with a single bathroom, four tiny bedrooms, no dishwasher (of course), an oil furnace with its hellish smell, without any modern comforts.

How can I explain that this is the place where happiness lives? And how can I be sure of this?

I believe there is something magical about big families, families that know and share a lot of human warmth. But sometimes I tell myself that maybe we have forgotten the difficulties and hardships, and that we've remembered only the good times we spent together, and that we exaggerate them more each time we talk about them.

Big families have lots of shared history. And lots of historians, of course. Each of the older children has his version of the facts, her memories, his point of view, and her interpretation. I certainly always want to hear the stories, especially when they go back to the early sixties or even to the mid-fifties, long before I showed up to turn my mother's life upside down.

As time passed, I began to know some old stories almost as well as if I had really lived them—because I heard them talked about so much. For example, sometimes I feel as if I really knew my grandfather Dion, to whom fate dealt a "low blow." Just a couple of steps from the house where we were living at the time, he was hit and killed by a train. By "we" I mean my family, but actually I never lived in that house, which my father built from the ground up. After the terrible death of his father, he couldn't stand being in that house. Even today, he doesn't like to talk about what happened.

"Your grandfather had just left the house. There was a terrible noise. And through the kitchen window I saw my father's car hitting the train. When the train stopped, the car was just a heap of scrap metal. I went up to it and stayed there, unable to move."

Afterward, my father couldn't stay in the house and see the train that had killed his father passing by every day. So we moved.

This was several years before I was born, but even so, I can tell the story of our moving as if I'd been there. It had begun to rain, and there was no canvas covering the truck. The men had delivered the furniture and a mattress was completely soaked. The kids liked finding themselves in a new house, especially because it had a large yard on the banks of the Assomption River. There were big trees from which my brothers hung tires to make swings.

It was an old Canadian house with the kitchen next to the main building, like in the old days. At the front, a very narrow porch ran along the entire front, from which you had direct access to the sidewalk of the rue Notre-Dame, which was very busy and noisy. On the ground floor, next to my parents' room, there was a large living room that actually looked more like a music room. Often there was a drum set in the middle of the room, guitars, mikes, amps, tape recorders, wires running in all directions, records, tapes. There was also, on the side facing the street, a sitting room where you barely set foot unless there were important visitors. It was a cold, dark place, and I didn't like to go there. Even today, I prefer kitchens to living rooms, for talking and playing cards.

The children's rooms were on the second floor, two for the girls, two for the boys. In the larger, which I shared with Pauline and Manon, the walls were covered with posters of actors and singers. The beds, which occupied almost the entire room, were so close together, you had to squeeze through the space between them, and between the beds and the chests of drawers, and between the dormer window and the big mirror on the door of the wardrobe.

I liked watching my sisters when they put on their makeup, got dressed, and posed in front of the mirror. I thought they were beautiful. And I was impatient to grow up and do what they were doing.

They also sang a lot, imitating Mireille Mathieu, Dalida, Ginette Reno, Barbra Streisand, Aretha Franklin. Before I even started school, I already knew all these singing stars.

I particularly remember one rainy day. Ghislaine, who must have been about fifteen years old, had turned on the record player in our room and she was mimicking a singer's performance over and over again. I listened to her all afternoon. She held an old mike without a wire or a plug, but she made use of it as if she were on a stage, facing an audience that she was welcoming and thanking. And I felt as if I, too, could hear the applause.

I've forgotten the title of the song—it was in English—and I can't remember the name of the singer. But I remember my sister's concentration and determination. She would ask me to set the needle back to the beginning of the song while she got her breath back. Then she'd start again. I was sitting on the floor next to her. I watched her sing in the mirror. And I was as excited and happy as she was when she succeeded in duplicating the intonations of the singer.

That evening, my brothers (probably Clement on drums, Jacques on guitar, and Daniel on keyboard) found the music for the song, and Ghislaine sang along with them. Everybody listened, even my father and mother, even Grandma Dion, who'd come to live with us after my grandfather's death.

She was already very old and nearly infirm. She didn't speak very much. She had a phobia about open doors. She told us all the time to close them to keep out the flies, even the cellar door, even in the middle of winter, when there were no flies anywhere.

Maman was wonderful to her. She gave her her own room, on the first floor, and she moved to the second floor with Papa. She took care of her, washed her, changed her like a baby. She even helped her eat and get dressed.

I don't know if I'd have the courage and the strength to do something like that, but I absolutely admire those who do it, whether for family members or as a profession. I'm certain that they find pleasure in some part of it. Doing good does you good; it makes you a bigger person.

Once more I see Grandma, huddled in her rocking chair, lost, completely lost in her thoughts. She would smile all the time. Even when you couldn't hear yourself think in the house, because there were several kinds of music playing at the same time. For example, Ghislaine and Claudette, my godmother, would be singing upstairs in the girl's big bedroom. Down below, Jacques would be playing the guitar, Clement the drums, Daniel the piano. Michel was listening to his jazz records. Another of my sisters was talking on the telephone. And sometimes the TV was playing over all of that.

But most often, someone, my father or my mother, imposed some order on the chaos and everybody ended up making music together. This could last hours, all evening, if not through part of the night. Grandma stayed in her rocker and watched her son's family make music, playing reels as old as the earth itself or doing versions of the big hits of the Doors, Hendrix, or Joplin. She seemed delighted. And maybe a little deaf, as well.

All of this made me feel great, free. I wanted this life to last forever. It was sweet and good. I must say I had a very unfettered childhood. It surprises me today that I didn't become a lazy, spoiled woman.

I never got a spanking in my whole life, neither from my parents nor from any of my brothers and sisters. Not a slap either, nothing physical. We didn't do that kind of thing. To me or to the others. My mother did, however, have a way of punishing me that was just as efficient as a smack on the cheek. One day, when I must have been four or five, I was with my parents at the shopping center in Repentigny, which was near us. I wanted to go to the toy store. I'd been a few times with my mother or with one of my sisters. Several Barbie dolls that I owned came from that store.

But on that day, my parents were in a hurry, especially my father. There was no way we were going into the treasure chest. When I saw that there was nothing to hope for as far as my father was concerned, I began begging my mother. But she said no too.

"Listen, Celine, money doesn't grow on trees. And you've already got enough toys at the house."

So I threw a real tantrum. I cried my heart out, stamped my feet, and yelled. You could hear me from one end of the mall to the other. I was so angry I no longer saw anything around me. Suddenly I realized I was completely alone. I turned around and saw my parents heading for the exit. They'd simply left me there.

I had the scare of my life! In thirty seconds, I'd caught up with them. And I hung on to my mother.

That's the kind of lesson she gave me when I acted like a spoiled child. She punished me with coldness or indifference. Never by hitting me, or hollering at me or shouting at me. Her authority was enough to set things straight.

*also cried my heart out the day I entered nursery school. I like to hear my mother recount that scene of horror. I had to leave the cozy, comfortable family nest and live every day for hours far away from my mother.

It was the same, only more dramatic, the following year, when I left for grade school. This time, however, my memory has retained a few precise snapshots.

I remember my mother went with me on foot and I held her hand very tight. Once we were in the schoolyard, she had to pry open my fingers to separate herself from me. She took several steps back and then left me all alone. She positioned herself behind the fence and watched me. Never, I think, has my heart been so heavy. Because I knew that I couldn't go back and remain a baby. My mother had told me this was coming. And I was, and continue to be, a very obedient girl. I do what must be done. I do, have always done, and will always do what I'm asked to. As long as those who are asking are people I love and in whom I have confidence.

I know every child has had to go through the first day of school. At five or six years old, all of us have been torn from our families and found ourselves all alone on an asphalt playground full of strangers. For me, it wasn't fear of a hostile or strange world, but rather a feeling of boredom. A profound sense of boredom, an immense sadness.

I had always lived surrounded by adults and children a lot older than me. I learned everything I needed to know from them. As far as I was concerned, real life existed around them. Not in the middle of a schoolyard full of terrified children who knew nothing about nothing. From that day on, I detested school. Forever.

I'm not setting myself up as an example; I simply believe I wasn't made for this.

My whole life had been turned upside down. Maman had found work in a department store called American Salvage in east Montreal, where she sold boots, raincoats, etc. I would eat dinner at my sister Louise's, who lived near the school and at whose place I had to stay and sleep on Thursdays and Fridays when Maman worked evenings.

At Louise's everything was modern, ordered, polished, and comfortable. What's more, Louise is sweetness itself. But in the evening, alone in my bed, I thought about the house. I wanted to wait up in the kitchen with Manon and Pauline. When Maman came home from work, we could make toast and hot chocolate. And even if I'd been sent to bed, there would have been those familiar noises, those voices, those smells, all of that world that I so loved. At Louise's, like at school, I felt that I'd been exiled.

I didn't hide my suffering from my mother, who was soon eaten up by guilt (was this exactly what I wanted?). So that I could travel between school and the house, she bought me a green bicycle. From then on, I went to eat dinner at Louise's but slept at our house.

One night I had a dream. I was coming home after school. I didn't have my bicycle. I was running. Very fast. All of a sudden I felt incredibly light. And everything started happening in slow motion, my strides got larger and larger, as if I were running on a rubberized surface. And I was extraordinarily happy.

I have never forgotten this dream. Even today when I think about it, I can still recapture a little of the extraordinary sensation it gave me.

When I think of that time, I can easily see that in some way, I always found it difficult to connect with children of my age. I don't think their world interested me. Today, I'm fascinated by it. But at the time, although I myself was a child, I didn't understand anything about it. I didn't feel capable of finding a way to connect with tiny children and become part of their games (or I thought it was useless to try). I preferred to be alone. Even when I played.

Near the shed next to the house, my brothers had put up a punching bag like those used by boxers in training. I spent hours hitting it, sometimes with one of my sisters as sparring partner or with my niece Cathy, the daughter of my sister Claudette. But most of the time I was alone. Sometimes I punched the bag until my fists and wrists were swollen. I just kept punching, without being able to stop. When I came in to eat, my hands were bleeding. My mother wrapped gauze around my wrists, just like they do for boxers. And I'd go back to my punching bag, find my rhythm and stroke once again, forgetting about everything.

I also played with dolls. Especially during summer, and usually outdoors. I'd set myself up at the foot of the staircase leading to the backyard. I'd wash my Barbies, change them, one after another, and put them into poses, talk to them, and scold them. Then I'd put them to bed the proper way in an old wooden chest my uncle Valmont, Maman's brother, had made for me.

I was my mother's and my sisters' doll. They did my hair up in buns and braids, they put polish on my nails, and made up my face, even when I was only seven or eight years old. Claudette, Liette, and Linda often took me with them to stores and had fun having me try on dresses, coats, shoes, and hats.

We fell in thick very quickly. I became part of their games, their conversations, and especially a part of their music and songs.

That was the game that I got the most pleasure from. The one I still play today: singing, putting on a costume and makeup, wearing a disguise, playing comedy, "doing" show business like my parents, brothers, and sisters did.

My father and mother had formed a musical group, A. Dion and His Ensemble, which gave shows in Lanaudière and east Montreal. Maman had bought a new violin. Jacques played the guitar, Clement was on drums, and Daniel was playing the accordian-piano; Denise sang folk songs and current hits. They even did some TV shows. I was almost always with them, in the studios, clubs, and bars, even when I was only six or seven years old.

Later, with a friend of the family named Michel Desjardins, Ghislaine, Jacques, Michel, and Daniel formed a real rock and rhythm and blues band. On weekend nights, they played in a club in Charlemagne: the Bord-de-l'Eau. They were called "Les Décidés" (the Determined Ones) and they had T-shirts made with two *D*'s separated by the note "si" ("ti" in English). I was their number-one fan. When they went on tour in Quebec (to Trois-Rivières, Berthier, Joliette . . .), I was in mourning. When they were near us, I never missed a show.

I have some very clear memories of those evenings, the sound of the Hammond organ, the Les Paul Gibson guitar they were so proud of. I even think that today I could recognize the smell of the Bord-de-l'Eau with my eyes closed. It's a mixture of cigarette smoke and potpourri, very fruity, very sugary. And it was damp and warm. Ghislaine, who called herself "Penelope" then, had taken up Clement's drums. She sang so well, with so much heart, that everyone in the club grew quiet when she launched into "Me and Bobby McGee" by Janis Joplin or Barbra Streisand's "The Way We Were." My parents came to these shows often. And they brought me too, of course. When I'd had enough, I went to sleep on a bench.

I often went to bed very late. I ate when I was hungry, I slept when there were no more people playing music. I missed school regularly, or if I did go, I was so tired that I nodded out during class.

I was never a good student. In school I really didn't look for friends, try to get ahead, or to attract anyone. Nor did I even let it be known that I sometimes sang with a band. In the playground, I didn't talk very much. I stayed apart. I must have seemed like a lunatic to some of the girls in my class, a lonely person paralyzed by shyness, or a complete snob. Everything that interested me was somewhere else, at home or at the cabaret. Or it was at the little club on the riverbank that my father and sister Claudette had bought. It was called the Vieux Baril (Old Barrel), and my family played music and sang there.

The evenings when I didn't go with them, I'd hear them coming home: they went into the kitchen, made toast and coffee. I was above, in my bed, and I listened to them tell Maman about their evening. They were giggling, happy, leading the most exciting life you could imagine. I wanted to grow up as soon as possible so I could go with them.

The Vieux Baril was the place where I saw real shows for the first time. It was also the place where I first experienced being in a crowd and had my first successes outside of the family circle. After the applause, they'd find me, at four in the morning, sleeping on a bench. Maman had warned me: "You can stay up as long as you want, if you get up in the morning for school."

So in the morning, I got up despite my fatigue and went to school to sleep.

I could hardly open my eyes and follow what was going on in class, so I dreamed. Like my brother Michel and my sisters Claudette and Ghislaine, I dreamed that I'd be on a big stage one day, the doors to recording studios would fly open for me, and I'd be a singing star.

The D si D (Décidés) fell apart, so Michel formed other groups. The Eclipse, which didn't last long, then the Show, which had a certain following in the cabarets and clubs. Then he recorded two 45s, and one of his songs rose quite high in the charts.

One autumn evening, my parents took the twins and me to one of the group's shows. The Show was preparing for a big tour of Quebec. The fashion at the time was for frock coats and long, tailored double-breasted jackets. Maman had made a white satin one with coattails and lapels for Michel. I sat admiring my big brother, the lead singer of the group, talking onstage under the spotlights. Michel has a strong, steady voice, and he moves well. I wanted to stay right to the end of the last set. As long as there was action, something to see and hear, I refused to go home.

I knew an incredible number of songs by heart. At the Vieux Baril, the customers asked me to sing some songs and gave me pennies. My parents were astonished to discover that I was no longer afraid of strangers, that I could face an audience without a problem. I became accustomed to crowds, to applause, to laughter and bravos. I couldn't do without them any longer.

At school, I remained a stranger, an exile. As soon as lessons started, if I didn't sink into a half sleep, I left for the moon and started making little movies in my head. The decor was usually the same: inside the Vieux Baril. The action was simple: I was singing in a big rock band directed by Daniel or Michel. And the people at the tables stopped talking and listened to me. Just like they did for my idols, Ghislaine and Michel.

Sometimes, as well, I went to Africa as a missionary, into the darkest part of the jungle. I saved children from misfortune, hunger, fear. I was unstoppable. I always succeeded. Or instead, I was a gymnast, like Nadia Comaneci, who'd become my absolute idol, the most beautiful girl I'd ever seen, during the Olympic Games in Montreal in 1976. I was eight years old. I'd plastered the walls of my room with her photos. I loved her intense look and her very serious manner. I thought there was nothing more beautiful on earth. Most of all, I admired her rigor and precision, the concentration she put into all her movements. For me she represented perfection—and she still does. She was also the first Olympic gymnast to achieve the highest possible score. Having the will to reach the top by training and discipline was an idea I could totally understand. I thought I was also capable of accomplishing what I wanted to do.

For me Nadia Comaneci was a model and an inspiration. I met her in 1996 at the Olympic Games. I was already a famous singer, but even so, I was so moved I was trembling and almost cried.

I don't know if it's because of my mother, but I was never treated like the very youngest in the family, the one that the oldest can barely tolerate. The one they hide certain things from, to whom they say, "You're too young for this, go to bed," or, "You'll understand when you're older."

I don't remember being excluded from adult conversations, no matter what the subject, whether I was four, five, or ten years old. I hadn't even been to school before I learned about all of life's mysteries, the birds and the bees—at least in theory. At twelve, I lacked the typical curiosity of a girl of that age about matters of love, and I felt no need or urgency to discover them. I knew them already. Perhaps that explains why I waited so long, until the age of twenty—longer than the average—to put my theoretical knowledge into practice.

The only thing they tried to hide from me was misfortune. I was nine years old when I learned that my niece Karine had cystic fibrosis. But in a big family, it's really difficult to hide anything from a child. All around me were faces on which I could read the sadness, the long silences, instead of music, in the evening after supper. My mother's eyes were filled with tears. She was talking on the phone with my brothers and sisters who no longer lived with us; she was telling them in a low voice that something terrible had just happened.

That's how I learned—through my mother's and father's tears, through their silence and whispering—that Karine, the rosy, fresh-faced baby of my sister Liette, had been diagnosed with a very serious illness. She'd been taken by ambulance to Sainte-Justine, the hospital for children, where I'd gone when I was hit by a car. The doctors had said to have Karine baptized as soon as possible because she might not live more than a few weeks. And if she did survive, she'd never grow, and she'd have to take medicines every day of her life. She probably wouldn't go to school, she'd suffer a lot, and she'd need constant care.

It was the first real misfortune to strike our family. The oldest children remember the violent death of our grandfather Dion. And we had just lost Grandma Dion. Everyone cried a lot, of course. But it was a part of life. Grandma went easily, at the end of a long life. Toward the end, I don't think she really wanted to live. Death had become a kind of deliverance, as much for her as for us.

But when death makes itself known at the beginning of a life, to a very little baby, you can't really talk about deliverance. It's more like a cruel and unjust condemnation.

Karine didn't die in several weeks, as some of the doctors had predicted. For years, my sister Liette surrounded her with constant care, every day. Two, three, five times a day, she had to give her massages to empty her lungs of the mucus that had accumulated and was blocking her breathing. She had her take her medicines, had her follow a very strict diet. All that without any real hope. I think that was the worst part: to know that, from the beginning, it was a losing battle.

Within a few days, everyone in the family had become experts on cystic fibrosis. We who had hated studying now spent whole evenings absorbed in the information the doctors had sent to Liette.

Or with our noses deep in an old French dictionary, looking up unusual or scientific words that you find at the very bottom of the page in such documents, or else trying to learn the functions and locations of organs and glands that were affected by or responsible for the illness—the lungs, the pancreas, the liver, the whole digestive system. I remember all the anatomical diagrams we looked at in that dictionary in an attempt to understand.

You need to have a serious case of bad luck to develop that disease. This is true of all diseases, of course, but in the case of cystic fibrosis, the odds against getting it make it still more terrible: it's transmitted to the child only if both parents carry the gene.

My mother got information about everyone that she knew in her family, in my father's family, and in Liette's husband's family. She discovered that two of the seven children of one of her cousins living in the United States, whom she hadn't seen for more than twenty years, had the disease.

During the course of my family's study of cystic fibrosis, we learned that a lot of researchers are interested in that disease. But research is progressing slowly and costs a great deal. At the very beginning of my career, I helped raise funds for the Quebec Cystic Fibrosis Association. I know there's hope. I know that important progress has been made. The expected life span of children with this disease has more than doubled. But there is still a lot to do.

My mother and I were alone in the house more and more often. I was ten or eleven. The twins were already going out with groups of friends to skate or see shows or films. Aside from my mother, I didn't have any friends and I thought that I didn't want any.

Nevertheless, Karine was going to occupy an important place in my life. She was the first child with whom I really enjoyed communicating. She wasn't altogether like the other children. Even when she was a baby, because of what we knew, because she had this illness, she always made me think of weighty, deeply moving things—of death, actually.

She'd become a very serious little girl, with the look and the thoughts of an adult, burdened in a way that other children weren't. At five years old, she already knew how unjust life can be.

I never saw her run, swim, roller-skate, or climb trees like all the other children. She couldn't even pet a cat or walk in a field or in a blossoming orchard or along the riverbank, because she began to suffocate as soon as she was exposed to the least bit of dust or pollen, to the weakest breeze. She had a good appetite, but because her body couldn't absorb nutritive elements from food, she remained thin, pale, anemic.

I don't remember whether we talked about her illness. I don't think Karine talked about it to anyone. Except to Liette, I would think, who showed her the patience of an angel and an incredible sweetness. Karine must have known intuitively that all rebellion was useless. Or maybe she didn't really have the strength to rebel, to cry out the rage that she must have had inside her. The kind I think I would have had if I had been in her place. But I know that she had her periods of despair. And during these times, she didn't speak for days.

When she came to our place, she spoke to me the most, probably because of the closeness of our ages. We'd both go up to the girls' room. We'd listen to music for hours. She'd watch me sing before the big mirror that Ghislaine no longer used because she, also, had moved out of the house.

Soon Papa, Maman, and I were the only ones left. After being the youngest in a family of fourteen children, I'd finally become an only child.

Maman was still working outside the house. But now she had a big plan to turn me into a singing star. She'd never been very interested in my homework and school lessons. But she'd followed my singing progress closely. She gave me advice, she suggested I try new songs. Or she said to me: "Don't imitate that singer, she has a beautiful voice but she doesn't make good use of it."

Our absolute model was Ginette Reno, who was then the biggest star in Quebec. I knew all the songs in her album *Je ne suis qu'une chanson* (I'm Only a Song) by heart. I knew not only the words, but every note, all her intonations, and I spent hours trying to reproduce them as faithfully as possible.

I would watch myself in the mirror, and as Ghislaine had taught me, I would imagine that behind me, behind my reflection, was an entire audience, full of people watching me. As soon as my song was finished, I lowered my mike, swept the cord behind me, and let them applaud, sometimes giving me a standing ovation, as they did for Ginette Reno at the Place des Arts.

One evening, after the dishes were done, with the two of us sitting at the kitchen table, Maman told me about her project. And her project was: me.

2

By the time I was twelve years old, Maman already had big plans for me. She wanted to make me into the kind of singer who could pack the Place des Arts in Montreal for three weeks in a row and who could tour Quebec and Canada for several months at a time. She wanted me to be like Ginette Reno, who had become one of Canada's most popular singers.

"And why not even all the way to France someday," Maman told me.

For me, this was a dream, but my mother had gone further than dreaming. She'd thought it through carefully, and she had a plan of action.

"If you want to get ahead, you'll need an agent," she told me. "Your brother Michel knows some. It's just a matter of choosing a good one—I mean, being chosen by a good one. But first you need your own songs. A good agent won't see much of anything in a girl who just imitates others."

I don't know how such an idea came to her, but today I realize the extent to which my mother has an artist's mind. Even in those early days, her intuition and her instincts were very sharp. She had a deep understanding and an innate sense of show business.

She knew that you can't really judge the value of a singer when she is interpreting a song that people already know. That's why she knew that I needed to produce several of my own songs, so that the good agent would find—or rather, the one who'd discover me would realize—that I knew something about music, about the structure of a song, and be able to see that I really could sing.

What my mother said that evening, at the kitchen table in our house in Charlemagne, seemed completely obvious to me, even if I'd never thought of it in such a clear way. And she was also telling me that it was time for me to take a big leap forward toward singing for real, in my own voice.

My brothers Jacques and Daniel put together some tapes with the latest hits for me to sing along with. At first, I'd inevitably fall back into the style of the girl who'd sung the song first. I sang like Ginette Reno, Barbra Streisand, or Aretha Franklin. But over time, I began to find my own intonations, my own stuff, my own voice.

Maman signed me up for some amateur contests, for all the festivals held in playgrounds in the area, for every neighborhood party.

That summer, I was obsessed with Olivia Newton-John. My brother Michel and my sister Linda, whom we used to call Dada, took me to see her at the Forum in Montreal. I started going through her songs using the instrumental arrangements. I didn't speak English yet, so I didn't understand a single word of what I was singing. But even so, I put every bit of emotion I had into it, often willy-nilly. I was determined to put my own imprint onto these songs. At times, I would use raging anguish for words that should have been sung tenderly, or use honeyed whispers where there should have been a cry of rage. I wasn't interpreting the songs, just showing what my voice could do. I was doing what my interim agent—my mother—had recommended.

One Sunday afternoon, I sang "Let's Get Physical" at a party on a golf course. Michel had brought his friend Paul Levesque, who handled the careers of several big rock groups in Quebec.

They ran into me and Maman under the big maples that bordered the golf course. Paul Levesque said I'd really impressed him. I was so glad that someone other than my family members had heard me, and had seen what I was capable of doing.

Paul also said I needed my own original songs in order to get a record company interested in me. He knew as well that the producers wouldn't come to see me sing on a golf course. I'd have to prepare some demos, and Paul said he would get them heard. But he didn't know any lyricists, except the ones who wrote in English for his rock groups. Nor could he find any musicians to compose melodies that were right for me.

What's more, at the tender age of twelve, I couldn't just jump right into heavy metal and start screaming like the big, tattooed rockers that he was sending all over the world. And I couldn't sing the torch songs that an adult would do either. I needed ballads that would sound right coming from the mouth of a teenager.

As a matter of fact, Paul wasn't sure exactly *what* to do with me, where there was a niche for me in show business.

Then one day my mother told me: "Little one, I'll write you some songs."

She had already written some lyrics in one of my school notebooks. So she had me listen to a melody she'd sketched out. That night I went to bed with the refrain of the song in my head. I was really excited, because, for the first time in my life, I was completely free. Not only could I choose which key to sing this song in, but I could decide which notes to emphasize, which syllables to lengthen or trill . . . It would be my first real song.

Though just a dream, so beautiful,
More real than I can say.

The refrain was perfect. But Maman couldn't seem to find the link between the refrain and the verses. She phoned my brother Jacques, who was working nights in a nearby bar. Like Daniel, Jacques has an incredible memory and ear for music. He can remember the individual parts of all the instruments after hearing a recording two or three times. Maman sang him her refrain and her verses over the telephone.

The next day, he came over around suppertime with a melody for the verses and some arrangements for the refrain. But we still didn't have the link between the refrain and the verses. It's called a "bridge"—a musical transition that takes you back and forth between the refrain and the verses. It's one of those technical requirements that can become the bane of any musician.

Jacques and Maman thought they could come up with one easily—by winging it—or *en criant lapin,* as we call it. They tried all sorts of things for an hour, but nothing worked. A couple of times they thought they had it. But I thought they didn't, and I showed them that it wouldn't work by humming their "big find."

"She's right, Maman, it doesn't work!" Jacques said.

The second time this happened, my mother added: "If you're so smart, Celine Dion, then find us something better!"

Actually, I thought I really had something, but I wasn't quite sure. Jacques was about to leave. I would have had to sing it out loud or have him play the melody on the piano.

"Let me try something . . ." I said, and hummed some notes.

"That's it, little one, you've got your bridge!" Jacques shouted.

We were so excited that we went through the song, the words, the music over and over, half a dozen times. Jacques left late but happy.

A few days later, my brothers and I put together some demos of "Ce n'était qu'un rêve" (It Was Only a Dream) and another song that Maman had written called "Grand-maman" (Grandmother).

Over the days that followed, every time one of my sisters or brothers stopped by the house, my mother had them play my song.

> *To a magic garden I did stray,*
> *And woke up one enchanted day*
> *To hear a harp and violins play.*
> *Though just a dream, so beautiful,*
> *More real than I can say.*

Naturally, my family thought Paul Levesque should be my agent. At the time, he was representing Mahogany Rush, a rock group whose guitarist, Frank Marino, was a virtuoso. A lot of people were comparing him to Jimi Hendrix. Paul was much more oriented toward this type of macho American hard rock than toward the sentimental ballads of a teenager. What's more, in Quebec there was already a girl my age, Nathalie Simard, who was singing in Montreal. She even had a television show! Paul really couldn't see how he could differentiate me from her. But he liked my voice, he thought that I knew how to sound moving, and he saw that I could put out an energy that couldn't be beat.

After a family conference, my parents signed with him. It was just before the holidays in 1980. Paul was less than thirty, but he was a responsible and meticulous man, who was very law-abiding and respectful of conventional values. He immediately began trying to find a good record company and a competent producer. But from the beginning, Paul was kind of culturally incompatible with our family, which complicated things. He was astonished, not to say horrified, by our very bohemian, artistic lifestyle.

For example, he was shocked that I often missed school without anyone at home being bothered by it. He knew the law did not permit a twelve-year-old singer to compromise her studies for her career. Personally, I wasn't interested in school. I was only hoping to be free to sing and to forget about math, geography, history, and all the rest. But Paul was worried that the school would report my repeated absences and that his agent's contract would be revoked. One day he even had a formal notice sent to my parents requiring them to send me to school regularly.

Nevertheless, in the studio he produced demos of three songs: "Chante-la ta chanson" (Sing Your Song)—a remake of the Jean Lapointe song—"Ce n'était qu'un rêve," and "Grand-maman." He sent these off to a number of record companies, with no response. He really wasn't sure what category to put me in or what I should be singing.

I don't know which of us—Paul, Maman, or Michel—had the idea of sending our demo to René Angélil. But I do know we all thought it was a good idea. Angélil was, at the time, the most important record producer in Quebec. He was Ginette Reno's agent, and she was my idol. He had produced her album *Je ne suis qu'une chanson,* with about three hundred thousand copies sold, the biggest-selling record ever in Canada. I knew all the songs on it by heart.

Paul was given the task of getting our little package to him, the demo containing all our hopes that my mother had wrapped in brown paper with a red ribbon and a little bow, like a present.

"Now just keep your fingers crossed," Maman told me. "And keep singing."

After about two weeks, there was still no news. Out of fear of missing René Angélil's call, my mother made sure that someone was in the house at all times. When she got home from work, she took over for Jacques or Ghislaine or Daniel. I was really disappointed that we hadn't heard anything, but she was furious.

"He could at least answer," she said. "He could at least be polite. If he doesn't like our songs, he should tell us why. And if he is too heartless to tell us, he should return the demo tape."

"The guy probably has other fish to fry," Ghislaine said. "He's Ginette Reno's agent. He probably doesn't have the time to listen to every demo tape he gets. Maybe he doesn't listen to any of them."

"I'd even be surprised if he was looking for new singers to represent," Claudette added.

What they said made sense. René Angélil was already the most important agent in Quebec. The gossip columns said his star, Ginette Reno, was about to hit France. She was already singing in Las Vegas and on American television. Why would Angélil want to burden himself with a second singer and get involved in a project in which everything still remained to be done?

"All he'd have to do is hear you one time, and he wouldn't think twice about taking you on," said Michel, who'd met Angélil a few times. Michel is very headstrong. Once he gets an idea in his head, there's no changing his mind. He called René Angélil's office again and again, until finally he got him on the phone. I was standing behind him and heard him say: "I know you haven't listened to the demo my sister sent you. 'Cause if you had, you would have already called us."

Angélil told my brother that he really hadn't had the time to listen to my demo, but he would do so in the next few days.

"How old's your sister?" he asked.

Michel didn't speak for a moment.

"Twelve . . ."

He knew this was no asset because Quebec already had Nathalie Simard.

"You know, don't you, that that niche in the market is taken," Angélil said.

"That doesn't make any difference," answered Michel. "My sister is twelve, but this is no little girl. She's a real singer. Listen to her and you'll see. What'll it take, ten minutes? And it could change your life, I'm telling you, it really could."

Finally, Michel hung up, turned to me, and said, "He'll call back, I know he will."

Ten minutes later, the telephone rang. Michel picked it up. "Well, didn't I tell you!" he said. Then he laughed, and, after a pause, replied, "Of course she can. Wherever and whenever you want."

He scrawled an address on the wall next to the telephone, then hung up and turned toward me.

"René Angélil wants to see you this afternoon, at two o'clock."

We didn't know it yet, but that telephone call was going to change our lives. Not only mine, but the whole family's. And René Angélil's.

*W*hen my mother had revealed the career she had mapped out for me, I knew that everything was logical, possible, sure and certain. I'd never doubted that things would happen like this, that things would be good, better than good. I was sure I had everything I needed to succeed. That I even had luck. And I was completely aware of what I wanted to do in life. Without a shadow of a doubt.

I was born into a very special environment, surrounded by adults who really took care of me. People who, above all, gave me a goal in life. As far as I'm concerned, aside from health, that's the most precious thing you can have in this world.

Ideally, school should give young people life goals and ways to attain them. But I got these things at home: a goal, the wish, and the means to reach it. For this reason, I carried a fully formed dream inside me. And I was ready to sacrifice anything or go to any extreme to achieve it. It was a dream that I hadn't created; I'd inherited it at birth. It had been conceived and carried by my mother and father, by my thirteen brothers and sisters. I had it in my blood at birth. Like the music that stays in my head. I also had a voice and an ear, which, I must admit, isn't given to everybody. For all of that, I thank God every day of my life.

My sisters Claudette and Ghislaine, my brother Michel, were singing onstage, making records, even doing a little TV. I would go to see them sing, and they were my idols. Truly. And to have known so intimately the people who were my idols would have a profound effect upon my entire life.

Most people think of their idols as unreachable, untouchable beings. I, on the other hand, saw most of my idols every day, up close. I ate with them, slept in the same room with them, played with their dresses and high heels. They took me to restaurants and stores; I went to hear them sing almost every night. They told me that one day I'd sing with them on television, at the Place des Arts, maybe even at the Olympia in Paris. They also told me about Broadway, and the big Las Vegas shows. They said we'd make records together.

So I wasn't the one who created this dream. It was my parents, my sisters and brothers, who brought it to me. And this dream, their dream, buoyed me along, like some powerful river that would carry the story of our family from one end to the other, from my father and mother, from my grandparents, my uncles and aunts, from the Dions as much as from my mother's family, the Tanguays, almost all of whom were singers or fiddlers, accordion or harmonica players.

In my mind there is no barrier or gap between the world of show business and myself. And for a long time I thought the whole world felt the same way. When I watched Ginette Reno on TV—or Aretha Franklin or Olivia Newton-John—or went to see my brother Michel or my sister Ghislaine singing at the Vieux Baril, I studied their vocal techniques, their body language. I told myself that with practice, I'd one day be able to perform as well as they did.

In the end, my goal of becoming a great singer seemed reasonable and accessible—maybe even inevitable. In other words, I believed in it. I had faith, which, I think, is as necessary as having a voice.

I also knew I had to work hard and this didn't frighten me. My brothers, sisters, father, mother, everybody around me has always worked hard. So, with understanding that only by working like a dog would I realize my dream, I began doing it with all my strength. I put all my talent, energy, charm, time, determination, will, hope, and most likely, all my ingenuousness and naïveté, into this enterprise, into this project that my mother had described for me one evening in our little kitchen. I made every sacrifice, loving it. And I was deeply happy.

I still vividly remember the first time I met René Angélil, the man who'd gradually occupy such an important place in my career, life, and heart. He wore brown shoes and a brown jacket. In the corner of his office, behind the door, there was a backgammon table, and by the window, there was a big sound system. But the story's been told so many times and by so many people that today it's hard for René, my mother, and me—who lived it—to remember all of what really happened. Each of us has his or her own version of the facts and a vision of the places.

I remember the office being kind of dark and somber. Maybe it was that kind of day outside, because there were large windows with a view of the roofs, but even so very little light entered the office. Diagonally across the street, you could see the boxlike building that was Télé-Métropole headquarters, where the television studios are. Farther on, the imposing iron structure of the Jacques-Cartier bridge looked like it had just sprung up on the city. The office smelled good, fresh.

René was standing behind his desk. He too seemed somber. He was extremely polite—"a gentleman," as my mother said. But he wasn't smiling. He asked us to sit down but he remained standing, with his back to the window. This made it hard to see his face. I remember that he seemed to address his words to my mother more than to me. He said he'd heard my demos and thought my voice was very beautiful. And then, suddenly, I felt terribly intimidated.

The man who was saying this about my voice was the same one I'd seen several times on TV or in the papers. During the sixties, René had been a big singing star with a group called the Baronets, who'd been the French version of the Beatles. I wasn't very familiar with the Baronets, who were ancient history for me. But as an agent for Quebecois artists, René Angélil was a part of the present. His wife, Anne-Renée, was also well known as a singer and a television host.

Finally, he sat down and asked me if I wanted to sing for him— right there, in his office, without music. My mother too was looking at me. There was a silence that lasted for what felt like a century. Then Maman said: "She's really not used to singing like that, without a mike."

René handed me an enormous pen and said in a very gentle voice: "Let's say that's your mike, okay?"

He still wasn't smiling. To me he seemed sad, but his voice had a soothing sweetness, very warm, very calming.

"Sing us your song, okay? Like you were singing it at the Place des Arts."

I'd done this hundreds of times in front of my bedroom mirror. But then I could see myself singing, and I had tapes for accompaniment. I'd also sung dozens of times in amateur contests and playgrounds. But I'd never sung into empty space, in front of two people, without music, in front of a sad-looking guy whom I hardly knew. I knew I just had to dive into it, start singing. There was no other choice.

I stood up and put myself in front of the office door, to get as much space in front of me as possible. My mother had to turn around to see me. I brought the pen to my lips and began singing.

To a magic garden I did stray,
And woke up one enchanted day.

All of a sudden I was feeling very good and confident.

Apparently (at least according to my mother and René), I sang as if I really were at the Place des Arts, as if I could see the audience in their chairs, and I was looking at them straight in the eye, in the orchestra, in the dress circle, the balconies. From time to time I even looked at him, at René Angélil. That I remember well. Because at one moment I saw that he had tears in his eyes. I then told myself that we had him. I'd never seen a man cry while listening to someone sing. I think that my mother too was really surprised.

When I finished, it was my turn to wait through a century of silence. René wiped his eyes. Then he said, as if we hadn't seen anything, "You made me cry."

I still didn't really know him, but I felt that that said everything.

You've got to be pretty "cool" and have a good sense of humor to be around our family without feeling hurt or scared. We really like to make fun of people. My father taught us that. When someone new turns up at our place we always put him through a kind of test. If he comes out of it unscathed, we adopt him for life.

I had watched my brothers and sisters leave home one after the other, but all of them still lived in the neighborhood, and we still played music together evenings and weekends. The first time that René set foot in our house, he was treated to a well-rehearsed parody of his old group, the Baronets. That doesn't mean we weren't proud, really honored to be visited by this man, who was known all over Quebec. We were certain that all our neighbors noticed his arrival at our door. He drove a Buick LeSabre. But since we're all a bit brazen at our place, famous or not, René had to put up with our tradition of teasing. My brothers had rehearsed one of his big hits, imitating the Baronets' voices, gestures, facial expressions. It was called "C'est fou, mais c'est tout," a faithful rendition of the Beatles' "Hold Me Tight." Luckily, René really laughed a lot when he heard this.

Then our family talked with him for a long time, about the Beatles, the Beach Boys, the rockers of the fifties and sixties. And about Elvis, of course. That first meeting told us to what degree René Angélil adored the King. He knew all of Elvis's songs by heart and sang whole verses of them with Clement and my mother, who were also great fans. He told us about going to Elvis's funeral in Memphis with Johnny Farago, whose agent he had been. At the time, Farago had made a career out of imitating Elvis. Both he and René passed themselves off as journalists for Radio Canada and were able to follow the funeral procession all the way to the cemetery, which was off-limits to the public at large.

René told all sorts of stories, with a lot of details. He could go on for hours, but we loved listening to him.

He passed our test with flying colors. From now on he was part of the family. My sisters and mother thought he was really handsome. It's true that he had magnificent eyes, and as Denise or Claudette or maybe Ghislaine said, his eyes had a "velvety look." He was always very elegant. And he had a mysterious, exotic side to him, like a quiet seducer, sure of himself.

The Dions had always lived in a tight-knit little world, peopled exclusively by French speakers, born and bred in Quebec. But René came from somewhere else, from another world. His parents were Lebanese, and he spoke several languages. In our eyes, he had an immense amount of class. For us he seemed a kind of prince in exile.

In the beginning, when he came to the house, he talked for hours about everything and nothing, except what counted for me. Then, before leaving, always discreetly, he would get serious. The first time, he had his coat on when he said to my parents: "If you put your faith in me, I can guarantee that your daughter will be an important star in Quebec and France within five years."

That evening he told us that he was no longer Ginette Reno's agent. Nobody dared to ask him what had happened. Later, we found out that she wanted to strike out on her own. And that René had been really wounded and humiliated when she left him.

One time, with one foot out the door, he told us about a lyricist that he knew, a man from France, who could write songs for me.

"He's the best," he told my mother. "He wrote for Edith Piaf, Yves Montand, Mireille Mathieu, even for Barbra Streisand. When he hears Celine, he'll write for her as well."

But in order for him to hear me, René thought we had to rerecord "Ce n'était qu'un rêve" and "Grand-maman." He said this time we would do them in a real studio, with real violins, new arrangements, and a slightly slower tempo.

He'd asked the pianist Daniel Hétu, whom we knew from television, to prepare some new orchestrations. One evening, René came to get us (my parents, Jacques, Michel, I think, and maybe Ghislaine) and took us to the Saint-Charles studio in Longueuil.

He introduced us one by one to the engineers and to Daniel Hétu, as if we were the most important people in the world. When he came to me, he told them: "Wait and hear her sing. It'll knock you out."

Sure, I was flattered, but I wished he hadn't made so much out of it. These were the best technicians (to hear René, you'd think all of us were the best of the best). They'd worked with Ginette Reno and a lot of other singers who had infinitely more experience than me.

I'd soon learn that René always had very high expectations, or should I say, expectations that are too high. It's pretty terrifying—even if it's motivating—creating for you the biggest challenges you can imagine. Telling everybody: "Listen carefully and see what I can do. You won't stop raving."

All this buildup definitely gave me the feeling that if I flopped that evening, if I "bombed" with such experienced people, maybe everything between us would come to an end. In that case, I would have only given half, a quarter of myself. But luckily I'm the type of singer who forgets everything after the first few notes and discovers an enormous confidence in herself. I let my voice go free. I don't have to push it; it just carries me.

Actually, I'm not sure anyone was truly knocked out by my performance, but I did give it my all, singing with all my strength, with restraint when it was necessary, and with confidence and heart. Today, nearly twenty years later, when I listen to that recording, I rediscover all the passion. The voice that I hear sounds awkward at times, but it's right, and it certainly has presence. Inside it there's somebody, a little girl of thirteen who wants to topple the whole world.

After this recording session, things started happening very quickly.

One evening René brought over his Frenchman, Monsieur Eddy Marnay. With them was Mia Dumont, Monsieur Marnay's "soul mate." Some of us were at the house, but I don't remember putting these particular people through a test. We were too impressed and terribly intimidated, a little worried as well.

At the time, in our world, everyone believed that all the French were contemptuous snobs who thought they knew everything about everything, when really they knew nothing about nothing. But Eddy was a refined, polite man, a type we'd never encountered before, always very considerate. Even if he spoke better French than any of us did, often using words whose meaning we vaguely knew but never used, and even if he had traveled the planet and knew the biggest stars of the century, he never looked at us with contempt or condescension.

On the contrary, Eddy was very curious about us. He asked us a thousand questions. He seemed really amazed that my parents had had fourteen children, that my father had built a house with his own hands, that my mother wrote songs, that we sang, and that all of us were musical. It wasn't long before we adopted him too. Permanently.

He was older than my parents, nearly five times my age. But he quickly became a real pal, a very dear friend, much closer to me than René was at the time.

I always enjoyed talking with Eddy. He knew how to approach me, win my trust, more easily than boys and girls of my age. I let him in on all my secrets and told him all my dreams. And everything I said to him seemed to fascinate him.

In order to write songs for me, he said he needed to know me deeply. My life as a teenager was easy enough to describe. I didn't have a boyfriend. And if sometimes I thought about love, I never connected it to the face of any of the boys I knew. I also talked a lot about my mother, who was my universe.

Sometimes he corrected me when I used verb tenses incorrectly or mixed up an adverb with an adjective. But he did this without making fun of me. Very quickly, just a few days after our first meeting, he brought us a song he'd written for me, "La Voix du bon Dieu" (The

Voice of the Good Lord). And he had me study the lyrics for several days until he was sure I really understood them.

"Never sing lyrics you don't own completely," he told me.

It even bothered him when I told him that, for years, like my sisters, I'd sung songs in English without understanding a single word.

"You shouldn't sing songs that aren't made for you, that you haven't really lived."

Like René, he told me I had a beautiful voice, and that I sang with a lot of emotion. But when we started to work seriously, he told me quite frankly that I had several bad habits I had to correct before going to a recording studio. We were alone in the living room. René was playing cards with my parents in the kitchen. I think all three of them knew what Eddy was telling me.

He explained that my voice sounded too nasal, especially some of my vowel sounds. And sometimes I used too many ornaments and arabesques, as he called them—too much decoration.

"They need to be called for and necessary," he said. "Too often you drown your words in vocalizations. To give all its meaning to a word, you've got to weigh each word carefully, think about what it contains, everything it can mean. Some words you can cry out, bite right into; others you can murmur. Some need to sound very detached. Others are only there as links between two ideas or for their sound quality."

I drank up his words. It literally demolished my interpretation of "Ce n'était qu'un rêve." And I was thrilled. He had a solution for everything, because he was there, reassuring, attentive, intelligent, in tune with me. I knew we'd go far together. He was my confidant, my counselor, my friend.

Before we went to the recording studio, he had me spend several days preparing everything in my head. Then he sang with me. His voice was unremarkable, but on-key. We went over every phrase, twenty, fifty, a hundred times. He told me where, when, and how to take a breath; where, when, how, why to pause, how to hold a word right to the end of my breath.

And we didn't notice the time passing.

*A*fter the new demos were prepared, René came to our house one day to say that he'd had the TV host Michel Jasmin listen to "Ce n'était qu'un rêve," and he'd been "knocked out" too. Jasmin was willing to do anything to have me on his talk show, the most popular in Quebec. We took advantage of the opportunity to launch my first 45—and to launch me too. In fact, this would be my first real public appearance, my first testing of the waters.

"It's the most important talk show in Canada," René told me. "A million people are going to hear you sing. Jasmin's the best, you'll see."

My mother made me a pink dress that was cinched at the waist, with puffed sleeves. Three days, or rather, three nights of work. My sister Dada found silk stockings the same color pink, but no matter how hard we looked, even in the big department stores on the rue Sainte-Catherine, we were never able to find matching shoes. Finally, Maman took an old pair of sandals and dyed them pink.

Manon did my hair and makeup, which she'd done a hundred times before, just for fun. My sister loves to do hair and makeup for people. But that day, I could tell she was nervous. She spent a lot of time making my face look right. In all honesty, my face isn't easy to do. My hair is as curly as a sheep's. And in those days it was very long. If it was badly dried or not arranged properly, it became wild. I looked like a clown!

My mother, René, and I got to the studio at Télé-Métropole at least two hours before the show was taped. René introduced us to the director, the floor manager, the cameramen, the researchers, and to the other guests. But this time he didn't tell anyone that my singing would knock them out. I was relieved but also worried. For a moment, I wondered if he'd stopped believing in me.

It was cold in the studio. When it was time to rehearse my song, I realized I was scared stiff in front of cameras. I couldn't figure out which one to look at. Luckily, René had a game plan for me to follow. I'd sing my first verse to the audience, then I'd do the refrain for the camera. Then I'd do it the opposite way round. But there wasn't any audience there yet, nothing but empty bleachers that could seat about a hundred people. And while I was singing, the cameras kept moving. When I watched myself in the monitor, I saw my profile, never full face, like I did when I sang in my bedroom mirror. I was totally disoriented. I put my best into it, I tried to concentrate, but the emptiness and the cold, black eye of the camera were terrifying.

You've got to dive right into it, René told me. Look at any camera at all and go inside it, be there. Tell yourself that through its lens you're talking to your mother and she's listening to you. And that she loves you.

I was afraid I'd forget my words, or that my voice would get shaky, or I'd dissolve into tears. I imagined myself running out of the studio. That would mean curtains for my career as a famous singer.

For good luck I wanted to knock on wood—something René often did. But I couldn't see anything wooden in the studio. René looked for some with me. Finally, he found the pipe of one of the guests, Fernand Gignac, in an ashtry. He asked him what it was made of.

"Briar," said Monsieur Gignac.

"Go ahead, it's wood," René told me.

I touched Fernand Gignac's pipe, and it reassured me a little.

When Michel Jasmin introduced me to the audience, I was standing in the shadows, shaking. René was behind me, his head very close to mine. And he said: "Go ahead, show them you're the best."

It was like diving into empty space. I couldn't see anything. I walked onstage as if everything were about to collapse around me.

But as usual, as soon as I started to sing, my stage fright disappeared. I felt really good. I stared right at the camera, aware that, through it, at least a million people were watching and listening to me. From time to time, I looked at the audience filling the studio. In the shadows I could see my father, my mother, my brothers with their wives, my sisters with their husbands, all watching me, loving me. And at times, I felt as if they were all singing in chorus with me.

As soon as the song ended, my fear returned fast and furious. Singing I knew. It was as natural as breathing. But answering the questions of a TV host, that was another challenge. Suddenly I realized I had nothing to talk about other than my love of singing. And that I wanted to do it all my life. Nothing else. It seemed a little too short to me.

Michel Jasmin mentioned my age, thirteen, and said my mother and brother had written the song I'd sung. He congratulated me warmly, complimenting me on my voice and politely asking if I planned to take singing lessons. I appeared astonished by the question and answered it rather abruptly, as if it were obvious that I didn't need any lessons.

I don't know why I answered like that. I was happy with my performance and my victory over stage fright, but I was well aware, as was Eddy, that I still had a lot of things to learn. My answer must have seemed ridiculously pretentious.

But I so wanted to become a great singer that I'd begun to think I had everything I needed to do so. I believed so strongly in myself that modesty seemed to disappear as soon as the subject was my voice.

Today I realize that unlike Eddy, René encouraged that attitude in me, and I don't think he was shocked or bothered by what I'd said to

Michel Jasmin. Although later he did want me to take voice lessons, he always pushed me to say loud and clear that I could knock everybody out.

"If you want to go far, you have to know what you can do and you have to tell it to the world. That way, you've got no other choice but to do it." That's what he thought.

A few hours after the TV-show taping, I watched the broadcast in my parents' living room, surrounded by my brothers and sisters. When I sang, it worked. But I utterly hated the interview. I did sound pretentious. And if there's one thing on this earth that I really hate, it's people who know it all, who've never been afraid, who have opinions on everything and think they have nothing to learn from anybody.

I have no memory of René's reaction. I don't even remember if he was in the room with us. However, I do remember that in the days that followed, at his office, I had to endure again and again the painful ordeal of watching myself sing and spout my idiocies to Michel Jasmin.

René wasn't judgmental about it. He didn't comment, except on the way I held the mike too high in front of my mouth and passed it back and forth from one hand to the other. Two little habits I had to get rid of.

What he really wanted was for me to get used to seeing myself and to become comfortable with looking at myself—as if I were a part of the audience. It isn't easy to do this. But you really have to. For years, René put me through this exercise every time I went on TV. I had to envision the broadcast and watch myself singing, which was more terrifying for me than facing big audiences. If certain things seemed like a disaster to me, I quickly corrected them and didn't think about them anymore. I've developed the ability not to keep endlessly looking back. I don't hold on to useless regrets.

Several times over the summer I sang the national anthems at the beginning of baseball games at the Olympic stadium in Montreal.

The emcee announced that "O Canada" and the "Stars and Stripes" would be performed by a young girl of thirteen.

"*Mesdames et messieurs,* ladies and gentlemen: Celine Dion."

Mike in hand, I ran right up to the pitcher's mound, and in front of the crowd and the television cameras, wearing the uniform of the Montreal Expos, I launched into the anthems. The next day, I watched myself five, six times. Without comment.

That summer, the best one of my life, we put together two albums: one of original songs written by Maman and Eddy, and one of Christmas songs. I remember every recording session as a real celebration.

At the end of the day, René came by to take my mother and me, and sometimes my father as well, to the Saint-Charles studio. René always invited a lot of other people—his cousin Paul Sara, his friends Marc Verreault, Ben Kaye, Jacques Des Marais, several others, people from the industry and the media. Sometimes he brought along his children, and his wife, Anne-Renée. Eddy and Mia were there, too. And with several of my brothers and sisters, their children, their friends, the control room was ready to burst with all these people who watched us working, sometimes until the wee hours of the morning. In the middle of the night, we had pizza or Chinese food delivered. One day René decreed that people who wanted to smoke had to go out to the parking lot. At the time, Maman smoked, as did my father and several of my brothers and sisters. But I didn't like seeing Maman smoke. I never liked the way cigarettes smelled.

On the days I didn't sing, I went shopping either with my sisters, Anne-Renée, or Mia. René had given Mia the responsibility of teaching me how to create a look for the album photos.

I've always loved fashion. When I was little, I watched my mother sew and knit. I cut out patterns from magazines, I designed dresses and coats for myself. And I had fun dressing up in the clothes and high-heeled shoes of my sisters. For my birthday and other holidays,

Claudette, my godmother, always bought something to wear. My sisters Dada and Liette often took me shopping with her.

With the very first money I had earned as a singer, in the summer of 1981, at thirteen, I bought some high heels, made out of black patent leather. My passion for shoes had only begun. For me they're jewels, the indispensable accessory to complete an outfit. Although I haven't counted, I must have more than a thousand pairs today.

My collection includes everything—candy-pink rain boots, shoes with feathers and sequins, wooden clogs, alligator-skin bootees, other footwear in plastic. And of course, I have a lot of high-heeled shoes that are very chic, in every possible and impossible color, even transparent and fluorescent. And I've worn them all at least once, even the ones that hurt my feet. I don't know where I got this obsession from. I just know that the moment I walk into a shoe store I'm not altogether myself. And I can behave in ways that are completely irrational. Several times, I've bought the same shoe in every available color. Then, when I get home, I realize that what I did was crazy, disturbingly so. And then one day I told myself that perhaps this was my only quirk. In every aspect of my professional life, I have to control my emotions to the maximum, all my impulses, my feelings. It's part of my profession. I've got to be extremely reasonable and disciplined about all that I do. Why, then, should I deny myself this harmless quirk that doesn't hurt anybody and doesn't harm my career in any way? Wherever I go, I look at the shoes of all the women I meet. The men too, although with them the universe of shoes seems less rich and less changing. With women the choice is limitless. And in this regard, all women are equal. Thin or fat, young or old, we all have a vast number of choices every time we go out, every moment of the day.

In my early days, I liked bright flashy clothes, frilly stuff. If my look had been left up to me alone, I'm sure I would have rigged myself out like a flamboyant rock star or like an aging vamp, with a boa, a long skirt slit high up the thigh, and high heels. Whenever I was with Dada, we always seemed to find something hilarious or provocative—I'd say almost sinful—about the outfits I chose, or that I would have liked to choose if I'd had the money.

I dreamed of seeing myself walking the runway like a model. I'd imagine myself singing as I descended the great staircase of a music hall, wearing a sumptuous dress that was all feathers and sequins. I guess every young girl has dreamed of that at one time or another. But keeping up with fashion costs a lot more money than we were used to having.

But that summer, really for the first time, we had quite a bit. To me, anyway, it seemed as if we were rolling in money. René always paid for everything—the studio, the taxis, the restaurants, even for the meals ordered in the middle of the night for the engineers and the audience at the recording studio. He was also going to pay for my look, for the photo session, the launching, etc.

But the point wasn't to do clothes and hair for laughs or to shock people. Mia, whom René trusted absolutely, explained to me how important it was that the first images of me presented to the public be right. She reminded me of the major themes of Eddy's songs.

"Your clothes have to match what your songs are saying," she said. "They've got to be in line with the story of a very young girl discovering life, asking herself about love, telling us about her grandmother, her dreams. It's a nice sweet girl who's only thirteen years old."

I might have been disappointed that I wasn't going to be flashier, but it didn't last long. As soon as I began working with Mia on the look I'd have on the album, I got really involved. I understood the logic of it. I also had confidence in Mia and René. So did my mother.

However, there was a problem. When I posed for the album photos, I refused to laugh or even smile, because I didn't want my teeth to show. My teeth were so long and prominent that even with my mouth closed, they hung over the corners of my upper lip. No one else in the family had teeth like that, not even my parents, from what I can tell from the photos of them in their youth. It's a distinction I would gladly have done without. For school photos I had gotten into the habit of keeping my mouth shut over my problem.

Whenever I had to smile–as I did for the album cover photo—I opened my lips as little as possible. In addition, the photographer created very soft lighting that considerably decreased the bumps my teeth made on my lips.

I remember the launch of that album more clearly than any other that followed. Probably because it was the first. But also because the journalists didn't really seek me out. At promotional appearances, after I sang "Ce n'était qu'un rêve" and "La Voix du bon Dieu," they all went to interview René and Eddy, as if I had nothing to say. Which was probably the case. I still didn't know how to speak to journalists. Or else they didn't know how to ask me the right questions. Even though I had the voice of an adult, I was barely a teenager. I guess they were taken aback by the discrepancy.

Eddy spoke to them about my voice, my spirit, my sense of discipline, and my family. Other than my mother, of course, he was the person who knew me best in the world.

Eddy was the first person, even before my mother and my sisters, to know that I'd kissed a boy. His name was Sylvain. It had happened on the porch at my sister Claudette's house in Lachenaie. It was a real kiss, not a long one, but I got very worked up about it. This was because, afterward, I couldn't manage to identify what I had been feeling. I didn't wonder if *he* loved me, but if *I* was in love. Besides, I wouldn't have understood it even if he had loved me. I didn't think I was very attractive.

Later, he brought me to the basement of his parents' place, where he spent hours playing Nintendo while I thumbed through hunting and fishing magazines, which couldn't have interested me less. And we never kissed again. We ended up almost not speaking.

That one kiss made me very mixed up. I probed my heart, I wanted to understand, to put my feelings in order. But the more I thought about it, the more confused I got.

When Eddy asked me one day if I was attracted to Sylvain, I realized I wasn't. And I began to cry. I so much wanted to love a boy. Even a boy who didn't love me back. Especially one who didn't love me back. But I had too many projects going to spend much time on a flirtation. I simply wanted to be in love.

Two or three days after this conversation with Eddy, when I went back to school, my mother told me that Eddy had phoned. He'd just written a new song for me. It was called "D'Amour ou d'amitié" (Lovers or Friends). When I read the lyrics, I cried again, a lot, because they were so close to me. It was almost as if Eddy had plucked them out of my heart.

And I am like an island
In the middle of the ocean.
You'd say that my heart
Is just too big.

These words were tailor-made for me. This was me, my story, the story of a teenage girl dreaming of falling in love. But apart from the love of my family, there wasn't any of that kind of love around me or in me. No great love possible. I was alone. And for a long time, I believed that I'd always be alone, my entire life. I told myself that perhaps love had forgotten me. This made me very sad, and I cultivated that sadness, pampered it, and when I sang, it passed into my voice.

At the same time, I had some great reasons to be happy. My life was changing. I knew that big things were in store for me.

3

*L*ess than a year after appearing on Michel Jasmin's show, I already had two albums out and was working on a third. I'd been on television about a dozen times. And I went on tour with the strangest show I'd ever been part of in all my life, almost a circus act.

A bunch of artists were in the show, all a lot older than me. There was Plastic Bertrand, a semi-punk rocker who was really outrageous, a real scream, and Nanette Workman, a super rock performer. They all had a lot of stage experience and knew how to stir up the crowd. My little rosewater ballads were at the opposite end of the spectrum from what they were doing. There was a world between "Ce n'était qu'un rêve" and "Lady Marmalade" (with its lyric *"Voulez-vous coucher avec moi, ce soir?"*), between "D'Amour ou d'amitié" and the rantings of Plastic. In other words, I was kind of out of place. My two albums had been selling well, but certainly not to the audience attracted by this tour.

"It's perfect," René told my mother. "She'll learn to look out for herself."

Each evening, before I went onstage, René was behind me, telling me I was the best and that I had to knock them out, as per his favorite expression, which meant I had really to get them to notice me. But the others had just finished their heavy-duty rock and roll when it was my turn. One evening, I turned to him and said: "Nanette's already knocked them out."

"Not me, she hasn't, Celine. I'm waiting for *you* to knock me out. I know you can do it."

For the first time, I sang for him. He joined the crowd just below the stage, staying where I could see him easily. But I didn't really look at him until toward the end of my song. I knew that I'd really moved him, even if half the crowd wasn't listening. I knew I'd sung like I'd never sung before, that I'd surpassed myself. And he knew it too. I think even the crowd was surprised.

"You made me cry," he told me when he found me backstage.

I didn't do all the shows during that tour. Halfway through the summer, Maman, Anne-Renée, René, and I left for Paris. I was going to record the first songs of my third album there. First the one I loved so much, "D'Amour ou d'amitié," also "Visa pour les beaux jours" (A Visa for the Beautiful Days) and another one that Eddy had written for Maman called "Tellement j'ai d'amour pour toi" (I Have So Much Love for You).

At least twenty-five of my family members—brothers, sisters, brothers-in-law, sisters-in-law—went to the Mirabel airport to see us off. Eddy and Mia were waiting for us in Paris with some friends of René's, Guy and Dodo Morali, who had a restaurant on the rue Cadet in the heart of Paris.

René hadn't ever really spoken much about his plans for me, but that evening on the plane to Paris, he spent a long time explaining that the French hadn't wanted my first album because they thought it wasn't commercial enough. I reminded them too much of Mireille Mathieu, a singer who also had a strong voice and came from a large family.

"That's why we're going to work over there in their studios, with their technicians, their producers, to get some idea of what they want," he said.

But a few days after we arrived in Paris, when René told me to take some diction and singing lessons, he informed me that the executives at Pathé-Marconi, our production company, thought not only that my recent albums weren't to the taste of the French, but also, most important, my voice had some flaws that needed correcting.

I figured that both Eddy and René, who were in agreement with the French producers, thought I sang badly. It really bothered me. But I made a point of not letting it show.

Eddy knew an elderly lady named Tosca Marmor, who had been teaching singers and opera singers for a half century. He took me to meet her, and then left, telling me he'd return to get me in an hour.

Deep down inside myself, I thought the old lady would be impressed by my voice and would say I didn't need lessons. But that's not, in fact, what happened.

The first session was pretty trying. Madame Tosca sat down at the piano and made me do scales for at least a half hour. Then she asked me to sing the same phrase for another half hour.

She made no comments, either positive or negative, nor did she show any emotion. As soon as I'd finished, she said: "Please begin again."

I did.

"Louder, more emphasis, please."

I sang louder, with more emphasis. No reaction. She merely seemed a little bored. I no longer knew if I was supposed to sing louder, lower, or higher.

I left there pretty worried and began asking myself questions about my voice, about what I'd been doing with her. It took some time for me to realize that I'd just had one of the most important lessons of my whole life.

I guess René and Eddy thought I was mature enough to handle this little trial. I still don't know if it was a deliberate strategy on their part. But I do know that my ego suffered quite a blow that summer. I was shattered and was no longer as sure of myself. I prayed that something positive would come out of this ordeal. I hate boxing and don't know much about it, but I do know that they say a boxer never comes into his own until he's been knocked out once or twice.

I found Tosca to be a fantastic, intelligent woman, very generous and attentive to others. I don't know what Eddy had asked of her, but she taught me a lot. Among other things, she taught me that I still didn't have enough of the tools and skills to become a great singer— far from it. I also learned that it wasn't enough to have a powerful voice, a big register, and vocal cords of steel. You have to find the emotion somewhere within you. And that can be a terrifying, painful experience. As much as Tosca upset me, she ultimately helped me attain a great sense of peace, and this helped me as I went into the studio.

Madame Tosca taught me not to be afraid of my emotions, even those I didn't understand.

"Don't let them take you over," she told me. "And don't be afraid of them. You have to tame them, become their master, make them serve you."

As our sessions continued, I would bring her flowers. Some days, all we did was talk—about the pleasure and the pain of singing.

Almost every evening while we were in Paris, we ended up at Guy and Dodo's, where we listened again and again to the recordings we'd made during the day. One evening, for laughs, we listened to old records by the Baronets that René had given to Guy, and to the Scorpions, the group Guy had belonged to in his youth.

The Family Song studio was very small, but always filled to bursting, like the Saint-Charles studio in Montreal. The musicians who'd made the orchestra tracks were there, as were the arranger and the composer. People from Pathé-Marconi were there, and sometimes a photographer, and friends of Eddy or Mia, French people, Quebecois passing through Paris, a lot of people who apparently didn't have anything to do at this studio.

"If that bothers you, we can leave you alone," Eddy told me.

I was preparing the recording of "Tellement j'ai d'amour pour toi," a very intimate song. But the presence of all these people didn't bother me at all. In fact, it reassured me, stimulated me. A lot of artists prefer to sing behind a screen, in the kind of booth where no one can see them. Not me. Not then and not today.

I stood right in the middle of the studio. I looked in the crowd for the face of my mother, pressed against the booth window, and I sang for her.

Time has its way
On your hair of gray,
But a child I'll stay
To my very last day.
I have so much love for you.

I know my mother well, and she doesn't cry easily. To spare others embarrassment, she keeps everything inside. René and I are big weepers, but not her. But it was clear she was very moved, proud of me, glad, happy about the path we'd taken.

After the second take, there was a short silence, then everyone in the studio applauded and shouted so loud that the sound reached me in the booth. And I applauded too, and burst out laughing. Something magical had happened, something bigger than all of us. It seemed to me that for a moment, we were all very happy together in that little studio. Even the people who had nothing to do there.

In spring, I finished my seventh year of school. I'd missed a lot of courses on a regular basis, and every time I went there, I noticed without much emotion how far I'd fallen behind. I quickly saw that I could never catch up with the others.

Once I'd realized that, I was somewhere else, on another planet. I made up little movies in my head. I returned again to deepest Africa or to the Amazon. Sometimes I also told myself really sad love stories or morbid, melodramatic romances that brought me to the edge of tears. But most often, I imagined myself as a star of show business and the movies. My name on giant billboards, opening nights, evening gowns, thunderous applause.

I wrote the stories, did the direction, costumes, scenery, dialogue. And I always had the starring role, usually playing a girl who looked like a sister of the heroine of *Flashdance*. I'd seen that movie at least five or six times, alone or with Manon, Dada, or Pauline, at a theater in downtown Montreal.

Flashdance is the story of a girl who dreams of dancing in a big Broadway show, but because she's poor and has to work hard to earn a living, she's never been able to go to a legitimate school of dance. She's had to learn on her own, all alone. To dance. And to fight. At every theater she goes to, they look down on her because she doesn't know anybody. And she never passes an audition.

One day, by chance, she meets an old lady who used to be a prima ballerina in a classical troupe. The woman sees her dance and tells her that she has a lot of talent and that she'll find the strength to realize her dream in herself and not somewhere else. She tells her never to let others impose their vision on her. And above all, never to give up her great dream. The girl never gives up, and at the end of the movie she wins a place at an elite dance school.

I loved everything in this film, beginning with the music and the song "What a Feeling." I'd learned it by heart, to Eddy's distaste, and promised myself that one day I'd sing it on tour. But above all, I adored the story of *Flashdance.* I took the old lady's advice to heart. I told myself that I no longer needed to go to school to succeed in life. I was convinced that my dream wouldn't happen through school. Fortunately, I didn't have to insist for very long before my mother let me skip school, especially if I had to rehearse a new song by Eddy or if I had a show that evening . . . or even the next day.

My mother never said it, but I'm convinced she believed I could learn everything as well at home as I could at school. She had been born in a town in the remotest part of the Gaspé peninsula, and had learned to read, write, and count with her mother and her elder sisters as her teachers. She wouldn't really say it out loud, but I'm sure she believed that when it comes to education your best teachers are yourself and those you're close to. I'd even go so far as to say that she had more respect for self-taught and self-made people than for people with a lot of diplomas.

Boys and girls at the school, and a few teachers, told me from time to time that they'd seen me on TV or in the newspapers or that they'd heard one of my songs on the radio. Some of them even asked me for my autograph. Everybody was super nice with me. I loved it. But I didn't really feel at home. And I never tried to make friends because I knew that I'd only be there for a little while.

The world has changed a lot since I was a teenager. Except for very rare exceptions, I don't believe that you can get by and feel good about yourself without an education. I'm also convinced that there's a lot of pleasure in learning and knowing a lot of things—how the world works, history, geography, art history, all that. And these days, I love to learn about new things. But when I was a teenager, I had other fish to fry.

At the Saint-Charles studio, I was finishing recording the final songs for my new album, which would be launched in the fall. René spoke about organizing a big promotional tour throughout the province of Quebec. But things turned out very differently, even more different than René had imagined in his wildest dreams. In fact, during the next few months, two important events—one in Japan, the other in France—were going to change my life.

One evening, maybe a month after school started, at suppertime, Eddy Marnay phoned from Paris. He told us that "Tellement j'ai d'amour pour toi" had just been chosen to represent France in a major international competition in Japan at the end of October.

I think I sounded very stupid on the telephone. In those days, when something very big and exciting happened in my life, I literally froze. Everyone around me could be jumping up and down but I stayed cool and calm, even though I was at the center of the whirlwind.

"Are you happy, Celine?" Maman asked.

"Sure I'm happy."

"You don't seem to be."

I don't think I know how to express my joy. Or I'm afraid that if I let myself go, I won't be able to control myself and I'll explode. Eddy couldn't have understood this because he himself was so overwhelmed with joy. He'd just pulled off a major coup in getting his song into the festival in Tokyo. Meanwhile, there I was cold as ice on the other end of the line. Still, Maman realized that something important was happening. She told me to let her speak to Eddy and asked him a thousand questions.

She congratulated him, shouted and laughed. She told him that of course I would be there, and she'd go with me. Then Maman added that I thanked him and that I was happy, even if I didn't know how to show my joy.

She'd just hung up and was getting ready to call my brothers and sisters to tell them the news when the telephone rang again. It was René. He had all the details, the exact dates, the number of songs that had been submitted (more than a thousand, if I remember correctly), the number of songs in the finals (about thirty), the list of participating countries, the names of the winners from previous years.

He asked to speak to me. First to tell me that the Yamaha World Festival of Popular Song was the most important event of its kind in the world. That he'd gone to it a few years back with René Simard, who was then about my age, and who'd won the grand prize. Afterward he had become an enormous star in Quebec. Even *Time* magazine had talked about him.

"Frank Sinatra was the one who handed him his prize," René told me. "And I was there. Do you realize, I shook the hand of Frank Sinatra? . . ."

Then he began to speak to me in a low voice, as if he were sharing a very important secret, very intimately, as if he and I were all alone in the world.

"I know you're the best singer who'll be over there. And you know you'll win first prize—you do, don't you?"

I'd always loved his velvety voice, so calm and gentle, but that night he really shook me up. Not only because of what he was saying but because of his tone, which sounded close enough for me to feel his breath against my ear. It was an incredible moment of intimacy.

In an even lower, gentler tone, he told me: "It'll change our life, Celine, you'll see."

Our life!

*S*o I had to stop going to school.

"We don't have any choice," René told me, as if he were announcing bad news.

He came with my mother and me to see the school principal to explain to him that I couldn't take regular courses because I had a "career" that was too demanding. I say "explain" because I'm certain that in René Angélil's head there was never any question of asking permission. Out of politeness, he simply wanted the principal to know that I wasn't coming back. And he wanted him to know why and to be in agreement as much as was possible.

He asked him to prepare a special program of studies for me. He said he would be personally responsible for my following this program and passing the examinations of the Quebec Department of Education. He also spoke about my mother. He said she'd always be by my side, that she was an incredible, intelligent woman who'd raised fourteen children. She too would oversee the education and studies of her daughter.

Feeling very intimidated, I was seated a little off to the side on a small, straight-backed chair. Actually, I was only pretending to be intimidated. I was hearing René say that the experiences that I was living were at least as rich in instructional value as the courses I could take at school. As usual, he spoke quite calmly and gently. He was saying that I had engagements not only in France and throughout Canada, but also in Japan.

"And she has an accountant, lyricists, composers and arrangers, a lot of people working for her," he was saying. "All these trips she's taking and people she's meeting are certainly as valuable as the geography courses and history or economics courses that your school offers. Surely you agree with that, Monsieur le Principal."

He even said that I was very intelligent, that he'd seen me learn songs by heart—words and music—in just a few minutes.

Listening to him, I could barely contain my happiness. For the first time, René was paying some attention not only to the singer he was managing but also to the girl I was.

He was saying that though all the boys and girls in my class had spent the summer in Charlemagne or its environs watching TV or working on a farm or at McDonald's, I'd gone to Paris, where I'd recorded an album with established artists, that I'd sung on a dozen stages throughout Quebec and met journalists, that my songs were played on the radio.

"You do understand me, don't you, Monsieur le Principal?"

He even told him that I earned more money in a month than my father made in a whole year.

I was overwhelmed and, of course, flattered by his words. I was sure that René knew how to convince the principal to let me leave. And that I'd never set foot in school again.

Meanwhile, I did my Little Miss Perfection routine, being very well mannered on my straight little chair with my eyes lowered.

But when the principal took out my school records and held out my report card to René, I thought of running away. I probably had the worst marks in the class, in the whole history of this school, almost all below average, near failing.

What would René think of my performance in school? He was so intelligent and well educated, he spoke English as well as he spoke French, probably he knew math, history, and geography. One look at my report card and he'd conclude that his little singer was not very intelligent. I was deeply humiliated.

But at the same time, I was jubilant. I was finally getting out of school. I wouldn't even have any friends to miss. The only pleasant memories I could keep were those times Mademoiselle Senechal had asked me to clean the blackboard after class. I wiped that blackboard with intense concentration until there wasn't a single trace of chalk left on it. Sometimes Mademoiselle Senechal took advantage of this situation to review with me the various lessons we were studying. I tried my best to repeat them, but I never could understand how these things could help me in real life.

René didn't even open my report card. Today I know him. I know that once he's made up his mind about something, he goes right for it; and anyone who wants to change his mind had better get up pretty early in the morning and had better have some very good arguments. In the principal's office, he'd weighed all the pros and cons. And he was taking action. He wasn't there to find out about my academic performance or even to learn the principal's opinion of me. He was there to take me out of school. And this is exactly what he did.

And *that's* how I finally became a studious and hardworking young girl!

René never pestered me to follow the education department's study program. But he was determined to teach me show business: the methodology of show business, the history of show business, the geography and economics of show business. For hours, especially when we were touring, in his car, at the restaurant, he'd pick up the story of Colonel Parker and Elvis Presley again, the Beatles and Brian Epstein. He told me the legend of Edith Piaf; the legend of the "French Elvis," Johnny Halliday; of Barbra Streisand. He described all the good and bad shows that he'd seen in Las Vegas or on Broadway.

I became the most studious little girl in the world. He took me to every show that passed through Montreal. He said that this was part of my work, my homework. I saw Ginette Reno quite often, Stevie Wonder, Nana Mouskouri, Manhattan Transfer, Anita Baker, Liza Minnelli; French stars Yves Montand, Michel Sardou, and Julien Clerc; Julio Iglesias; the Stones; McCartney; Metallica . . . My mother went with us quite often.

We had to leave for Japan at least a week before the festival so that I could rest after the trip and wouldn't be too affected by jet lag. Mia and Ben Kaye went with us.

Mia, as my enlightened advisor, knew all the rules—of etiquette, good taste, dress, behavior. She always knew what to say, how to react, what to wear, for every circumstance.

Ben Kaye had been the agent for the Baronets. He was fearless, and what's more, he had a terrific sense of humor. One of his most amazing stunts consisted of forming a chorus with everyone who happened to be in a particular restaurant. He had them all sing, even the waiters, even the people who at first didn't want anything to do with it. If they refused to sing, he'd have them make noises with their mouths or play percussion. The result was tremendous. I'd seen him at work in restaurants in Montreal. I knew he was capable of doing the same kind of things in Tokyo.

Eddy was going to come directly from Paris. But two days before his departure, Mia informed us that he'd hurt his back badly. He'd been to see a doctor, a chiropractor, and an acupuncturist. Nothing and no one had succeeded in providing any relief. The next day it was worse, and he was practically incapable of walking. Mia went to stay with him in Paris. Now only four of us were going: René, Maman, Ben, and me.

Out of the four, I think my mother was the most excited. She'd always dreamed of taking big trips, and here finally was her chance. She'd sleep in luxury hotels, visit exotic locales; she'd have a lot of people doing her bidding, guides, interpreters, chauffeurs, chambermaids; she'd see her daughter sing—or "triumph," as René put it—before an immense audience.

"I really don't know if I deserve all of this," she told me the night before we left for Tokyo.

The next day, just before boarding the plane, she turned toward my brother Paul and held out her pack of cigarettes.

"You can smoke them, give them away, or throw them out; I don't want them anymore. I'll never smoke again in my life."

Once on board the plane, she explained to us that by this gesture, she was trying to "deserve the trip."

I never saw her smoke again. And I never heard her complain about missing her cigarettes. Throughout the trip, René didn't stop congratulating her. He'd never dared tell her that her cigarette smoke could be harmful to my voice. But starting that day, he began to control my environment more and more strictly. Smokers were banished, even Papa, who quickly got the idea and took up the habit of smoking his cigarettes outside, under the veranda, when I was at the house.

Often, very often, I've thought of the symbolic gesture that my mother made on that day—and about her idea that we have to deserve what happens to us. And I want to believe that she's right. Certainly, chance favors some people and not others. Then too there is talent, gifts that heaven makes to some and not to others. So I must—and must always—deserve the voice that God has given me.

I've always been very disciplined. I fulfilled all my obligations as a singer, and every day I practiced and did my singing exercises with all the application I'm capable of. Without cheating, I followed all the regimens I was given, staying silent for long periods to rest my voice. I never broke the rules, not even for one day or one hour. If I had done so, I would have been practically incapable of going onstage, I would have been too afraid that my voice would become hoarse.

This kind of concern and unwavering dedication comes from my mother. She knew it instinctively. Or perhaps because she had been raised as a Catholic. It doesn't matter how. Today, for me, it's an absolute truth, which doesn't come from instinct but from reason: What we don't deserve, we have no right to; it doesn't belong to us.

In Tokyo, I was still too young, I think, to become preoccupied with such thoughts. I was impressed by what was happening, of course. And I also had moments of stage fright. But I probably didn't really understand this need of my mother to "deserve" what was happening to her, all the joy and happiness. In Tokyo, I merely wanted to knock them out.

The Yamaha festival lasted several days; the finals were Friday and Saturday and the grand finale would be on television Sunday. It took place in an amphitheater where I've since sung several times. It's called the Budokan; it holds about twelve thousand people and is located in a magnificent park near the Imperial Palace. You're in the heart of the city, yet everything is peaceful, even the crowd, which is very well behaved, quite different from the excited crowds I'd been part of at the Forum in Montreal, for example, when I'd gone to see Olivia Newton-John or Elton John.

In order to determine the order of the performances, each participant has to pick a number at random. On Friday morning, I ended up with five. Our interpreter told me that the word for this in Japanese is *go*. René, who has always loved omens and coincidences, was thrilled.

I sang well, without forcing my voice, though I performed a little distractedly. For the first time in my life, I found myself on an unbelievably vast stage in front of an enormous audience. I was accompanied by a large orchestra of more than fifty musicians with whom I'd rehearsed for only about ten minutes. I felt a little out of place and disoriented. I didn't know where to look, and I couldn't hear myself very well. It took me a while to gain full control of my voice.

But as I left the stage at the end of my song, I heard the applause of the crowd, which seemed more intense than it had been for the two boys who had come before me. However, some of the participants who followed were given applause just as loud as I had, if not louder. I started thinking that there was a good chance I'd be eliminated before the grand finale.

On Saturday afternoon, after the last competition, the judges announced the names of the ten people who'd be in the grand finale on Sunday afternoon.

I was one of them. This time, I ended up with number five again—*go*. And this time again we looked at it as a good omen. But I was still very nervous.

In addition to the twelve thousand spectators who filled the Budokan Sunday afternoon, there were several million watching the event on television. Reason enough to feel weak in the knees.

Waves of anguish washed over me as I thought of the moment when I'd have to go onstage and launch into my song. I imagined the crowd I'd have to face as a heartless monster capable of devouring me. And I tried to forget, to tell myself that this wasn't so important, that I'd survive very well without taking home first prize.

René didn't try at all to convince me that I had no reason to be afraid. On the contrary, he kept telling me that this was a crucial, decisive moment in my life, that the monster I was about to face was terrible. He knew it was. But he added that I had no choice, that I had to win.

Instead of diminishing this monster, as I'd been trying to do, he told me that I was strong, determined, capable of facing it. When he spoke to me, I really felt like a great person, a real professional. That evening I went to bed convinced that once I got onstage I'd know how to master my voice. And tame the monster. Maybe even knock it out.

The next afternoon, while waiting my turn to sing, I remained standing in the wings so that I wouldn't crease my dress. It was white and made of heavy cotton by Josiane Moreau, my stylist at the time, who used a pattern Maman and I found in a magazine. It was magnificent, but a little out of season. We'd both imagined that Japan was a warm country, that the climate was like July in Quebec all year long.

Right at the foot of the stairs leading to the stage, and right at the moment when the announcer spoke my name, I saw something on the floor that at first I thought was a medal, but was actually a coin. I picked it up. When I saw that the number five—*go*—was engraved on it, I decided to keep it. For good luck. My dress had no pocket, so I slid the coin into the side of my shoe. As I walked under the lights to sing "Tellement j'ai d'amour pour toi," I felt it sliding under the arch of my foot. It would be my good-luck charm; I knew it. I would keep it with me always. From now on, five would be my lucky number. I was sure of it; thanks to the coin I was going to win first prize.

What I'd seen the previous night and the next morning as a horrible monster—the judges, the crowd, cameras, millions of television viewers—now seemed like a warm, friendly presence.

When the awards were announced, I tied for first place with the Mexican singer Yoshio. The musicians, who also voted, awarded me the special orchestra prize. Before I rehearsed with them on Friday afternoon, René told me to greet them and thank them, and if possible to shake hands with the conductor and the pianist as well as the first violinist. I think they really appreciated those polite gestures.

I cried a lot. On the stage, in front of the audience at the Budokan and the Japanese television viewers. Then in the wings, I found René too crying as though his heart would break. And Maman and Ben.

Our interpreter and the Japanese people around us looked like they were in shock. I don't think they were used to seeing such public displays of emotion. Out of propriety, they turned away and withdrew. The four of us stayed hugging each other and crying for quite a while.

Then, as if he'd suddenly come to, René took my hand and led me into the auditorium, in front of the stage. A telephone was placed on a pillow between two monitors. He handed me the receiver.

"It's for you."

It was Eddy and Mia in Paris, where it was dawn; they'd watched me sing "Tellement j'ai d'amour pour toi" and then heard the president of the jury announce the name of the winners. René and Ben had had this telephone installed by the organizers of the festival. This time, I knew just how to express my joy. And I gave Eddy something to celebrate by telling him how much I loved him and how much I owed him. Mia, as well. Of course I kept crying and crying. This time I knew that I deserved my happiness.

Maman and I had promised René that if I won the Yamaha first prize, we'd eat raw fish.

It had happened on board the plane. The passengers had been given a choice between a Western meal—beef, pasta, or chicken—and some Japanese dishes. Without hesitation, both of us chose the chicken. But as was to be expected, because that was always what he did, René tried to convince us to try the Japanese dishes. He was convinced of it: "Just taste it and you'll love it," he said.

"Not on board an airplane," Maman answered.

Maman loved cooking for people. And René really liked her pies, pastas, chopped steaks, and meat loafs, but we knew that they were never spicy enough for his taste. He always wanted marinades, spices. And there wasn't enough variety, either.

René always wanted everybody around him to like what he liked:

gambling, exotic cuisine, Elvis, the Beatles, Coca-Cola. He was always trying to convert his friends. At every chance that presented itself in Montreal or Paris, he took us to Lebanese or Moroccan restaurants. He had us try everything—falafel, babaganoush, hummus, shwarma.

So while he ate his sushi and sashimi, he extracted that promise from us. I had to eat raw fish.

I'd have the occasion to do so a few days later. Since I'd won the festival, I'd been invited to sing at a big gala for high officials and ministers of the Japanese government. At the banquet that followed, I was sitting at the table of honor, as were my mother and René, but I wasn't next to them. As soon as he could, René made a sign to me by raising a piece of raw fish between his chopsticks, as if to say: "It's now or never."

I had to keep my promise. I'd already managed to swallow a heavily flavored soup when the worst arrived: slices of raw fish on little balls of rice—sushi—which delighted my tablemates. There was also a small bowl of black sauce into which they would dip their sushi. And wasabi mustard, which looked to me like the split-pea puree found in Lebanese restaurants. I took a mouthful. And I really thought that my head was going to explode. It was as if I'd just received a strong electric shock. Through my tears, I saw all heads turn toward me, even the guests at the other table.

My mother and René had gotten up to help me. I was brought damp towels to wipe my tears and blow my nose. When my interpreter explained what had happened, everyone burst out laughing. But René wasn't laughing at all. He stayed near me, on his knees next to my chair, until I could speak.

"Are you sure you can sing?" he asked.

"Yes."

"Try it, let's see."

To reassure him and make him laugh, I sang him a tune that was passing through my head. It was a love song, in a velvety voice. Right up against his ear.

"Are you lonesome tonight?"

He didn't cry. He became very serious. He held me very tight in his arms and then went back to his seat without looking at me.

I refused the steak and grilled fish that was offered me. After what I'd just lived through, I was ready to swallow fire! I managed to grab a hunk of very red fish, a corner of which I dipped in the soy sauce, then I brought it to my mouth. Strange texture, smooth, oily. And not bad tasting at all. The people next to me kept silent, their eyes lowered to their plates. They'd understood that I was a beginner and, I think, wanted to politely overt their gaze in case I spit the piece back onto my plate. "Mmmm," I said, signaling in an exaggerated way that I thought it was good. All of them smiled.

That evening was magnificent. My little blooper with the sushi had created a marvelous atmosphere and put everyone in a good mood. The people sitting next to me began to hold forth about the treasures of Japanese cuisine; they showed me how to hold the chopsticks. Then they asked me a thousand questions about my family, the snow and forests of Canada, the Eskimos, the wolves and bears, the Canadian Mounties.

Since that time, I've loved Japan. I always feel at ease, at home, even if there are language and etiquette barriers, rules and protocols that I often don't understand. I love the order that reigns in this world, the special humor of the people, their discretion.

At the time, I kept a diary that I'd brought with me. It was my mother's idea, to keep me occupied. In it I'd listed the birth dates of all the members of my family and my friends. For days, farther away from our home than I'd ever been in my life, I questioned my mother about her childhood, about how she met my father, the birth of her first children, my birth.

Then I set about writing in my diary what happened each day, describing this country that was at once so strange and so familiar. But I didn't succeed in finding words to express what I was feeling, or even to describe what I was seeing. The phrases were all knocking about in my head. It was all happening too fast. Faster, farther away, and at a higher altitude than those little movies I used to film in my head when I was in school.

Now I no longer had the time or the inclination to make my home movies. What I was living was as exciting as what I'd dreamed of for such a long time.

Arriving back in Quebec was unforgettable. At the Montreal airport, a crowd was waiting for me with flowers, teddy bears, and velvet frogs. TV cameras were pointed at me and microphones were thrust toward me. My brother Paul had brought us the newspapers. All of them were talking about the grand prize I'd won in Tokyo.

"On TV too," he told me. "They're talking about you everywhere."

Reporters had come to our house in Pointe-aux-Trembles, where we had just moved, and interviewed my father. They'd asked for photos of me. They wanted to know how old I was, if I had a boyfriend, what color my eyes were. The prime minister of Quebec, René Levesque, asked to meet me and congratulated me in the name of all Quebecois. I was also invited to join a dozen artists who were part of a mega-show at the Montreal Forum. When I climbed onstage, even before I began to sing, the ten thousand people filling the auditorium stood up to applaud me.

That day I made a strange discovery. Most of the people applauding me hadn't even seen me sing onstage. A lot of them probably hadn't even known my name ten days before. They gave me their applause and ovations not because my singing had impressed them, but because I'd achieved something on the other side of the world.

This made me feel, in a way, like I owed them something. As if I'd been paid in advance. Their applause and shouts stimulated me. And for that reason, I sang with my heart, with incredible pleasure. The next day my photo appeared in all the Montreal papers.

René was jubilant. It couldn't have been a better time to launch my next album, *Tellement j'ai d'amour pour toi.* With Mia, he prepared an enormous publicity campaign. They wanted me to meet all the print, radio, and television media so they'd talk about me more.

But I never felt I had anything to tell them. The only thing I knew how to do back then was sing.

The main thing that intrigued the reporters was that the most brilliant manager in the country was interested in me and me only. By this point, René had broken all professional ties with Ginette Reno and was occupied solely with my career. He'd known how to surround me with the best writers—Eddy Marnay, to be sure, but also Luc Plamondon, who had written one of the songs for the new album. Also, we had the best arrangers, composers: François Cousineau in Quebec and, in France, Hubert Giraud, who'd written the music for one of my most cherished classics, the very beautiful "Mamy Blue" (which I used to sing when I was five years old) as well as the song for my mother which gave the album its name: "Tellement j'ai d'amour pour toi."

For the holidays, René, his wife, and his children went south. And for the first time in months, I had nothing to do for more than two weeks. No engagements, no promos, no TV appearances. After three days, I was at a complete loss as to what to do with myself. When René was around, he always created a kind of ferment around me. I always had a lot of things to do, concerts to see or give, interviews, TV shows, new songs. I was learning things too, discovering them, having all kinds of exciting experiences. I had been sucked into a veritable whirlwind, and he was its cause, the engine, the initiator.

Once he was gone, everything around me became dull and flat. I didn't even go out, except to visit my brothers and sisters with Papa and Maman; the only times I came alive was when we were all singing together. It was like old times, but now I had a real voice, a real place in the family choir.

My brothers and my sisters were all happy about what was happening to me. However, certain of them, notably Claudette and Michel, my godmother and godfather, were realizing that when my career took flight, it would probably end their chances of having their own careers in show business. It was as if all the dreams of the family had been given to me, who really possessed nothing more than the others, except luck and an attentive, intelligent, daring manager.

For some time, I'd seen my career change not only my own life but also that of the others around me, especially my mother. But also the life of my father, who, because of me, was often left alone in the house. My mother had quit her job and always accompanied me everywhere, even when it was only a minor TV appearance. She even came along when I went shopping with Mia or Anne-Renée. I wanted her to be there. I needed her to be there. Later, I wondered if my father had born me a grudge for having stolen his wife in that way.

But during these holidays, the last I'd experience in our house in Charlemagne, my father was always very gentle with me. He saw that I was sad, but he didn't try to understand why, like Maman did. He simply tried to make me laugh, to put some other thoughts in my head. One evening when we were alone in the house, he took out his accordion and played for me for hours.

It must be said that I had all the reasons in the world to be happy. I was becoming everything I'd dreamed of. Every day, I listened to "D'Amour ou d'amitié" on the radio and also the songs on the

Christmas album I had recorded a year before. But it seemed as if that was a thousand years ago, that I'd sung those songs in another life.

I explained my sadness to myself as a result of having nothing better to do. Only later would I understand that it was really something else.

Even before René returned to Quebec, he unleashed a new whirlwind that would carry me even farther away. One evening he phoned to tell me I was going to sing at Midem, the international fair that the record industry held each year in January or February in Cannes, France.

"You'll be singing for professionals, nothing but show-business professionals. From all corners of the globe."

This was the biggest market for the record business in the world. And the best producers, lyricists, composers, and journalists on the planet would be there to hear me. On board the plane, he once again told us that my songs didn't always sell that well in France. They weren't played anywhere on the radio. Not even "D'Amour ou d'amitié," which Pathé-Marconi had brought out as a single and which Eddy and René had thought was tailor-made for the French.

"Eddy doesn't understand," he told us. "He sees it as a personal failure. He's humiliated. But I know what the problem is. It's that they've never heard you over there. When they hear you once, just one time, things will change. You'll see."

Once again he was right.

In Cannes, all the artists had to lip-synch using orchestra tracks. For a lot of them, this was hell. Not only did they have to be perfectly synchronized with the music, they also had to simulate the effort and the emotions. In other words, they had to become actors. But I'd done this thousands of times in front of my bedroom mirror.

Besides, I'd always loved singing for people who were in the business. So I was perfectly at ease.

At the same time, I knew that I had to give it my best. Pathé-Marconi had pulled out all the stops. "Lay all our cards on the table" was how one of the executives put it. All over the Palais des Congrès, where the gala took place, I could see big posters and banners with my face and name in giant letters. All the disc jockeys, producers, and record archivists from every radio station in France were there.

I understood that, this time, if my song didn't make it in France, I wouldn't even be going back to square one; I'd be out of the game altogether. And surprisingly enough, I was excited by such high stakes, by this last and only chance I had no choice but to seize.

Before I even finished my song, I knew I'd done it. I could feel the crowd becoming attentive, captive, holding its breath. The house was brightly lit. I could see the faces turned toward me, everyone motionless until my song was finished, at which point they leaped to their feet to applaud.

That very evening, we met the executives of the big radio stations in France, who assured us that they'd add my song in their playlists. A very polite gentleman and lady came to our hotel to present us with an invitation to the Michel Drucker TV show *Champs-Élysées*, named for the most famous street in Paris.

"Drucker's program is the biggest variety show in Europe," René made sure to tell me.

I was told to do two songs. Maybe there'd even be a short interview with Drucker. But what excited René even more was the fact that I'd been invited to appear on the very next broadcast, which was to air in a few days.

"That means they've bounced someone off the show for you," he said. "Drucker's really important, you know. He's the French Ed Sullivan."

He had to explain to me who Ed Sullivan was. We were in Paris, in the sitting room of a big hotel on the Place de la Concorde as, fascinated, I listened to him recount the life of Sullivan, whose Sunday-night show—"the biggest TV show of the fifties and sixties"—had had featured all the greats—Elvis, the Beatles, the Stones. Then, standing up, he imitated Sullivan, with his hunched back, rubbing his hands together as he announced in a nasal voice: "Ladies and gentlemen . . . Celine Diooooon."

Overnight, I found myself surrounded by a crew of publicists, producers, all kinds of advisors. The whole thing made us so edgy that I think we were within a hairsbreadth of losing our marbles.

In my suitcase was the cotton dress that had brought me luck in Tokyo, the black pants and white blouse that I'd worn at Cannes, the houndstooth jacket Josiane Moreau had designed for me, the red dress Mia had bought for me. And the girls were still discussing my look. The day before the recording session, they went around to all the stores again and had me try on sweaters, dresses, jeans. A hairdresser played around with my hair for hours while a press agent spoke to me about Drucker.

"If he comes over to see you when you've finished singing and if he takes your hand, or, better yet, if he puts his arm around your neck and says nice things, if he speaks to you even for only thirty seconds, you'll know that you've become a big star in Europe."

The day of the recording, we all met as usual at Guy and Dodo Morali's restaurant. Even though everyone was unbearably nervous, René and I didn't leave until late. He was driving Guy's little car, and Guy was in the back. At the time, René liked to drive. Especially in Paris. For him it was an exciting game. With Guy in tow, he'd make up challenges for himself, such as driving around the Place de l'Étoile in the opposite direction from the flow of traffic. But today he was just too nervous.

At the circle at the Champs-Élysées, René hit a car. Right away he turned toward Guy. "I'll let you take care of this."

And then the two of us started running between the cars. We could still hear the other driver yelling as we climbed into a taxi that would drop us several minutes later at the Champs-Élysées studio, where Maman, Eddy, Mia, Anne-Renée, and the entire Pathé-Marconi staff were waiting for us.

There was an unbelievable crowd in the studio, in the dressing rooms, and in the wings. Each of the artists who were going to be on the show had his or her own staff and friends. Nicole Croisille, Herbert Léonard, Francis Lemarque, and other well-known French singers were there. I found this reassuring, I was happy to rehearse in front of all these people. I've always felt that show-business professionals were kind to me, even those who performed in a completely different genre, like the English punk group who was also part of the show.

First, I sang "D'Amour ou d'amitié." Drucker, who was following the rehearsals on a monitor, came out of his box and walked toward me, congratulating me very warmly. He told me he'd ask me a few questions at the end of the broadcast.

So, had I won the prize? Was I going to have my "thirty seconds"?

René really didn't want me to declare victory too soon. I could see he wasn't too pleased that Michel Drucker had come to congratulate me so quickly. He wanted to up the ante.

"That doesn't mean that you've made the grade," he said. "You have to impress him even more. This guy's been rubbing elbows for years with the greatest stars in the world. You've got to really move him, stun him."

More and more, that's what René was asking for. I was still very young, but I knew that the higher the ante, the higher I'd go.

When the broadcast began and Drucker introduced me, René

stayed very close to me, his head bent toward mine. It had become a custom, a sort of ritual that I wouldn't have wanted to do without. Every time I did a TV show, he whispered in my ear that I was the best—with that voice that I loved so much.

"You're the best. You're at home here. Everybody loves you."

And then he'd push me gently toward the stage lights.

"D'Amour ou d'amitié" is a song that is full of nuances. I had worked on it a lot with Eddy. For days, I performed it over and over in my head. I owned it. It was tailor-made for me, for a girl who was beginning to wonder about love.

I think I impressed Drucker. He came toward me clapping his hands, hugged me, took my hand, and spoke to me for a good while.

That evening, we celebrated at Guy and Dodo's. René was wild with joy.

"You know what he said when he introduced you?" he asked me.

I didn't have the foggiest idea. Offstage in the wings, it's another world, where you concentrate and don't really hear what's happening onstage.

"I suppose he said: *'Mesdames et messieurs, Celine Dion,'* or something like that."

"Not at all. When he introduced you, he said: *'Mesdames et messieurs,* you'll never forget the voice you're about to hear. So remember this name: Celine Dion.' "

René marveled at these few words and repeated them a hundred times that evening. Years later, when we launched my first album in English—*Unison*—he turned it into a slogan that the publicity department at CBS used.

In less than a week, Midem and Drucker had made me a star in all the French-speaking parts of Europe. "D'Amour ou d'amitié" played everywhere and was at the top of all the charts, and stayed there until the summer. I was giving interviews left and right. In Paris, as in Montreal, people recognized me more and more often in the street.

That year I had to cross the Atlantic about twenty times to do promotional work or tape TV broadcasts or record new songs. In France and Quebec, my records went gold, platinum, and diamond. And I was still only fifteen years old. I was already accustomed to luxury hotels, expensive chic boutiques, airplanes, and chauffeur-driven cars.

It was a style of life I'd wanted, dreamed about, but even so, it was rough, puzzling, and sometimes really agonizing. Sometimes I really missed our house in Charlemagne, and especially Papa, of whom I saw so little, and also my brothers and sisters. I missed those sweet moments we had all shared in the past when we were part of a very unified family chorus.

I knew that it would never be the same with us, that from now on I wouldn't be able to do anything more than pass through. I already lived a different life, wasn't living in the same world. And I'd left with the best they had, with their dream. I'd taken Maman, who was always with me, whom I always needed so much, when I was away from them.

Eddy had me talk about all these things for hours. He took me for walks through Paris a lot. He was the greatest walker I've ever known in my life. We'd go to the Luxembourg Gardens or to the banks of the Seine, or to a trendy part of Paris called Neuilly. And I'd tell him about my moods, dreams, fears. This really helped me.

Sometimes, when he'd worked out a few lines of a song, Eddy got so excited he'd phone me at eight in the morning to have me listen. Especially in those days, I didn't exist at eight in the morning. I was in limbo. And I hated to talk, especially on the phone. But he was so elated that he managed to pull me out of my torpor and out of my bed. When he arrived at the house an hour later, I was awake, all worked up, and his song was running through my head, with or without music.

One day he called me from the Mirabel airport, where he'd just landed: "Listen to what I found in the plane."

Over the telephone, he hummed the first few bars of what would become "Les chemins de ma maison" (The Roads That Lead to My House). He was really excited about it.

"I've found the thread," he told me. "Your next album is in my head. It will be the last trace of your childhood, the childhood which you are leaving. After that, you'll be singing about the life of a woman."

In Eddy's songs, I saw myself as if in a mirror. He made me conscious of the changes I was going through. By talking to him about what I was feeling and by singing the songs he wrote for me, I was able to pass smoothly through the stages of mourning for my disappearing childhood and the cozy life I'd lived in the bosom of my family. I was watching myself grow up, little by little becoming a woman. A strange woman, however. I was a professional artist who could confront large audiences, endure great pressure, but I still needed to hide behind my mother's skirts.

I'd had no moonlight romances or kisses stolen in corridors. No female friends either. No time. More than ever I was surrounded by adults. And I was living like them, thinking like them, working like all of them at my career, exclusively, seven days a week, fifty-two weeks a year. At the time I wasn't capable of doing anything else. I was putting all my time, my energy, into my profession. Even when I ate or slept I had only one goal: to be strong and healthy enough to sing better. It was grueling discipline.

Was I happy in this hellish place? I think I was. I was doing what I'd always dreamed of doing: I was singing. René took care of all the rest. He planned out everything, negotiated, organized. He found me the words and the music, the musicians and the stages, all kinds of venues. He was obsessed. He wanted everybody to hear my songs and to see me.

We were always on the go. One evening I'd sing with the Montreal Symphony Orchestra and the next, by suppertime, I'd be doing a TV broadcast with country-music performers. I'd give a concert on a raft on a lake in the Laurentides in central Quebec. At night I'd record a Christmas song with a chorus of forty people, all from my family. Then Maman, René, and I would leave for a distant region of Quebec where I was performing in a festival.

I was asked quite often to perform on the variety shows on Télé-Métropole, the most popular channel in Quebec. We always accepted these invitations. But René wanted the audience of Radio Canada to see me and hear me as well. So he pestered the producers and programmers of public television until they agreed to produce a special broadcast, a kind of portrait of me, which they were contracted to air during prime time.

For days they followed me everywhere, right into the kitchen of our house in Pointe-aux-Trembles and into my bedroom. They even included shots of Paris. Interviews with Papa and Maman, with Eddy, with my musicians and technicians, with René, obviously, who said in front of the Radio Canada cameras that one day I'd be "the greatest singer in the world."

"It just slipped out," he said as a way of an excuse. "But by saying it, I realize that I really believe it. One day, you'll see."

In the meantime, he was working to expand my audience as much as possible. When he found out, for example, that the Quebec Department of Cultural Affairs was preparing a big show for the inauguration of the Félix-Leclerc Theater, he got it into his head that I ought to be there.

"You'll sing a Félix song," he said. "That'll surprise them. You'll see."

At the time, however, the Quebec show-business world was divided into two major clans who were often at odds with each other. There were the intellectuals, and there were the "others." Obviously,

I was part of the second group. And the "others" hadn't been invited to participate in the show inaugurating the Félix-Leclerc Theater. Nevertheless, René arranged for me to be there.

"You're going to show them that you're capable of singing not only songs that are tailor-made for you but also classics," he told me.

He had me sing "Bozo" in a very slow tempo, very soberly, practically without gestures. And we practiced it together for several days.

"Think of him," he told me. "Think of Bozo. He's a poor nut who loves a girl who doesn't exist."

But actually I just thought of myself. I wanted to love and be loved. But I was alone, a poor loveless nutcase, like Bozo. When I finished my song the evening of the inauguration, a tear rolled down my cheek and I didn't bother to wipe it away. The next day the critics were full of praise and frankly astonished, all of them saying I'd sung with a great sense of inner meaning. Of course I did: I was singing my life, my pain. Bozo was me.

A few days later, at the Adisq awards ceremony, I won four Félix awards, including best new star of the year and best female performance of the year. The Félixes are to Quebec what the Victoires de la Musique are to France and the Grammies to the United States. Adisq is the Association of Recording and Performing Industries in Quebec.

I cried a lot when I went up to accept my first award, and even more the second and third. What a thrill!

But when I heard my name the fourth time, the entire house was seized by a fit of giggling. And I began to sob and hiccup in the aisle leading to the stage.

The next day, the main paper of Quebec showed my face swollen with tears and all puffy from sobbing.

A lot of girls are moved to tears when they walk up to receive a prize, but I think I hold the absolute crying record. For two or three years, my crying jags were the delight of critics and commentators in Quebec. Several times I was the butt of hilarious imitations in the end-of-the-year television revues.

I had to exercise control over my emotions. Rather than waste them in crying and hiccuping, I had to put them in my voice, in my songs. If I cried too much, I wouldn't be able to sing, I'd lose control of my voice.

But nothing moves me as much as an ovation. Even today, when I see a crowd stand up to applaud an artist or athlete who has just given a fine performance, I automatically start to cry. On a few occasions, I didn't succeed in getting control of myself and missed doing the next song.

It is difficult to sing while crying. I've had to work long and hard to channel my emotions and hold back my tears. It's grueling work. You've got to manage to smile, to accept the applause and the ovations gratefully and prevent your throat from trembling, squeeze your eyes shut on that tear that threatens to flow.

From the very beginning, when René began to look after me, he got into the habit of sitting in the audience to watch all my shows. He'd always done it. He never stayed in the wings, like a lot of managers.

Afterward he'd come into my dressing room or my hotel room and tell my mother and me what had happened, song by song, during my show.

"Honest to God, he acts as if I hadn't been there," I'd say. "He's giving me a blow-by-blow description of what *I* just did and what *I* just said!"

But I loved listening to his accounts. And soon, I couldn't do without them. Usually, these commentaries took less than a half hour. Then René stood up; he'd kiss my mother and me on both cheeks and leave us to ourselves after unfailingly asking my mother every evening if everything was in order, if we were eating well, if the beds were comfortable, if everyone on the staff of the hotel and the restaurant had been nice to us, etc.

I'd go to bed with my cheeks softly tingling—and with a little of his cologne on my skin. He'd leave to meet his friends. Whether we were in Chicoutimi or Val d'Or in Quebec, or in Ottawa, he always had some people to meet. He would play cards or go see a show at a nightclub. He lived in a mysterious world that I dreamed of entering, a world that seemed very glamorous and exciting. But I was just fifteen or sixteen years old, and I hadn't even lost my baby teeth, as my mother used to say.

For the first time in my life, I was hiding something from Maman, hiding my budding love for René. I must have told her at least a hundred times that he was dear to my heart, but I never dared tell her that I dreamed of him every night: how he would come to my bed to get me and take me away to a desert island where we made love. I never told her about the torrid movies that he was starring in more and more often.

I'd found—where I don't know—a photo of him that I gazed at a thousand times a day without my mother knowing and that I covered with kisses at night, in my bed. I rubbed it against my cheek. It slipped onto my neck like a kiss and slid onto my shoulders. Before I fell asleep, I slipped it under the pillow, out of fear that my mother, who always shared a room with me, would find it.

One morning, I woke up with the photo of my love on the pillow, in full view, next to my head. My mother had already gotten up, washed, dressed, and even opened the curtains. She must have seen the photo. I was scared stiff that she'd talk to René about it, that she'd tell him that I had a crush on him and that he'd better be careful with me if he didn't want any trouble from her. And that it would be best for me to get over it as soon as possible.

If she'd seen that precious photo, she must not have believed there could be anything serious between René and me. I understood her. René's head and heart were somewhere else.

As soon as I left the stage and work was over, he didn't see me. It was as if I no longer existed. In his eyes, I turned back into an ordinary little girl who wasn't very pretty, with inordinately long and prominent canines (some humorists had nicknamed me Dracula), bushy eyebrows, too long a face still encumbered by baby fat, with a big nose and lips that were too thin.

If he ever spoke to me in a personal way, it was about what I was onstage and TV, about Celine Dion the singer, never about me in real life.

And so, I never wanted to leave the stage because it was the only place I felt I existed for him.

Probably it was his watching me that started to make me love being onstage or in front of the cameras or even in the recording studio, singing. Just to fascinate him more.

I say that now, but I no longer really know what went through the head of the teenager I was. I don't even know any longer how or when my love for René began, when his hold on my emotions became too obvious to ignore.

Sometimes I saw him standing so attentively in the shadows, in the audience that was watching me and applauding or gaping. And each time it was magic; I sang for him so that he'd think I was good, so that he'd tell me again and again, "You're the best." And so I could make the tears come to his eyes.

I was sixteen. I no longer knew how to get over him. I was already hopelessly in love.

4

To be the opening act for a show is a formative and necessary experience. Everyone knows that. But it's also a very painful lesson that demands a lot of energy as well as a good dose of humility. The audience has come to see and hear the big star, the name at the top of the poster; how interested could they be in the little singer who tries to win them over with her sentimental ballads and between-song patter about her childhood and her dreams. Sometimes the audience doesn't even listen at all. They get up, talk, laugh, read a program, or just aren't there.

It's a tough lesson!

In the fall of my sixteenth year, for five weeks, I was an opener for Patrick Sebastien's show at the Olympia in Paris. I was starting to do well on the French pop-music scene and was no longer a total unknown in France. Several of my songs had received a lot of radio airplay, I'd done several important TV shows, which hadn't passed unnoticed, but I still hadn't proven myself on the Parisian stage.

Quebec was another story, a done deal. In the past weeks I'd appeared in two very big outdoor shows in front of tens of thousands of people. The first was in Quebec's Vieux-Port, where we celebrated the 450th anniversary of the discovery of Canada by Jacques Cartier. I had sung, one August evening, with about thirty extraordinary musicians and chorus members. The weather was lovely. It was a magical, magnificent evening, which nevertheless managed to turn into one of the funniest situations you can imagine.

When I approached the floating stage, I noticed that millions of mayflies, attracted by the lights, were circling the musicians. I soon had some in my hair, nose, ears, eyes, and mouth. I could feel them buzzing under my skirt, tickling my legs.

Several times, to keep from choking, and because I really couldn't spit in front of fifty thousand people, I had to swallow the insects that had flown into my mouth. I could see my sisters—Claudette, Denise, Pauline, Louise, Ghislaine, Dada, and Manon—sitting in the very first row, horrified yet doubled over with laughter as they watched me swallow and return to my song as if nothing out of the ordinary were happening.

It was harder for me to keep from laughing than it was to keep from retching. And I couldn't look at my sisters anymore, for fear of bursting out laughing if my eyes met those of Ghislaine or Dada, with whom I'd always loved to laugh.

Two or three weeks later, in September, when the pope came to Montreal, I sang at the Olympic Stadium of Montreal, which was packed. Before Canadian, American, and French TV cameras, we narrowly missed being part of a big disaster. Instead, we got to witness and be part of a real live miracle.

It was the end of the afternoon on a windy, rainy day. An hour before the ceremonies, the weather forecasters predicted the worst. But when the emcee, Michel Jasmin, who'd had me on his talk show the first time I appeared on TV, stepped up to the podium, the sky suddenly changed. A gust of wind chased away the clouds. And at the very moment when Michel said my name, sunlight filled the stadium. Before I even opened my mouth, the crowd began to shout and applaud.

While I sang "Une Colombe" ("A Dove"), a song written for the occasion, two thousand young people in the stadium held up white banners, forming a giant dove that slowly flapped its wings. It was magnificent, truly grand, deeply moving. I finished my song, weeping heavily because of the glaring sun, because of the pope, the dove, and the crowd.

At the time I still didn't know how to hold back my tears, despite all my efforts. But I somehow managed to cry while singing (or sing while crying) without my voice breaking or quavering. That showed marked progress.

For me, these big shows at the Vieux-Port in Quebec and at the Olympic Stadium in Montreal weren't really challenges, like the one I was about to participate in at the Olympia. I certainly had a major case of stage fright as I walked onstage in Quebec. But I knew that I'd triumph over my fears. After a few minutes, the stage fright would disappear and I'd really start enjoying myself.

At the Olympia, on the other hand, it was a whole new ball game. I had to prove myself.

Patrick Sebastien and I belonged to two totally different universes. There was little chance that our audiences overlapped. Patrick told spicy stories to a rowdy audience that was loud and eager to laugh. They'd come to the Olympia for a knee-slapping good time. I liked to make people laugh, but not really in the same way as he did.

René warned me. And, as usual, he took the opportunity to raise the ante as high as possible.

"Obviously, this isn't your audience," he said. "But you can be sure that here and there in the house are a few spectators who'll want to hear you. Who'll like what you do and will help you. But don't worry about them too much. First and foremost sing for the ones who aren't listening, for those who aren't at all interested in you. Pick them out one by one if you have to . . ."

I had never had to fight for anything in my life. Certainly not to attract the attention of others. More like the opposite. But because of René, because he wanted it and required it, I spent every evening fighting for five weeks. I nearly went hoarse I tried so hard. It was tough, difficult, and draining. But each night it was a victory. Not necessarily over the audience, but over myself, my fears.

When I was little, my father told us: "If you're afraid of it, do it. Begin by doing what you least want to do."

So I aimed straight for my fears; I sang for the audience members who didn't want to hear me, and who made it clear by talking in loud voices until it was time for Patrick Sebastien to take my place.

Some evenings, however, I really made contact with the audience. These sudden turnarounds remain among the most beautiful experiences I've known onstage. It would only last a few seconds. All of a sudden people stopped talking and began to listen, without moving. It was like the calm after a storm. And when my song was finished, they applauded and shouted bravo. Was it because they'd really been enchanted and moved by the little Canadian singer? Or because they were impressed by her will, her nerve. It doesn't really matter. From then on, they knew I existed. And at the time that was what counted for me. They never went wild. But at least I knew that for a minute or two, I'd put everybody on the same wavelength.

Probably I never would have succeeded at this, even if I'd tried with all my strength and determination, if René hadn't been in the house, in back, somewhere in the darkness. No matter how many times he told me that you don't preach to the converted, all that really mattered for him was that I was singing and struggling with that audience and with my fears.

My stint at the Olympia as an opening act remains an unforgettable experience for me. I don't think it marked a turning point in my career. But during those five weeks, I changed deeply, I learned, and, even more, I realized that I had grown up.

A year earlier, when we were putting together "Les Chemins de ma maison," Eddy had told me that it would be a swan song for my childhood. And that fall in Paris, as I struggled with an indifferent audience at the Olympia, I felt that my childhood actually was very far behind me.

I'd become a young woman who could play hardball, who was becoming better and better at controlling her emotions, capable above all of not giving up, not turning her back on fame and success. It wasn't easy. To accept success is in a certain way to accept the fact that you must leave behind those you love, brothers and sisters who didn't have a chance of making it.

I was only sixteen, I didn't really understand that fear of causing pain or betraying others, or even of being taken for a swelled head, but I felt it. And thanks to René, I knew that I couldn't let it get to me, that I had to vanquish that fear like all the others.

I had to harden myself in a way. Like a boxer, or any kind of athlete who builds up his muscles, who works at developing his endurance. At the same time, I had to remain a sensitive artist, capable of feeling and expressing the emotion of a song. I was discovering that it was necessary to fight not only onstage but also in life.

Right before my eyes was the example of my niece Karine, whom I often went to see when I was in Montreal. She too was fighting. Every day. Desperately. And despite all the care her mother, Liette, surrounded her with, she grew sicker and sicker, gravely so, murdered again and again every day by cystic fibrosis. She was the one who'd inspired Eddy to write the title song of my last album, "Melanie."

I owe Karine a lot. Though she certainly didn't want to, she opened my eyes to the saddest realities of life. At the time, I never read the newspapers or watched the news on TV. I lived in the sealed-off universe of show business. Just by her presence, Karine constantly reminded me that in this world there is suffering, misery, and injustice. And reminded me as well of an insoluble mystery that troubled me endlessly on certain days and for which I will never find the answer: "Why her and not me? Why does the world and life have to be so unjust?"

I'll never have the answer to these questions.

I was working hard. "You get nothing for nothing," as my mother would say. I agreed completely. But I was always winning, everywhere. Maybe I didn't know love, as I so would have wanted, but I had my health, wealth, and fame. One of my songs was regularly climbing to the top of the Quebecois charts. My career in France was more than promising. A host of competent people took care of me, advised me. I had a fan club, a wardrobe full of glamorous clothes. I traveled, sang; one by one, I was realizing all my dreams.

Karine was waging a lost war and she knew it. We all knew it. No matter what she or we tried, she'd end up with nothing. Or almost nothing. Just a too short life filled with constant suffering. The only hope, and it was a slight one, lay in scientific research.

For several years, I was the sponsor for the fund-raising campaign for the Cystic Fibrosis Association in Quebec. Like all the members of my family, I closely followed the discoveries of researchers whose work had been funded by the organization more or less all over the world. But the life expectancy of a child with cystic fibrosis—which today is thirty years—was only about fifteen in the mid-eighties.

Karine, at eight, was already in the middle of her life, halfway through her journey on this earth. And she continued to fight with all her strength. Liette as well. As if they really believed they could beat this illness.

That summer, I got to know a professional athlete, Sylvie Bernier, who at twenty had just won a gold medal for diving at the Olympics in Los Angeles. We saw each other only about half a dozen times, and never for very long, but the intuitive bond and mutual understanding between us was always very strong. I felt like we'd always known each other. I discovered some disconcerting resemblances between us, not physically, but in our souls; we were sisters, two people who really connected, who were always on the same wavelength.

She had Karine's blue eyes. And like Karine, she was very kind with others. And very hard on herself—very disciplined, strong.

At twenty, Sylvie was a mature woman, very sure of herself, very thoughtful. She knew her own skills, her strengths and limits. Like all top athletes, she had a strength of character and a power of concentration that were beyond the ordinary. She too had been fighting every day, for years. Without ever letting up. Like Karine. But Sylvie had reached the stars. She'd won. And Karine dreamed of meeting her.

Sylvie and I talked about our training, the diets we followed, our tricks for fighting stage fright, how we prepared for a public event, for an ordeal. And I realized, as I think she did, that our professions had a lot in common. With her I found out about the terrible life led by great athletes, a life made of perseverance and solitude.

She told me how she prepared for a competition, by doing her dive a hundred thousand times in her head, after having done it a hundred thousand times in the air. She practiced every somersault and twirl to perfection. Maybe even beyond perfection. Before a concert or a recording, I did exactly the same thing, a hundred thousand times in my head.

Karine especially wanted to know how Sylvie trained, and if she ever got discouraged on some days. If she'd ever had a desire to just give up.

I'd never been interested in sports. Aside from golf. But after I met Sylvie I felt a closeness to athletes. And I often felt that I had infinitely more in common with them than I had with a lot of show-business people. I like athletes' mind-set, their temperament, their determination, their desire to win, and something else, something hard to define that you could call purity—of action, effort, and ideals.

René was as close to the world of sports and athletes as he was to that of show business. Actually, for him, there was no difference between the two worlds. For two weeks, from morning to evening, he'd follow every competition at the Olympic games in Los Angeles. He knew the names of all the star athletes. He told us in detail about their feats, even if we'd just seen them on TV. He'd always spot something we'd missed, a look of complicity between a trainer and an athlete, fear in someone's eyes, a premonition of victory in another's.

He sometimes told reporters that I was training myself like an Olympic athlete. He told them how I practiced my songs in my head, and said that a singer, like an athlete, has to train every day so that her vocal cords stay in shape. And he made them laugh by making his voice as hoarse and scratchy as possible while saying: "See what happens when you don't train?"

René hadn't sung since he was in the Baronets, who'd broken up fifteen years before. And his already husky voice had become even huskier.

A short while after the holidays, hardly a month after my five weeks at the Olympia, I started on a long tour of Quebec. René created a program with Mia and Eddy and had it printed up. It showed me with Sylvie the shining athlete and Karine the haggard child.

Two soul sisters, two warriors, who had had a profound effect on me, and from whom I'd learned a lot.

celebrated my seventeenth birthday on the stage of a liberal-arts school in Val d'Or, in Abitibi in Quebec. We were right in the middle of a tour, the first really big tour of my life, which had already sent us from one end of Quebec to the other, throughout eastern and northern Ontario, and into New Brunswick. There seemed to be no end to it. We didn't want it to end, we were so in a groove, so excited.

Our show got larger every day and the tour was extended, adding one city after another. We caused a stir before we arrived and after we left. We were sold out everywhere.

I had a completely new orchestra directed by Paul Baillargeon, who'd composed the music for "La Colombe," which had become an enormous hit in Quebec. I worked out the content of the show with René, Paul, and Eddy. I sang a mishmash of all kinds of songs that I liked, in all sorts of genres.

"This is your first real tour," René had said. "You have to present them with the complete menu of your talent."

So I did rock, lullabies, opera, blues . . . I sang Giraud's "Mamy Blue," Félix Leclerc's "Le Train du nord," old classics like "Over the Rainbow," my eternal "What a Feeling." I also sang an aria from Bizet's *Carmen.* And "Up Where We Belong" in duet with Paul, whose voice sounded a lot like Joe Cocker's. Eddy had introduced me to the music of Michel Legrand, who was a friend of his, and he put together a medley of his songs that I adored. Of course, I also sang my biggest hits, like "Ce n'était qu'un rêve" and "D'Amour ou d'amitié."

But these songs weren't always so easy to perform. To sing the same song for the hundredth time, putting your heart and soul into it, even a song that you cherish, demands a power of concentration that I didn't always have.

Without realizing it, I would put myself on automatic pilot, and let my song wander off by itself. René noticed it every time. In the analyses he made for me after the show, he reminded me that I lacked concentration and presence in my best-known songs. These songs became the most difficult to sing and to live in.

"You've got to fight against habit and routine. It's part of your profession."

René watched over everything, from the stage direction to the scenery, from the musical arrangements to the lighting, the order of songs, even my clothing and hairstyle. He worked on my transitional material between songs, sometimes even on what I would say to reporters or the poses to strike for the photographers. Quite often during the tour, he took charge of the direction and the lighting, posters, and publicity.

And almost every evening, he played cards with the musicians and technicians. He'd perfected a system, he claimed, for winning all the time at blackjack. He told everybody about it. Even me, who wasn't at all interested in gambling. He had a green felt mat, some chips, everything needed for a card game. He could play through part of the night. He was thrilled by his system, on which he put the finishing touches by using the people who accompanied us or friends who sometimes joined us.

He also told us about his theory of patterns.

"In gambling, just as in life, there are patterns," he said. "A bad event never comes alone; neither does a victory or a defeat. You have to keep track of the patterns. Bet heavy when you have a chance of winning. And withdraw, pull back, when you're in danger, unlucky."

"But how do you know when you're in luck?"

"You feel it. When luck is with you, you can really feel it."

My career and gambling occupied him more every day. At one point, a few weeks into our tour, his wife, Anne-Renée, had had enough and threatened to leave him.

We were in the Gaspé peninsula at the time, about seven hundred miles from Montreal. That night René returned all alone to the city. The tour was interrupted. And for several weeks, I barely saw him. Obviously he was working to repair the damage. I fell into the worst state of inactivity. Without him to motivate and inspire me, I had no desire to do my voice exercises, to practice and keep in shape. It was the coldest and darkest of winters. I stayed at my parents' without going out, just sleeping, watching TV, waiting.

My close friends Eddy and Mia, who came by to see me from time to time, were about to make some troubling revelations about René. Since he'd begun to work on my career, four years earlier, he'd never let on that he had any financial, romantic, or family problems. He'd always kept me in an ivory tower, away from all danger and any worrisome subject other than dealing with a mike or an audience. In other words, I'd been a spoiled and overprotected artist, without the least material worry, the least financial stress. I was seventeen—four years into my career—and had never thought that a particular project (a show, recording, or trip) was impossible because of money. I lived without consideration of a budget.

During that time I read about the lives of artists in magazines and watched them recounted on TV without ever finding an example comparable to myself. I never heard them talk about an artist—Streisand, Piaf, or Tina Turner—who had been this sheltered and protected, and who at the beginning had been free of all material worries. René had taken everything on himself without ever letting himself appear the least worried. Never in my life would I have believed, for example, that he'd had to borrow large sums and that he'd already declared bankruptcy. Because of me.

During this entire time, I'd lived like a princess. I'd bought a big house in Duvernay into which I'd moved with my parents. I had a car, furs, jewels, everything I wanted and more.

Then, two years after the fact, I suddenly learned that he'd had to mortgage his own house to finance one of my albums, and rather than paying back the mortgage, he'd reinvested all the profits in producing another album. The year before, he'd chosen to file for bankruptcy rather than accept the very interesting financial offer of a promoter who wanted to produce a big tour with me. He thought that I wasn't ready and that I hadn't yet developed a broad enough or original enough repertoire.

I could understand why Anne-Renée had had enough of it. René probably hadn't been the most faithful and attentive husband on earth. And he gambled a lot. His numerous trips to Las Vegas and Atlantic City were sometimes disastrous, sometimes great successes. He won a lot of money. And he squandered his money as if it were an inexhaustible resource.

Eddy told me that René had always acted like a millionaire; then, after he really did become one, his habits merely stayed the same.

But at the time, besides gambling, I certainly was part of his problems. In any case, I was hoping to take some responsibility for them.

Anne-Renée, who'd been very close to me at the beginning, had gradually grown distant. She no longer came to see my shows, even when they were in the Montreal area. Deep down inside, I was very happy about this. Less and less could I hide from myself the fact that I was in love with René; I had all the symptoms. And seeing the two of them together depressed me. Despite myself, I would sulk. I don't think I gave a good performance when she was there.

I had no doubt after Eddy's revelations that I was now the center of René Angélil's life. He'd sacrificed and risked everything for me. Even if his first interest in me had been as a gambler, he must have really believed in me, believed that I was a sure thing, to have invested all that he had, all his time and money.

When we went back to the Quebec tour, I knew things would never be the same between us. I couldn't prevent myself from thinking of everything he'd done for me, of everything I represented for him, of what I'd changed in his life and the enormous importance I had for him. And I looked at him in a completely different way. I was intimidated as I'd never been before. I was waiting for him to speak to me about his life. I thought he'd know how to establish a different, more adult relationship between us.

But to my great confusion, his attitude hadn't changed in any way. He never told me what sort of arrangement he'd made with Anne-Renée. But it seemed obvious to me that she couldn't be very happy about him taking off on tour and spending his days and nights in the studio or on the telephone with producers, writers, composers, musicians, all in the name of a single goal: to make me a star, a big star.

He still came into our room every evening and reviewed for Maman and me the show that I'd just given, song by song. Every evening he told me that I'd done well, but he always had some comment, it was never perfect, I always had to do better or try to do better the next time . . . A certain note I had to sing louder and hold longer; a gesture I needed to do less often; maybe I needed to change the key of such and such a song.

Do better, be better. Each evening he persuaded me that I could. He gave me the inclination, the desire, and the need to surpass myself. Then, after having upped the ante a little higher, always a little higher, he said good night to Maman and me, told us to sleep well, and gave me two pecks on the cheek. As if I were still thirteen years old. And then he went out to live his life. Without me.

Everybody in my family had been suspecting for a long time that I was in love with René. Unconsciously, I'd done everything to give it away. Even before I realized that I was in love, a lot of people, in the recording studios, on television sets, or in the auditoriums where I performed, understood that something was happening between René and me. I had eyes, ears, smiles, thoughts only for him. Whatever he said I took as gospel. I couldn't spend a quarter of an hour without mentioning his name. If he wasn't around, I looked for him everywhere and waited for him.

At the beginning, my mother wasn't overly worried. She figured that I was bound to get over it, that sooner or later I'd meet a boy of my own age, fall in love, and get married.

We never spoke openly about it, but I could sense my mother watching like a hawk, ready to protect me against what she could only see as an unrealistic kind of love. Meanwhile I continued to go to sleep with René's photo pressed to my cheek, against my neck. I wore out several of them. Some days I felt horribly alone. I was locked up all by myself in this love about which I couldn't speak to anyone.

And I knew very well that I wouldn't get over it. I was a real woman, had become a woman, I'd be eighteen soon, and I wanted René to take me in his arms, to kiss me, to make love to me. For real.

"But maybe he isn't aware of it at all," I told myself. "Maybe he simply isn't interested in me."

I tried to understand why I loved him so. I thought he was handsome. I loved his soft eyes, his gestures, his voice, the color of his skin, his hands, his cologne, the quiet strength that he exuded, his calmness, the authority that he exercised over everyone, even over my parents, even over the executives at the record companies. I loved his passion for gambling, and his laugh, and his ways of analyzing situations, of making and putting into practice decisions—above all of course, I loved the way he looked at me, the confidence he gave me, and his hopes for my future.

I had a surge of hope when the tabloids said that Anne-Renée had asked for a divorce, which René had granted. But I quickly realized that he was devastated by what he considered a major and irreparable failure on his part.

René had always managed to maintain a healthy contact with Denise, the mother of his eldest son, Patrick, who was within several weeks of my age. But with Anne-Renée, with whom he'd had two children, Anne-Marie and Jean-Pierre, who were then only eleven and eight years old, things didn't seem to be working out as easily. He believed that his children were going to suffer as a result of the breakup. Later, I realized that this was almost exclusively what was bothering him, knowing that his children wouldn't know the comfort of a stable home. It took me some time to realize it. At the time, I believed that he was suffering from being abandoned by a woman he still loved.

"He still loves her," I told myself. "She can still cause him pain."

I wanted so much for him to forget the pain of love. I wanted to console him. To hear him say that he loved me, to know that he was suffering because of me.

I retreated into my little movies, which I endlessly scripted for myself. He loved me, but I ignored him. He was unhappy because of me. Sometimes I was even in love with someone else. He did everything to seduce me. I resisted him. And then in one magnificent scene, I gave in. I consoled him. We made love, he took me far, far away.

A great classic, to be watched over and over again!

The most extraordinary part of all this was that rumors about us had begun to circulate. Friends or colleagues sometimes asked my brothers or sisters if there was something going on between René and me. And the rumor quickly reached the scandal sheets, which suggested all kinds of possibilities, and which took opinion polls on the subject from their readers. A lot of people said they were shocked because of the difference in our ages or thought that René had abused his authority and power as my manager.

He himself never mentioned the rumors circulating around us. But later I knew that they had troubled him deeply. And because of them, he and I lost some of the time we could have spent in love—a lot of that time.

The rumors certainly didn't make things easy for me.

They were, however, not unfounded. At least half of them. More, perhaps. I really was totally in love. And he was too in a way. I knew it, felt it, saw it. And above all, I wanted it.

When we were together, he was captivated, fascinated by me. He had eyes only for me. He too couldn't stop looking at me. And we felt as if we were alone in the world, even if twenty people were around us.

At the studio, when we listened to my recordings, or at a restaurant, where we ate almost every day, in Montreal or Paris, we were always seated side by side, very close to each other. We talked to each other without bothering with other people. We laughed a lot. Quite often I'd lean right against him, I'd let my head fall on his shoulder. I told myself that other people would think that it was completely innocent. But it wasn't. I felt as if René was participating in this game and also getting a lot of pleasure out of it. It was clear that he liked being with me. He liked to talk to me, he loved me, I was sure of it.

But he fought it.

One day in Paris, in a restaurant we went to often, I was seated at the end of the table and waiting for René to sit down next to me. But when he came in with the others, he passed by me, by his usual place, and went to sit at the other end of the table. I was shattered, destroyed. My legs began to tremble. Everything collapsed around me.

It was a dreary meal. I obviously couldn't swallow a thing. I kept seeking his eyes, which avoided me. My mother was sitting with us somewhere, so was Eddy, Mia, and some others, composers and producers who'd been at the recording session.

And then everyone left, leaving us alone. He got up and came toward me. He seemed tired.

"Come on," he told me. "We'll walk back together."

I thought he was going to tell me something terrible. I was shaking so much I had difficulty standing up. Outside, he immediately told me we couldn't let ourselves be seen that way anymore. We had to break off that familiarity between us. I think he'd prepared a speech and rehearsed it. My head was spinning. I wanted to sit down on the sidewalk. I wanted him to go away, to leave me alone. I would have stayed there until the world ended or I would have kept walking until I dropped.

"Did Maman ask you to do this?"

He didn't answer.

So I said: "I know that you love me, René Angélil."

He didn't say anything. I thought he was going to cry.

"If you don't love me, I want you to say it. Tell me: 'Celine, I don't love you.' If you don't say it, I'll never believe you. I can't believe you. Because I know that you love me, understand me. Tell me I'm wrong if you can."

He was never capable of telling me he didn't love me. That's what kept me, I think, from completely falling apart.

I knew he loved me. If he'd said he didn't, I would never have believed him. And I just couldn't understand why he was refusing the love I had to offer. Why he was rejecting me and rejecting our happiness.

I myself had never had the slightest hesitation. Not for a fraction of a second had I ever thought of doing harm to anyone. I knew his marriage to Anne-Renée was over. Not because of me. There was no longer any love between them now, either on René's side or on Anne-Renée's. Finally I realized he was trying to patch up his marriage for the sake of the children. And I said to him: "Do you really think making yourself unhappy can make your children happy?"

He didn't answer.

"Your happiness is with me, and you know it. Tell me it's not, if you can."

He was walking next to me. But he was far, far away.

Maman was waiting for me at the hotel. She knew perfectly well what had happened. She ran a bath for me. She helped me to undress. She patted me lightly on the back like you do a terrified, grief-stricken baby that you want to console. We didn't say anything to each other. I didn't hold her silence against her. I never held anything against her. She was doing what a mother has to do. She was watching over me. I was crying not just because of René but also because of her pain and worry, her fear of having to see my life shattered.

My mother held René responsible for the love that consumed me. She tucked me into bed, and before letting me sleep she came out with: "He could have kept this from happening."

I wanted to answer her: "He wouldn't have wanted to keep it from happening, because he loves me too."

But she would have answered: "Did he tell you that?"

And I would have had to answer no. But in my heart, there was no doubt.

For the first time in my life, my mother couldn't and didn't want to find a solution to my problem. Worse than that, and despite herself, she'd become an obstacle to my happiness.

Far from supporting my love, she wanted to cure me of it, she wanted me to forget René. She even got angry when I talked about him. I must have caused her a lot of pain by reminding her, one day, that I was eighteen years old.

"I'm not a minor. This is a free country. No one has the right to prevent me from loving whoever I want to."

She'd written a terrible letter to René accusing him of betraying her trust. Saying she wanted a prince for her princess, not a twice-divorced man who was two and a half times older than her daughter.

But at the same time, my mother, a woman of heart, knew that you can't stop a heart from loving. She knew me well enough to understand that I wasn't going to let my feelings for René drop. I had wanted to become a great singer and I was becoming one. I wanted that man in my life; I was going to put as much stubbornness and strength into getting him as I had put into my singing.

That fall, at the Adisq gala, we won five Félixes—best song, best show, best singer, etc. A triumph. I've never cried so much in my whole life. Some tears of joy, of course. But more than that, tears of sadness, a deep sadness that I'd felt growing in me for several months, the end of which was not in sight.

Professionally, I had every reason in the world to rejoice. Everything we'd tried in the course of that year had been a resounding success. The tour had ended beautifully with three shows in the main auditorium at the Place des Arts before a captivated public and thrilled critics.

But my heart was aching, broken. I was in love with a man I couldn't love, who didn't want me to love him, who didn't want to love me. Even worse, he didn't want to see or believe that I was really in love with him, despite all the proofs I'd given him.

"I love you and I'll love you my whole life. No one but you."

Meanwhile, I was sure that he loved me. But then, why was he resisting me? Why did he enjoy making me suffer?

I was having horrible doubts. If two days went by without seeing him, without hearing his voice or feeling him looking at me, I began to believe that I was living an illusion. He didn't love me, hadn't ever believed that I really loved him.

If he'd loved me even a little bit, he would have seen that his wife's request for a divorce was a deliverance. But instead he seemed devastated. His suffering and distress were killing me. His efforts to save his home appeared to me as proof that he did not love me, that I had been mistaken about his feelings for me.

By the beginning of summer, he'd already made up with Anne-Renée. And they'd started living together as a couple. I sank into my own private hell.

It seemed clear that Anne-Renée had demanded that he be at the house more often, because he abruptly stopped spending evenings at our house or taking my father, mother, and me to restaurants. We saw him now only when there was some specific work to do.

That summer I recorded a new album, *C'est pour toi* (This Is for You). René was there at the sessions, but he didn't seem altogether present nor as exacting as he'd been before. He no longer said to me, "You can do better," or "Make me cry."

Because of this, I decided that he was losing interest in me, or worse, that he felt I wouldn't be able to respond to his demands because I seemed so sad. Apart from that assessment, I concocted all kinds of theories, one more twisted than the next.

"He can feel me suffering because he knows I love him. Or maybe he sees that I'm suffering but doesn't want to know the cause. But if he doesn't, then he really doesn't love me. Maybe all this bores him, and he really doesn't want me to love him. Maybe he's been telling himself that because of this we can't work together."

This time, as he did before, Eddy told the story of my life in the songs he was writing for me. He'd been observing me. It was obvious that he too had seen everything, understood everything. He'd found the lyrics for his songs deep inside me. What's more, they seemed so familiar to me that I only had to read them once or twice to learn them by heart.

> *Sometimes my words sound so bizarre;*
> *On and on they go about the things I've felt.*
> *Then comes your look to make my poor heart melt.*
> *Sometimes I laugh just a little too much.*
> *You don't get it at all.*
> *You look at me appalled.*
> *Don't ask too many questions.*
> *The answer's in my eyes.*
> *Between us lies the reason why.*
> *Don't make me tell you everything,*
> *'Cause you already know.*
> *Everything I do today I do because I love you so.*

As I sang, I'd tell myself: "He can't not understand." I spent my days and nights wondering what he was thinking, where his heart was, if he knew that I loved him, and how he could ignore it, and if he still loved Anne-Renée, if they made love together a lot . . .

For the first time in five years, we had no upcoming project or tour, no show in France or Quebec, no TV appearances. We made the album *C'est pour toi* almost mechanically, without putting much heart or time into it—and without much hope inside ourselves. What is more, René didn't seem to be in a hurry to organize the publicity campaign as he had been in the past.

It was because he had other projects in mind for me that he had been thinking about for a long time. One evening he revealed them to me, a few days before the Adisq award ceremonies where I'd triumphed as the crying machine that couldn't be turned off.

He had decided that we were going to stop things cold.

"For how long?" I asked.

"For as long as it takes."

"As long as what takes?"

"For our luck to return."

"It's your wife that's left you, not luck."

He laughed. I liked his laugh, even when he sounded sad.

He reminded me about his theory of patterns, about bad things never coming alone, as well as victories and defeats. And that you needed to hide away for a while, take some time off, not act when you knew you were in danger, when you knew you'd make some foolish mistakes.

"At the moment, as you can see, I'm going through a bad period. And instead of making mistakes, I'm going to step back. You're going to stop for a few months too—for a full year if necessary. When we start again, it'll be in a big way, we'll be going far, you'll see."

The day after the music-award ceremonies, he was going to leave, unhappy in love, happy in business, for Las Vegas, where he'd spend the major part of the next year. It was great to have won five Félixes, but without him my arms felt empty. He had, however, given me some homework to do: learn English and take some dancing and singing classes.

Well, he wasn't abandoning me. On the contrary. He was asking me to pretty myself up, to grow, to become stronger than I was. I saw this as a promise of the future. If he was so interested in having me learn English, it was because he'd decided to have me record an album in the United States. If he was imposing this hiatus on us, it was because he had some big projects for us both. And I held on to that idea.

"To start, we're going to fix your teeth and you're going to change your hair and your look. Then you're going to listen to everything that comes out—all the music, all the new singers, even the bad ones."

I knew that I'd be apart from him for several months. "Out of sight, out of mind." I knew that out there, in Las Vegas, there would be other women, other pleasures to preoccupy him. And that he wouldn't be thinking about me very much. Maybe not at all, for days and days, and for nights.

I started making up little horror films for myself. I imagined him at the casino surrounded by dazzling redheads or sexy blondes in low-cut knockout gowns. Blonde, redhead, or brunette—I could always try a new hair color. As for the low-cut part, I had to be content with what nature had given me and that wasn't really much of a knockout.

No problem, I'd work out the rest. I'd tighten up the muscles and learn to move my hips when I walked. All things considered, I was thin like my brothers and sisters and father, and thanks to that thinness, I could get away with acting the part of supermodel.

He wanted me to pretty myself up. All right, I'd do it. I was going to leave behind the guise of bashful teenager in love and confront this lothario with equal weapons. When he got back, he'd discover a changed woman. I would put all my cards on the table, and when he came back, I was going to knock *him* out.

But for now I needed to go it alone. That's why I had cried so much at the awards ceremony. I was getting ready to begin a period of my life that terrified and thrilled me at the same time. I was going to break that wonderful contact I'd established with my audience during the tour. And above all, I was going to be living far from the man I loved.

For the first time in my life, I was facing an important challenge alone. I was going to undertake a large-scale project without the support or the advice of my brothers and sisters, my mother, or René Angélil. In fact, it would be my very first personal project as a responsible, adult woman: to seduce a man twenty-six years older than me.

When my beloved manager came back for good, I'd sing better than ever. I'd speak English. I'd dance and move gracefully onstage. He'd be pleased. But I wasn't counting solely on doing that. Above and beyond anything else, I wanted the changes in me to get me to the man. He was the one I wanted to impress, the one I was going to go after with my new look, my perfect teeth, my new hairstyle and appearance. I'd have a new, provocative way of looking at him, a bewitching smile, an air of mystery, a lot of strength, charm, and sex appeal. Give yourself a goal and reach it, that's the only thing I would believe in. I was going to train myself in the art of seduction, like a top athlete, and snag René Angélil once and for all.

And so, I enrolled in a language school for nine hours a day, five days a week, for two months. At times, it was a nightmare. I stopped understanding words in any human language at all. I started talking nonsense and all my ideas got mixed up. And then all at once, everything became clear and intelligible. I watched a talk show in English on TV and understood all the conversation for long stretches. Or almost all. I discovered a new meaning in the songs that I'd known since early childhood.

I quickly got used to life out of the limelight, but I was working just as hard. For months, I wore braces, which made me look like I had a gigantic orthodontic scaffold in my mouth. I could still be heard regularly on the radio, but I wasn't seen anywhere. In fact, after this period, I never saw any photos of me that dated from that time, never with the braces, in any case. I was really out of the limelight.

All kinds of rumors began circulating in the tabloids. I'd become a nun, I was a missionary in Africa, I'd lost my voice . . . The next day, I was pregnant; three days later, I had just had twins; I gave them up for adoption, one went to Switzerland, the other to California.

During the winter, René returned regularly to Quebec, mostly to see his children. But he too had some homework to do. He had decided to revamp our whole enterprise. He wanted to change every-thing—our record company, the distribution company, the musi-cians. He was talking again about broadening my repertoire to attract a bigger audience. He especially wanted me to make an expensively produced record in English. So he was going to go into partnership with a multinational record company. He was meeting people in Toronto, New York, and Los Angeles and making plans.

Every time we saw each other, he told me stories, as he had always done. From him, I knew the adventures of Elvis and Colonel Parker, Barbra Streisand and her manager Marty Erlichman, and many oth-ers. But from this time forward, his stories took place in the future and they featured him and me as the heroes. He saw me within two years on the Johnny Carson show, in Las Vegas, on Broadway. These days he was talking less about France. He seemed to be interested only in the American market.

I would have followed him to the ends of the earth.

And it's a good thing that I was willing to go to such lengths, because in the end, that's where he was intending to go.

Finally, one day, I noticed that I'd gotten him really flus-tered. It was almost summer, he'd come to get me at my place in the town of Duvernay to take me to see a show at the Place des Arts and meet some people from CBS, our new record company.

During his absence, I'd changed my hairstyle and look. I no longer had those extra-long canines that had won me the name Dracula. I was wearing shorts and a camisole, my shoulders and thighs were bare and tanned. I love to get a tan. I had muscles too, because for several months I'd been taking dance lessons. Added to that I had a smile that I'd practiced for a long time, the smile of a woman who was very sure of herself.

He remained standing on the doorstep looking at me, without saying a word. I could almost see him reeling. For the first time, I felt him looking at me the way a man who desires a woman looks at her, not just looking at me the way an impresario looks at his artist. I'd really flustered him, and it was sweeter and more intense than it had ever been in my little scenarios of unrequited love. An invisible shiver went through me from my head to my feet, the sensation of having power over a man. The seducer was being seduced.

I told myself our relationship was finally changing. From then on, René Angélil would be not only my impresario but also my inspiration.

Starting with that day, he'd be involved on two levels of my life. He'd guide and manage my career, make all the business decisions, choose my songs. Songs that told a very simple story, the story of a very determined girl who thirsted for love, who loved a man she wanted to seduce. He had become the object of the love that I sang about, he was the man of my songs. How could he not know it?

For quite a while after this, out of decency, and also out of fear of public opinion, which seemed unfavorable to him, he refused to take on this role.

One thing I was sure of at least: I could get him all flustered. I felt it in his look. Sometimes while he was speaking to me, he got lost in his thoughts and he couldn't find the thread again.

"Now what was I saying?"

From then on, I tried to fluster him every chance I got. I wanted to surprise him, shake him up. I became confident about my power. Often I stayed very close to him, positioned so that he saw my bare shoulders or legs—my whole arsenal of weapons of seduction. And I was happy, a state of mind that is practically as powerful as sex appeal when it comes to seduction.

We weren't lovers yet. But we had to hide so that no one could see us together.

I loved the secretiveness and the kind of ambiguity this created around us. I found it exciting and extremely romantic. People's looks, the innuendos, what everyone around us was wondering. René and I finally had a secret life. And I had no doubt that one day or other we'd be lovers.

And I knew it would last a lifetime.

I don't know where my need or desire to experience a complete and absolute love came from. It was no longer a fashionable thing to crave, I well knew. But I've never imagined that love could be any-thing but grand and exclusive. I wanted only one man for my entire life. I knew that one day it would be René. And from then on I didn't hold back. That love became the major project of my life.

The only thing that upset me was that I still had to lie to my mother. I consoled myself by believing that one day she'd understand that I was serious. She'd accept our love. Then I'd admit all my little lies to her.

I never know how to answer when someone asks me today how I'd have reacted if my mother demanded that I break off completely with René. Or rather, that I give up trying to seduce him. Actually, I never imagined such a thing happening. I figured that she'd try to dissuade me, that she'd be against it. As would my father. But not for a fraction of a second did I think that they could act in a way or demand something that would have made me unhappy.

For my parents, as well as for all my brothers and sisters, René was a very formidable and impressive figure. He'd realized very quickly that in order to work with me, to have a professional relationship with me, he'd have to have the complete agreement of my family. Beginning with my mother. And with her he'd developed real ties of friendship. He consulted with her about everything and listened to her opinions. I don't think he wanted to lose that mutual understanding; it would have been practically impossible to manage my career without it.

My mother found herself in an untenable position. She was his ally in a professional sense, but she was also his adversary in the evolution of our love story. In order to carry out my seduction, it was crucial that I convince my mother that what I felt was more than just the passing fancy of a young girl.

I remember one critical moment when I found the words and the tears that really touched her.

We were at home in the kitchen. Maman was busy preparing dinner. There was somebody else with us, maybe Papa, or one of my brothers. I said: "What you don't understand is that I love him, I love him."

And I burst into tears.

"It's true. I love him for real. For life."

Maman wiped her hands on her apron. She came toward me and took me very gently in her arms. I put my head on her shoulder and she said: "I believe you, my little girl, I believe you."

I understood then that she was no longer opposed to my project. Maybe she wouldn't go so far as to encourage it, but she had admitted that my passion for René was not just a passing phase. After that day, everything changed. Even my voice, my heart, my whole life.

René wanted me to do my next video, "Fais ce que tu voudras" (Do What You Want), with François Girard, who was already recognized in Quebec and in English-speaking Canada as one of the most brilliant video directors.

He was barely older than me, about twenty years old, but he had a will of iron. He demanded that René give him absolute freedom, and obtained it. Not only in composing and editing the images he wanted, but also in working on my image, my own look.

"I want you to be a sensual, sexy girl," he told me.

I couldn't have asked for better.

René understood that François was doing fresh, original things. That was the reason he had pursued him. And it was the reason he had given him all the freedom he wanted. From then on, that's how René would proceed. He'd find creative people, ask them to work with me, then give them all the technical and financial means as well as all the latitude they needed.

A few days before the shooting, François took me shopping for hours in all the secondhand clothing stores and shops I'd never even set foot in. He had me try on all sorts of things it never would have occurred to me to try on.

Mia had taken me a few times to the great couturiers of Paris. She'd guided me through the fascinating universe of fashion. Now, with François, I discovered that you create a look as if you're working on a canvas, or like you create a song. And that the look you choose is also a tool. It takes into account the spirit of the times, of the world in general, and its general mood. And, of course, it takes into account your own vision.

François saw that I wanted to seduce, at any cost. That's what the song "Fais ce que tu voudras" was saying. Once more, Eddy had seen right into my heart with astonishing clearness. He'd penetrated my head and my heart.

I'll even fight,
I'll bet my life,
My last card to keep you.

Of all the changes and reenvisioning plans René was making, one thing deeply bothered him. He was afraid to hurt Eddy by seeking out young songwriters whose styles were more rock, more pop than his. I think Eddy definitely saw me as part of the tradition of French singers Mireille Mathieu or Nana Mouskouri, who specialized in ballads. He didn't see me as a pop singer and even less as a rock singer. But René wanted me to be a part of that universe.

He especially wanted to work with Luc Plamondon, who was already the most innovative and visible lyricist in the francophone world. He'd had hits with dozens of French and Quebecois performers, including Charlebois, Diane Dufresne, and Julien Clerc. And with Michel Berger, he'd written a fabulous opera called *Starmania,* which had been having a good run for several years.

One day in the fall, Plamondon invited us to his place in Paris. I'd already met him briefly in the wings of the Place des Arts after a performance of *Starmania.* He's a big cheerful guy who looked very elegant and unkempt at the same time. By then he already wore those famous black glasses he later was known for.

The windows of his apartment opened directly onto the Eiffel Tower, with the river Seine in the background, and the Palais de Chaillot, the trees of the Champs-de-Mars. He'd invited several important people from Parisian show business, including Gilbert Coullier, who'd later become the producer of all my shows in France and Belgium, and his wife, Nicole, my future partner in shopping jaunts in the rue Faubourg Saint-Honoré.

On the day of this meeting, I became terribly intimidated about being with these people and quite unsure of myself. But when the evening arrived and I was in their presence, I don't know what devil got hold of me, but I was uninhibited, confident of my charm, my makeup, of everything that I was wearing and saying. I felt self-assured, surrounded by these people who seemed interested in me, genuinely. I talked a lot. And I think I gave them quite a show. First at the table, then in the sitting room full of curios, books, paintings of the masters, and sculptures. To make them laugh, I told them funny stories about my family and imitated Streisand and Joplin, and Edith Piaf. Luc Plamondon was really taken with it. Especially when I sang the songs from *Starmania,* imitating the female roles of the opera one by one. I could see René a little to the side watching me proudly. I knew at that moment that I was making him happy and that he could never do without me. I also knew he was in love with me, or would be very soon.

We had entered the period in our life I call our silent love, our platonic love, which was chaste and completely idealistic. And practically unspoken. Since that scene in the Paris street when he'd wanted to break things off, I'd never reminded him that I loved him. It was painful and exquisite at the same time.

We were always together. He was considerate and gallant, always gave me his arm, and always opened doors and car doors. We walked together through Paris. We were often alone, even when there were a lot of people around us, even if Maman was there, as she still often was. We had moments when we thought we were alone in the world. He talked to me about his projects, the agreements we were going to sign with CBS, about the album in English that we'd do in a year or two (at most), right after the one we were working on, which he said would be a big hit.

"It has to be a hit," he said. "I had a clause put in the new contract. As soon as we've sold a hundred thousand copies of the next album in French, CBS is going to give us the means to produce a record in English."

He was so proud of his clause! He spoke to me about it for hours. And about the musicians and lyricists he was lining up to produce this hit album that would win us the record in English.

A few weeks later, we met again with Plamondon in his house in Montreal, which overlooked a very lovely park. It was snowing. Under the trees, there was a skating rink, where some young people were playing hockey. Luc had written two songs for us, "Lolita" and "Incognito." The lyrics were handwritten on scraps of paper that he handed to René.

René took his time. I could feel that Luc was nervous. He offered me some champagne and canapés, and rose to arrange some books, to turn a lamp off or on, to move a curio. Then René handed me the scraps of paper without saying a word. But I could tell from his eyes that he was really happy.

When I saw what Luc had written, I was bowled over. Like Eddy, Luc had explored my inner life. What he had written was so close to me that I couldn't help being really unsettled by it.

Luc sat down at the piano and, as well as he could, sketched out the melody that had been composed by Jean-Alain Roussel.

The first time I sang the words to "Lolita," I was in front of René, and I sang it to arouse him:

> All those nights I spent alone wanting to touch you,
> you've got to return them to me one by one,
> all those nights all alone in the gloom,
> dreaming you'd come to my room!
> Will you make me wait for days, for months?
> If you don't come, it will be another.
> And you'll bear the blame for a lifetime of regret
> for my first night of love.

As I was singing, I heard René tell Luc that the song was exactly what he was looking for. And inside myself I wondered: "What game is he playing? If he thinks that song's perfect for me, it's because he knows how much I love him, how much I need him."

I sang the refrain in a very low voice. I think I was angry. René had read it before me. He must have known what I was thinking. It was weird, a kind of public, shameless declaration of love.

Lolita isn't too young for love,
Isn't too young to surrender
When desire devours her body,
Right to the tips of her fingers.

We were silent for a long time. The message was clear. I was past the age of fairy tales, and at the age to jump into bed with the man I loved.

A few days after my nineteenth birthday, we launched the album *Incognito* in the most fashionable discotheque in Montreal, where I was getting my first real media exposure in more than a year and a half. New look, new sound, new team, new record company, new Celine Dion . . .

Je recommence ma vie à zéro ("I'm starting over at square one"), the song "Incognito" rightly said.

Very quickly, the rumors took on a new form. One day they'd say we were engaged. The next, that we'd gotten married in Las Vegas, after having lived in sin for months. They let everyone know, however, that I wouldn't ever be pregnant because René had had a vasectomy; then, miracle of miracles, they announced that I was pregnant and that we were expecting twins.

Someday I hope I'll understand the gossip columnists who for more than ten years have insisted that I was going to have twins.

In Quebec, no one doubted that René Angélil and I were in love. Scads of people claimed to have seen us kissing on an airplane, in the streets of Paris, in a restaurant in Montreal.

Sometimes my greatest happiness has come when life imitated the rumors that were being spread. As if life wanted to make the gossip true or to fulfill our most cherished dreams.

The album *Incognito* attracted a wide spectrum of the public. As the people in marketing at CBS said, "We've never cut such a wide swath." The rock stations, who'd always stayed away from me, as well as the more genteel, family-oriented stations, who stayed faithful, shared the songs so completely that for months we had two, sometimes three hits topping the charts at the same time. At least in Quebec. Elsewhere things were going to move a lot more slowly.

In France, the programmers and marketing specialists didn't think that two of the songs would work there. Strangely enough, these were the songs that did the best in Quebec—"Incognito" and "Lolita"—the two that had been written by Luc Plamondon.

René, who had always wanted to keep me away from critics and problems, probably would never have told me about the difficulties in France if it hadn't been necessary for me to go to Paris to record some replacement songs for the album. Since Mireille Mathieu, who'd become a forgotten page in the history of show business, French fashion tended to favor the "breathers." A wispy voice like Bardot's or Zazou's was now all the rage.

What's more, when I went to the studio to record one of the songs Eddy had written, Romano Musumarra, who'd composed the music, told me that I overdid songs. I can still hear him saying: "Hold back your voice, don't give so much."

Ironically, the song I was recording was called "Je ne veux pas" (I Don't Want To). I was disappointed, frustrated, and shocked.

France wasn't interested in the kind of pop singer I wanted to be. They couldn't accept that I'd changed. They wanted me to remain the ingenue, the somewhat starry-eyed and dreamy little girl I no longer was and I no longer wanted to be.

I later discovered that it was the artistic milieu that was wrong. These were record magnates we were working with, people who, I think, lacked judgment, daring, and imagination.

In English-speaking Canada, I didn't fare any better. I was treated with total indifference. Which wasn't surprising. In this country, there have always been two record industries, two star systems, two solitudes, as they say, which, at that time more than today, were completely separate and distinct. For the rest of the Canadian public to listen to a Quebecois artist, a stroke of great luck or a miracle was required.

But two such miracles happened to me. They were the result of events I had the luck to participate in and that allowed me to get recognized by the Canadian public very rapidly. Then some American decision makers opened some doors for me down in the United States, some big doors.

At the start of summer, CBS-Canada had its annual convention at the Esterel, a big hotel in the Laurentides, north of Montreal. I was part of that record company, so I was entitled to a short presentation, what one calls a "showcase." In the afternoon, I did two or three songs, which were politely received. Everyone knew they couldn't go very far. The vast majority of industry people, who came from Ontario and from the western provinces of Canada, didn't understand any of the words. And even if they had understood, even if they had found me interesting, there wasn't any place for my songs in their market or on their radio stations. French songs were rarely played.

The big star of that convention was Dan Hill with his hit song of the summer, "Can't We Try," a duet he did with Ronda Sheppard. I don't know why Ronda hadn't come to Esterel. A few days earlier, as soon as René learned that she hadn't, he contacted Hill, Hill's agent, and the president of CBS and proposed that I sing with Dan in her place. He asked them not to talk about it, so it would be a surprise.

"It'll add some drama," he said.

On the day before the performance, I rehearsed with Dan. Our voices went well together. And the song was in a range where I felt perfectly at ease.

René had returned to his strategy of upping the ante. During the two or three days before the convention, he never stopped telling me that this would be a crucial moment, that I probably wouldn't have any other opportunities to show what I could do for a long time. Maybe never.

"If you can't bring the house to its feet, we go back to square one and stay there a pretty long time."

Square one was the Quebec area, where everything had gone as far as it could go. I was an established star, I'd sold several hundred thousand albums. My songs were played on the radio day and night.

But I too was intrigued by the idea of going elsewhere, seeing other audiences, facing other challenges. René and I wanted to get out of Quebec. And in France, I was being less well received than during the period of my first songs, like "D'Amour ou d'amitié." My last albums weren't selling well. René didn't talk to me about it. But I was no longer regularly invited to big television shows or written about at length in Parisian magazines.

That summer we were preparing both a big TV show for Radio Canada and a super tour of Quebec at the same time. But without the prospect of getting out of Quebec, these projects seemed almost trivial, even though we had access to enormous funds and technical support to produce them.

Some people think that ambition is a serious fault. Not me. In all the interviews I gave then, I never hid my great desire to succeed. I stated straight out that my goal was to one day be the greatest singer in the world. And a few good souls were shocked by that.

In the eyes of some, that ambition was somewhat shocking and vulgar. Intellectuals looked at me with a half smile. I didn't read what they wrote, but I guessed by their attitude what they thought of me.

To me, such ambition is essential and necessary, completely legitimate. I felt like a caged animal. I love Quebec deeply; my roots will always be there. But I did want to get out of the country and know other things. What they call ambition is for me just a need for air and freedom, open spaces, the need to be able to make choices.

So that evening at the Esterel, I sang that duet as if my life depended on it. I did it with all the passion within me. And we brought down the entire house. They all leaped up to applaud Dan Hill and me. This time it wasn't just to be polite, like the day before. It was a very small audience, about a hundred and fifty people, but they were the decision makers and executives of the recording industry throughout Canada, with some from the United States. From then on, the people at CBS knew who I was.

René was waiting for me when I left the stage. He took me very gently in his arms. We held each other for a long time—out of pure happiness. Surrounded by all these people. We were both so excited that we stayed in the Esterel long after everybody had left. As if we didn't want to leave the place where our future had hung in the balance. That's really the sense we had at the time. René didn't talk about it. He couldn't stay in one place; he walked back and forth in front of the little stage where I'd sung. He was laughing. I was waiting . . . but he didn't take me in his arms again.

We knew that CBS would in all likelihood honor its commitment to have me make a record in English. Now the projects that we had, the Radio Canada TV show and the Quebec tour, had me excited again.

During the weeks that followed, at Radio Canada, I worked with researchers and the director on the concept for that broadcast. While doing that variety show, I discovered the great pleasure that lies in doing comedy and becoming different kinds of characters. From the very first meetings, they spent hours asking me what I wanted to do and be. I answered that I wanted to do everything, which kind of alarmed them. I'd say to them: "I want to make them laugh, make them cry, I want to dance, I want to sing rock and opera, new songs and old hits, in French and in English."

I wanted to have a lot of costumes and play a Garbo-like vamp, a Lolita, a goody-goody, a suburban lady, a tomboy, an ingenue, a rock star.

Actually, what I wanted to do most was seduce René Angélil. The best way to do it was to be every woman at the same time. Maybe I didn't say it then, but today it seems completely obvious.

René always took care of everything. He obviously wanted to approve all my costumes. I'd prepared about a half dozen with the researchers, the director, and the wardrobe people. One day I did a kind of fashion show for him in a soulless space lit by neon, two or three floors belowground in the basement of Radio Canada headquarters. I had two very daring costumes that I really liked, but he nixed them immediately. He said they'd shock people. The show we were preparing was for a general family audience on a Sunday evening.

"You don't need to shock when you have a voice like yours."

I was disappointed. I really would have liked to shock a little. But I was consoled to know that he'd seen me. I hadn't left him indifferent. A girl can see these things.

The album *Incognito* still wasn't selling in English-speaking Canada. But it was doing so well in Quebec that it became the top seller in Canada, and as a result, it merited the Juno prize for the bestselling album in the country. Even if practically no one out-side of Quebec, French-speaking Ontario, and New Brunswick had bought it. This gave me the right to an appearance on the Juno awards show on television, the most important media event of the Canadian recording and performing industry. So that autumn in Toronto, I'd be the "token" French Canadian.

According to tradition, I would sing my most popular work. Either "Incognito," "Lolita," "Jour de fièvre" (Day of Fever), or "On traverse un miroir" (Through the Looking Glass), which had all topped the charts for months. Every year, one singer from Quebec performed his or her little song for three minutes in French at the Juno awards. It was an utterly wasted effort. Everybody knew it. The Quebecois didn't watch the Juno awards. The English-speaking Canadians didn't listen to the French songs on the program.

As soon as the invitation came to us, René informed the organizers of the show that I'd sing a song in English. That or nothing. They had to accept it.

At first we thought about doing an old classic. It's easier to move a general audience with a tune they already know. I thought of "The Way We Were" or "Over the Rainbow" or even a boogie-woogie "Chattanooga Choo-Choo," which I was planning to include in my tour.

Then René got it into his head that I ought to do an original song no one knew.

"Remember when Eddy heard you for the first time. It was because you'd created your own songs that he was really able to see your abilities. You need a new song, and one that will let you show them what you can do."

Barely two days before the event, we finally came up with "Have a Heart," which was actually the original version of "Partout je te vois" (I See You Everywhere) on my album *Incognito.* It's a very physical, spectacular, demanding song, which has the great advantage of exploiting the whole register of my voice.

We left for Toronto in a state of almost unbearable excitement. Yet again we were going to put all our cards on the table. Now it wasn't just the industry I was confronting, like at the Esterel six months earlier, but also the mainstream audience of Canada and especially the Canadian media, which always paid special attention to the Juno awards. Our future depended on their reaction.

I was in a trance when I left the stage. As always. I keep singing when I dash through the wings, when I get to my dressing room, when I climb into the limousine, as if the fire in me can't be extinguished.

The next day, René got up at dawn to get the papers. He waited patiently for me to come out of my room to tell me that I'd been a smashing success. He'd had the time to learn by heart all the articles that appeared in all the papers he could find. He even called Halifax, Montreal, Vancouver, to find out what the reactions had been in those cities.

"You stole the show," he kept repeating.

In the afternoon, he met with the big bosses at CBS. For them as well, he'd up the ante. He asked them to invest ten times more than had been anticipated for the English album. And he demanded as well that David Foster, the record-industry wonder boy from the United States, be the producer.

"The money's no problem," said the bosses at CBS. "As for Foster, Celine and you will have to find a way to approach him and get him interested."

Foster may not have been known to the public at large, but in the world of show business, he was a huge star. Originally from British Columbia, he had made a name for himself in Los Angeles, where, in the eighties, he was already working with the biggest of the big:

Barbra Streisand, Natalie Cole, Frank Sinatra, Neil Diamond, Paul McCartney. He wrote words and music for them; he arranged, produced, and conducted for artists who were making high-quality albums.

"He's the best," René said. "He's the one we need."

But how was another story. How to approach an artist of the stature of David Foster, who was already living on planet Hollywood?

"We'll find a way."

While waiting for David Foster and the blessings of the big bosses at CBS International, we continued to prepare our show *Incognito*. I'd say that of all the shows I've presented in my career, this was the most extensively and minutely prepared. We had quite a support staff in place—about fifteen musicians, a dozen technicians, lighting people, sound people, a director, a set designer, a writer for the texts between the numbers, a lot of costumes, and the inimitable Mego as orchestra conductor.

He and I had met in a rehearsal space at the Place des Arts. After ten minutes, we both knew we had been made to get along. I rediscovered with him the pleasure I'd once had in making music with my brothers and sisters. Even though René had to hold us back a little at the beginning. At each rehearsal, we launched into completely outrageous improvisations, boogie-woogie, and rock and roll. In addition to his crazy artist side, Mego also had a lot of discipline, and a keen sense of organization and leadership skills. In addition, he was a good showman, very funny, full of humor. To be onstage with him was always a great pleasure for me.

Starting at that time (a little before the holidays in 1987) and until I went on sabbatical in January 2000, Mego was at all the shows I did, without exception, good times and bad times.

Suzanne Gingue, Mego's girlfriend at the time, also did the whole journey with us, acting as director of the tour. She watched over everything, from the reservations for our hotel rooms to the fitting out of my dressing room, to the setting up of the sets and repairing of my moods. Suzanne is a workaholic. We always said to each other that she never slept, never ate. A pure spirit.

The memories that first come to mind when I think of the *Incognito* tour are filled with fits of laughter. From the beginning, in Abitibi, just like the preceding tour, we all knew that we had a good product. And an audience that had been conquered in advance.

When I speak of fits of laughter, I don't mean only among ourselves, but with the audience too. I did imitations (of Fabienne Thibault, Julien Clerc, Michael Jackson, Mireille Mathieu) that really went over well. I'd also had some hilarious monologues and several numbers that I did with Mego. Most of the time, the audience was laughing at my expense.

A few years before, for example, René and I had been given an audience with the pope. We had been sent to Castel Gandolfo, where the summer residence and farm of the Holy Father are located. In front of the reporters who accompanied us, I had had the idea of milking the pope's cows and drinking several mouthfuls of raw milk. The description of that episode in the Quebec media had unleashed a storm of laughter. That hadn't been our intent, but in such situations it's better to roll with the punches. So in my show *Incognito* I recalled my "papal milk-tasting experience," which drew big laughs yet again, this time without any contempt.

I also told how I had become part of Sobbers Anonymous. SA, like AA, met regularly to help people learn how to "stay clean and sober from sobbing."

"Next week will make one year without crying," I'd say in a voice filled with emotion. "I'm doing a lot better, I can control myself, I think I'm on the road to recovery. The proof: I'll now sing for you, without a problem, one of the saddest songs in my repertory, 'Mon ami m'a quitté' [He's Left Me], which used to make me cry so much in the past."

Everything had been written, not only the music and the lyrics of the songs, but all the transitional speeches, the dance steps, every gesture and smile. It was reassuring, and constraining at the same time, almost stifling. Some days I felt like I was in a straitjacket. It was with *Incognito,* however, that I really learned to become master of a stage and that I understood that it was a place of power. I learned, night after night, to react with the crowd, to become the master of my emotions—and of theirs.

And during this tour, I began seriously practicing what I call my little rituals. During this time, I accumulated a virtual collection of them. I don't really know how it began. But everything seemed to lend itself naturally to the process, even if it was completely irrational. We often added a gesture or glance to our routine, a detail that was sometimes almost invisible. But once we'd added these little nothings, they took on absolute importance. There was no question of getting rid of them. Finally, our ceremonies began to last several minutes.

For example, each time before the curtain rose, Mego, Suzanne, and I played a little game. When everything was ready, right before the stage manager gave us the signal and the house was plunged into darkness, we did a kind of incantation dance together. I pretended to strike a chord or to pull out one of the wires that connected Mego's keyboard to the amps. Mego pretended to freak out, acted as if he were furious, and gestured for me to go away. Then I went around the stage, touching right thumbs with each of the musicians and chorus members.

I'd find Suzanne below the stage. She'd hand me my mike. Before taking it, I'd squeeze her shoulder three times. Then I'd turn toward

René. He'd come up to me. He'd kiss me on each cheek, always the left first. Then he'd put his hands on my shoulders, and he'd shake me very gently while looking me straight in the eyes with a very serious expression; then he'd turn me around, position me facing the staircase leading to the stage and gently push me.

"Okay, go for it. You're there. Go."

These rituals evolved over time. But they could never be ignored. They were games, but at the same time, they were serious and essential. During a tour, things like the dressing room, the hotel room, the stage, the audience all change from day to day. I needed to have something permanent. In these rituals and rigorously repeated gestures, I found something to reassure myself.

For a long time I've kept in the bottom of my purse, in a small transparent plastic envelope, a coin I found years ago on the stage at Trois-Rivières in Quebec. As I always do after my second song, I was getting ready to talk to people, to thank them for having come, to tell them that I loved them, that I was happy, when I spotted the shining coin, tails up, easily visible, right at the edge of the stage. I could see the beaver, the symbol of Canada, found on Canadian nickels.

During intermission, when the curtain had fallen, I bent down to pick it up. But René had gotten it into my head that you must never pick up a coin that is tails up. Only heads.

"Don't touch tails. It's bad luck."

I nevertheless picked it up and tossed it a little farther, twice, until it fell heads up, the side with the queen of England. Then I picked it up and kept it.

I think you have to make your own luck. And in this domain, as in many others, you're best served when you do it yourself.

Today I know that rituals, good-luck charms, fetishes, even prayers can't always protect us and those we love. Misfortune strikes where it wishes. And when it comes, rituals lose their power. You have to act, fight.

One evening when I got home, I discovered my mother looking frightfully pale. She was short of breath, her features were drawn, and most worrisome of all, she was sitting down. My mother is always up and running all over the place. My father was at a loss to explain it. Unlike my mother and me, in this kind of situation, he was incapable of making a decision. He wasn't able to reason with my mother, who is rather authoritarian, hyperactive, who takes charge of making all decisions and doesn't take orders from anybody. She kept saying that it was only fatigue, that it would pass. I knew just by seeing her and hearing her weak, expressionless voice that she was in bad shape.

In the little movies I made up in my head, I'd often imagined my mother dying. I could see myself at her bedside, completely paralyzed by pain, crushed and distraught and completely incapable of reacting.

But faced with the reality, I reacted completely differently, without thinking, and with a coolness and authority that surprised me.

I called Dr. Gaston Choquette, whom René knew, and made an appointment for my mother the next afternoon at the Montreal Institute of Cardiology. The hardest part was convincing her to go.

"I'm your mother and I'm more than sixty years old. If I don't want to see your doctor, I'm not going."

Aside from Dr. Emile McDuff, who'd delivered her last ten children and who'd practically become a member of our family, my mother never had much respect for doctors. She didn't consider them infallible scientists and didn't think anyone should bow down before them. My mother didn't bow down to anybody.

My brother Michel was my supporter and my idol. Here I am at age five at his wedding, where I sang in public for the first time, discovering both stage fright and the unforgettable sensation a singer feels when an audience hears her and applauds. (Dion family photograph)

My childhood was very happy and carefree, and I spent most of my time with adults and children who were much older than me. Luckily, my parents let me be at every party. (Dion family photograph)

*W*hen I look at this photograph that was taken of me when I was eight, I see a lot of confidence in my expression—proof that I had a happy childhood. (Dion family photograph)

*M*y brothers and sisters always doted on me, and I loved making them laugh by putting on shows for them. (Dion family photograph)

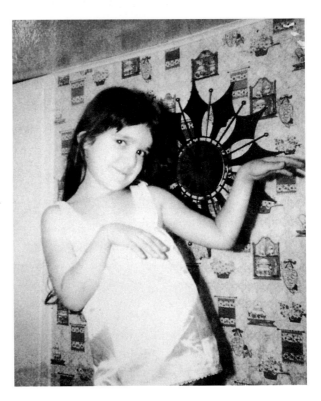

I was so fortunate to be part of a family that was crazy about music. Even today, they are both my family and my music—tightly linked to my happiness and my equilibrium. (Dion family photograph)

My mother and I shared the same dream that I would one day become a singer. She has been my confidante and my adviser. At the same time, she is always the irreplaceable and unique person who is my mother. (Dion family photograph)

I've never been able to get enough of the sea, the beach, the sun, and the heat. (Dion family photograph)

*H*ere I am at age fourteen with René and Mia at a maple-sugar party, when the future was nothing more than a dream. (Photograph by François Rivard)

World Popular Song Festival in Tokyo '82

*I*n Tokyo at the Yamaha Music Festival in 1982. Before taking the stage, I found a five-yen piece on the floor and slipped it into my shoe. I've kept it ever since for good luck. (Feeling Productions archives)

*O*nstage at the TV show *Champs-Élysées* in Paris. This was my first meeting with Michel Drucker, who opened the doors of show business for me and who has remained a close friend. (Feeling Productions archives)

❧

*I*n the fall of 1984, Pope John Paul II granted René and me a private audience at the Vatican. We asked him to bless our families. (Photograph by Arturo Mari)

Eddy Marnay was a master at knowing my thoughts. He knew better than anyone how to read me, and he wrote songs that were made-to-measure for me. (Feeling Productions archives)

I owe so much to my beloved niece Karine. She opened my eyes to the sad realities of life. And she gave me an example to follow. (Dion family photograph)

When I was on *The Tonight Show* for the first time, Phil Collins said to me, "We'll see you again," to which I replied, "You bet!" (Feeling Productions archives)

Princess Diana, so beautiful and elegant. At a dinner in Ottawa, we spoke about fashion and happiness. I found her very warm, but there was something deeper and very serious about her. (Feeling Productions archives)

𝒨uhammad Ali is a warm, emotional, and physically affectionate man. I joined him in his crusade for the protection of children throughout the world. (Feeling Productions archives)

❧

𝒥 love fire as much as water. I love its reassuring presence, its color, and its scent. (Feeling Productions archives)

Mr. and Mrs. René Angélil. This photo is one of René's favorites. (Feeling Productions archives)

Despite the enormous pressures of his position, President Bill Clinton appeared relaxed, funny, attentive, and unquestionably happy each time I was fortunate enough to see him. (Feeling Productions archives)

$\mathscr{I}$'ve always loved working in the studio. I feel that I'm away from the world and that time stands still. Whether I'm in Paris or Los Angeles, whether it's noon or midnight, I always feel the same. (Photograph by Laurent Cayla)

$\mathscr{D}$uring the recording of the album *Let's Talk About Love* at the Hit Factory, I was surrounded by (left to right) John Doelp, head of Sony-USA; Ric Wake; René; Vito Luprano, our artistic director; and Umberto Gatica. (Photograph by Laurent Cayla)

At the Hit Factory studios with Luciano Pavarotti. We were recording our duet, "I Hate You, Then I Love You," for my *Let's Talk About Love* album. Having Luciano around put all of us in a good mood. "If not," he'd say, "what's the use of singing?" (Photograph by Dimo Sefari)

Far left: Tommy Mottola, the CEO of Sony; on the right the Bee Gees surrounding actor Joe Pesci. We were all laughing wildly after that photo session. (Photograph by Dimo Sefari)

$\mathscr{I}$ realized my greatest dream when I sang the duet "Tell Him" with Barbra Streisand. She has always been my hero, and since working with her Barbra has become my friend . . . and is still my hero. (Photograph by Herb Ritts)

$\mathscr{W}$ith Oprah Winfrey things clicked fast and forever. (Harpo Productions)

ℋere I am performing at the Stade de France in June 1999. A satellite hookup let a convalescing René watch the show directly from our house in Florida. This outfit was designed for me by Annie Horth and is one of the most beautiful that I own. (Photograph by Steve France Studio)

$\mathcal{I}$ always travel with photographers, especially those who know how to reveal my inner soul. (Photograph by Dominique Isserman)

After I finish a show and everything has gone well, I'm still so full of energy that I can't stop singing and laughing for hours. (Feeling Productions archives)

Karl Lagerfeld, the head of Chanel, guided me through the fascinating world of fashion and haute couture. He is supremely elegant. (Photograph by Bertrand Rindoff Petroff)

Golf is more than a sport, it's a way of life, a constant search for perfection, equilibrium, and happiness. For René and me, it's a way for us to be together— and is always a very intimate experience. (Photograph by Pat Krause)

The joy of victory. (Photograph by Marc Gassman)

A marvelous gift for my thirty-second birthday: learning that René had regained his health. (Dion family photograph)

Even so, I didn't understand her reluctance until my father told me she was supposed to watch my sister Linda's son the next morning.

Five minutes later, I'd found a baby-sitter. I'd convinced René to put off for a day our departure for Chicoutimi, where I was supposed to sing two days later, in the evening. And I went with my mother to the doctor, who diagnosed heart failure. He sent her to the emergency room and had her operated on the next morning: a quadruple bypass.

Several hours later, I went on stage at Chicoutimi. I knew that Maman was out of danger. And we went back to touring.

When we returned to Montreal, after touring through Quebec, our show, words, music, and rituals were going along just fine. There was a wonderful sense of togetherness in our group. The force was with us. Happiness, triumph. All of us felt it.

"Talk about it," René told me when I started doing publicity in Montreal. "You don't have to be ashamed to say that you had a good show."

I didn't hesitate. I hate people who boast, but I don't like false modesty either. I was happy with my show and I said so, on television, on radio, in the papers. It was like René's approach, upping the ante. You have to be sure of yourself, of your luck.

I supposed that intellectuals would avoid me a bit more now. I think I remember that they accused me of being a little too commercial, meaning that I was successful and enjoying it. But I could see people of all ages in the house, which was always filled to bursting. Every evening after the show, in my dressing room, I was visited by show-business people, but also by people in sports, politics, and business.

One evening, a smiling and hospitable Carol Reynolds, who was responsible for the variety shows on the English-speaking network Radio Canada, was among those who came to see me. She waited until everyone had left to come to say hello and to tell me how much she liked the show. All three of us—René, Carol, and I—went to a restaurant. An Italian one on the rue Saint-Denis in Montreal. Carol wanted to produce a TV show with me for English-speaking Canada. I talked to her about my album in English and how we hoped to work with David Foster.

"David? I know him well," she told us. "I'll be seeing him next week in Los Angeles. If you want, I'll talk to him about you."

If I want? And how!

Carol left with the album *Incognito* and a videocassette of my version of "Have a Heart" from the Juno gala.

"I'm sure he'll love what you do," she told me. "But he's really busy. He may not be available for months."

Shortly after, a few days before my twentieth birthday, we were doing a sound test at the Saint-Denis Theater when I saw René coming toward me, almost at a run. He came up to me and whispered in my ear: "I just spoke to David Foster. He listened to *Incognito*. You know what he told me? That you have everything it takes to get into the U.S. market. Listen! He said that you have 'that little something extra' that makes great stars. And that he wants to work with us."

"When?"

"Not until the fall."

"But that's six months away."

"The time will fly, believe me."

Then he went to tell his secret to Mego and Suzanne. Then on the telephone to his friends, to Ben and Marc.

I really needed to arm myself with patience. But I thought I'd already given a lot. In the heat of action, love really hadn't progressed. René was always very loving and gentle with me. But I think he was totally on to me. He avoided being alone with me for too long a time. He knew he wouldn't escape. And I knew it too. It

was only a question of time, a few weeks, days. It was almost unbearable. And wonderful at the same time.

fter René and I admitted that we were in love, we
talked a lot about the months when we were so in love
without even saying it.

"Remember the day you came to pick me up at Duvernay. And
how shocked you were to see me."

"Do you remember what a lovely moment we had in each other's
arms at the Esterel when you sang with Dan Hill for the people at
CBS?"

"You know, I've never forgotten that depressing evening in the
restaurant in Paris when you decided to put some distance between
us."

"You know, I'll never forget the fashion show you put on in those
rooms in the Radio Canada offices. I could describe every one of the
costumes you wore."

"Even the ones you thought were too daring for television?"

"I'll never forget the time when you fell asleep on my shoulder in
the plane that took us back from Paris."

"But I wasn't asleep on your shoulder, darling. I was pretending to
be asleep."

I'd let my head slide against his shoulder because I felt good and
because I was hoping to possibly seduce him. I looked at his hands,
which excited me so much, strong hands with nails that were always
well manicured. And he smelled so good, so fresh. I had a terrible
desire to take his hand, to place my lips on it.

"If I'd only known," he said to me.

"You wouldn't have done anything. You knew I loved you for a
long time and you did nothing."

Unlike him, I'd never had even the shadow of a doubt. That day, in the plane taking us back from Paris, I knew I was in love with him forever and that something had to happen sooner or later. I had no experience (other than theoretical) of love, but I was really determined.

René had a lot of experience, but at the time, he acted like a scared adolescent, a hundred times more intimidated than he would have been in front of a woman of his own age. He was afraid of what people would say, afraid to hurt me, afraid that at thirty I'd find myself with a man of fifty-six.

But I knew I had him. And I bided my time. Finally it came.

It was in Dublin, on that unforgettable day of April 30, 1988, the evening of the Eurovision competition in which, though French Canadian, I was representing the Swiss! And singing a song written by an Italian and a Turk.

My mother had had open-heart surgery a few weeks earlier. I wanted her to take some rest. And I no longer wanted her to go with me on tour, especially not if it involved a trip overseas.

That day the suspense was unbelievable. Until the last minute, we thought that first prize would go to the performer representing England. I remember his song was called "Go," my lucky number in Japanese. And in this I saw a bad omen. What is more, I didn't really like the song I was going to perform. I found it too pompous.

After I'd sung the song, I'd remained in the wings with the other contestants. We were watching the TV and stage director explain to the young Englishman how to come onstage when the winner was announced. It seemed that he'd won. I was resigned to losing. Only one thing felt urgent: I wanted to find René, who would probably be devastated. We were going to live through our first defeat together. I'd turn it into a personal victory. I'd hold back my tears and console him; I'd mother him.

But the judges from two or three countries hadn't announced their choices yet. In the end, I won by just one point.

As I went to collect my prize, I dissolved into tears in front of the audience at Simmonscourt and the hundreds of millions of Europeans who were watching the awards show on television. I made my thank-yous more or less coherently and left the stage almost at a run. When I found René, I threw myself into his arms and, still crying, hugged him very hard and kissed him on the neck. I was as happy as it was possible to be.

He let it happen. He was laughing.

As usual, he went back to my room with me, and he began recounting the day we'd spent together. How scared he had been. He reminded me of how important this victory was, since, according to him, it gave me a lot of visibility in Europe. For at least the hundredth time in two weeks, he told me that the Eurovision show was, after the Olympics and the Oscars, the most-watched TV program in the world. He also talked to me about the other participants, who had sung well and who wouldn't go very far. And then . . . I don't remember what he said. I wasn't really listening. I just let myself be cradled by his voice.

I was seated at the head of the bed, legs folded under the covers. I was happy about being alone with the man I loved. And I had a very precise plan.

I realized that he'd stopped talking, that we were enveloped by silence. He stayed there, sitting on the arm of the chair, very near my bed, without saying a word. I looked at him with my mature woman's smile. I think that at that moment he realized that I hadn't been listening to him for a while and that I was thinking of other things. He lowered his eyes. I could feel that I'd touched him emotionally. Right in his heart. He got up, then backed toward the door two or three steps, as if to escape my hold over him, and said good night.

I couldn't let it go like that.

Every night since our first tour three years before, he'd said good night to me by kissing me on both cheeks. For several months, especially during the *Incognito* tour, I'd had the impression that his kisses each day slid a few millimeters closer to my lips, until our mouths sometimes touched.

And on this night of glory and victory, he was about to leave without kissing me at all!

He'd already opened the door. I slipped off the bed and walked up to him; I pressed myself against him.

"You haven't kissed me yet, René Angélil."

I took his head in my hands and I kissed him on the lips. I put my arms around his neck . . . He held me tight, the door still open behind him. Then he removed my arms. He fled to his room. I stayed there for a moment all alone, my heart beating—trembling and dumbfounded.

I knew that I'd won. That flight was an admission of it.

I grabbed the telephone and called his room to tell him: "If you don't come back here immediately, I'm going to go knock on your door."

But there was no answer.

It was he who called me several minutes later from the lobby of the hotel. To ask if I was all right. And then he told me: "If you really want to, I'll be the first."

And I answered him: "You'll be the first. And the only."

5

Two days later, when we arrived at the Mirabel airport outside Montreal, we were greeted by droves of reporters, photographers, cameramen, and other people in the music industry. René had brought them the Irish and English newspapers, which he read to them. He showed them my picture and the headlines. Then he reminded the journalists how important Eurovision was, even though hardly anyone knew about it in Canada.

He couldn't resist telling them how I'd cried my eyes out. And everybody laughed when he reminded them how long it had been since I'd had a good cry like that.

He told them every detail of the press conference that had followed the competitions and how incredible he thought I'd been. He also said that all the journalists from around the world—"six or seven hundred," he claimed, which seemed like a big exaggeration to me— were amazed to learn that I was the youngest of fourteen children from a backwater town called Charlemagne.

"Afterward," René continued, "they had her sign autographs everywhere—the hotel, the Dublin airport, in the plane that took us back to London. The pilot even announced that she was on board and everybody applauded."

The reporters were fascinated by all of this, but to me, the biggest news—what gave me the greatest pleasure of all—was that we were in love. I looked radiant and I'm sure they all thought it was because of my success in Dublin. That actually had little to do with it.

René reminded the reporters that CBS had promised us an English-language record that we'd begin working on in the fall after the *Incognito* tour.

"With the best director, the best lyricists and composers, and under the best conditions you can imagine," he said. "It'll knock you out."

A reporter asked us if we were happy together, if we still got along well. I thought she'd guessed everything. In fact later, she told me she had. But René answered her before I could: "I wouldn't give this up for anything in the world," he said. "And Celine feels the same way, I'm sure. We share the same dream, the two of us."

"And the same bed," I was tempted to say.

But I wasn't allowed to. The day before, he'd convinced me to keep silent about our love.

"For how long?" I asked.

"As long as necessary."

"Necessary for what?"

"We've got to tell the people close to us about it, your relatives first."

He was right, as usual; he always thought of everything. Only, at the time, I didn't imagine that "as long as necessary" would be as intolerably long as it turned out to be.

I gave the reporters the proper answer about being happy with my professional association with René. For seven years, he'd made all the decisions that concerned my career. And he'd never been wrong.

"I have complete confidence in him."

But one journalist gave it another try.

"You just turned twenty, Celine. Don't you have a boyfriend? A lot of girls your age do."

Images passed through my head. I saw myself earlier, standing against the wall of my room after René had left, my knees shaking so hard I almost collapsed. I remembered the sound of his voice before that, as if in a dream: "If you really want to, I'll be the first." I heard myself answer, on the edge of tears: "Of course I want to . . . You'll be the first. And the only . . ."

Reacting to my silence, the reporter asked again: "Do you have a boyfriend, Celine?"

I swallowed my feelings, then calmly answered with a smile, while René kept his eyes on me: "No, I don't have time for one, my career's my top priority. I devote everything to it."

It was the first of a very long and very painful series of lies. I was beginning a happy, yet troubled period of my life, the period of my secret love affair. It would bring me great happiness; but despite professional success, the prison of lies I had to lock myself in would from time to time ruin all my pleasure.

On the other hand, in my family, things settled down quickly enough. I was, after all, twenty years old. My parents now realized that I wasn't going to give up a love that was making me happy. We knew other very successful couples, such as Eddy and Mia, with an age difference of fifteen, twenty, even thirty years. And there was the example of Charlie Chaplin and Oona O'Neill, who stayed happy together for more than thirty years. They'd even produced a strong, close-knit family.

René told me that when he realized he was falling in love with me, he'd tried to forget me. He'd left for Las Vegas at every opportunity. He'd even gone to Paris and seen Eddy Marnay, whom he'd always thought of as a father and a person in whom he could confide.

"You know Eddy. He and I walked for miles through Paris while I spoke to him about you."

"What did he tell you?"

"He said to me: 'Do you really love her?' "

"And what did you say?"

"I told him: 'I'm crazy about her. I see her everywhere, I think about her all the time.' "

"And he said?"

"He told me: 'If you love her, you've got nothing to fear. You can't hurt her.' "

"That's just what I told you."

But René was also thinking of my career. He thought about it even more than he thought of our happiness, an idea that really crushed me at moments. He thought that if people found out that we were in love, all we'd built would be destroyed.

So for a long time we loved each other only in the privacy and intimacy of our families. They adjusted to it pretty well, I think. But not me. I suffered and wept, perhaps because I was the younger one. And also because it was my first love. I wanted to shout it from the rooftops on the very first day. To be loved by René Angélil was more beautiful than anything I had known my whole life. But out of love, in fact, because he'd asked me to—to please him—I agreed to keep quiet. Except that it was for much too long a time.

At the very beginning of summer, David Foster told René that he'd be ready to work with us soon, but first he wanted to see me perform live. A week after Eurovision, I'd gone back to Europe for a quick tour. Ten cities in ten days. It was insane. Press conferences, interviews, TV, radio, some fabulous encounters, such as meeting Elton John in Munich, and a big show during the Cannes Film Festival with Julia Migenes-Johnson and Michel Legrand. When I returned to Quebec, I continued the *Incognito* tour, and the show couldn't have been in better shape. Not only were the musicians in great form, but I was in good voice as well.

But as luck would have it, at the time that David was passing through Quebec, the only performing I was doing was a show for a group of vacationers, under a tent at Sainte-Agathe in the Laurentides. René tried really hard to make him put off his trip.

"In two weeks, Celine will be performing at the most important theater in Montreal," he said. "Under ideal conditions."

David decided not to put off the trip. He came to the show with his new wife, Linda Thompson, who had been involved with Elvis Presley. It was a really hot day. And it was pouring. The air inside the tent was humid, suffocating. The sound was horrible. At times, the rain hammered so loudly on the roof that it was almost impossible to hear the music.

Nevertheless, I felt good, confident, and cool, despite the oppressive heat. The songs came off well. During the show, I introduced David Foster by saying that he was the greatest record-album producer in the world and that he'd worked with the most brilliant American singing stars. The audience at Sainte-Agathe, who obviously had never heard of him, gave him a polite standing ovation, something to which dear David is not impervious.

After the show, the four of us went to a restaurant in the Laurentides. David didn't compliment my performance at all—that's not his style. He has other ways of showing his enthusiasm or approval.

"Count me in," he told us. "Find yourself some songs and let me know."

With Vito Luprano, the artistic director of CBS, which had now become Sony, René began sorting through the dozens of songs we'd collected during the past months.

After the holidays, when the *Incognito* tour was over, René and I went to California. We settled into a little inn on Malibu Beach, not far from where David lived. At the time, he was the only person we knew in Los Angeles.

Years later, David told me that what he found most charming about us was how happy, how joyous we were. When he came to the inn with Linda, he'd find us in the parking lot playing basketball or on the nearby beach, where we took long walks. Sometimes he played or walked with us.

Relatives and friends from Quebec also came to visit. Mego and Suzanne came. Sometimes people from Sony came also. Usually it was Vito, who brought music for us to hear. Little by little, what would become our first English-language album took shape. It would be composed exclusively of love songs. Most of the approximately two hundred songs I've recorded in my life are about love—its joy and its pain.

We were alone a lot, far from all the rumors that were circulating about us. I was finally living intimately with the man I loved. We were a couple, a real couple.

For the first time in my life, I could be a lover and pretend to be a wife. I could slip into the kitchen at the inn, make some pasta or a cake. I'm not a very good cook. At the house, my mother did everything and knew how to do everything. Outside of spaghetti bolognaise, my talents are limited. René is a big eater. And at the time, he was a better cook than I was. He added spices to my sauce, changing everything.

He let me sleep very late. I'm a night person and he's a morning person. Around six A.M., he'd tiptoe out to buy magazines and newspapers to read on the terrace. He always wanted to know all the news and everything on the sports page, whether it was hockey, baseball, football, or boxing. He always wanted to know who'd won or lost in every game, every battle.

When I got up around noon, he'd get me back into the world. He'd have made some fruit juice for me. Sometimes we didn't do anything but walk on the beach and enjoy the sun.

That winter in California, our days were peaceful. They were the last days that were that way, before the great whirlwind once again swept us up.

In California, nobody knew us. We could let everyone see our love and our happiness.

Everything was new. Love, the landscape, the words, even my voice seemed new to me.

I knew my singing would sound different in English. When you change from one language to another, the very texture of your voice changes, even its register.

But there was something else. I'd changed too. And I was conscious of it. I could see it in myself, in my gestures, my thoughts, in my whole life. I was a woman in full bloom, confident of her femininity, of herself, of her power to attract the man she loved.

I felt freer than I'd ever felt before. At the Chartmaker studio where we spent our evenings and sometimes our nights, everybody knew that René and I were together. We had nothing to hide. We could kiss, hold hands, call each other "darling" or "my love" without surprising or offending anyone. I think the freedom and happiness I was experiencing also had an effect upon my voice. It felt more supple, closer to me, freer, brighter.

As usual, René considered this current project to be of the greatest importance.

"This album will give you an entrée into international show business. If you miss the mark . . ."

"Yes, I know, darling, if I miss the mark, we both go back to square one. And stay there probably for life."

I made him laugh. A lot. I've always made him laugh a lot. However, during the entire year when we were recording *Unison,* he was worried and preoccupied, always ready to rethink everything. Some days he felt like changing everything, beginning all over again, trying something else, changing the tempo, brass instead of strings, two pianos here, no guitar there, or a completely new song.

He and David Foster understood each other perfectly. Foster was detail-oriented too, a stickler, never completely satisfied. With himself, with the musicians, or with me. To hear him, you could always do better. You could always start all over again. And that's often what we did.

Sony's strategists were really excited that we were working with David, but to get a wider buying audience, they wanted me to work with other producers and composers as well, in other studios and cities. That was fine with me. With René too; he'd always been obsessed with the idea of enlarging my audience and varying my repertoire. Even David thought it was a good idea. Everyone decided that I would go first to New York to work with Andy Goldmark, then to London to work with Christopher Neil.

That's how we got caught up in the whirlwind that would never let us out of its grip, even though it would create some unbelievable moments in our lives for more than ten years.

When we left Malibu for New York in the spring of 1989, we both knew that from then on, we'd be living the lives of gypsies and nomads. From then on we'd only be passing through Montreal, Paris, Los Angeles, and Las Vegas. Passing through everywhere, never staying more than a few weeks in the same place. Then leaving on tour.

I don't think that Grand Prix Formula One drivers at the wheel of their race cars have much time to admire the scenery. But they live intensely, of that I'm sure. Actually, they see the scenery differently than we do. They see another kind of scenery. Like them, I was going to fly through the years of my youth like a bat out of hell. The stops would be few and short. But I'd see things that the majority of people don't get to see; I was going to lead another kind of very intense, full life. The one I'd always dreamed of living. So much so that I often had the feeling that I already knew all of it. I'd been in these studios, heard this music, worked with these musicians. In another life, maybe. At times, everything was like déjà vu; I knew it all already.

I was at home in Los Angeles. As comfortable at the Chartmaker as I was in the Saint-Charles studio in Longueuil, Quebec, or the Family Song in Paris, where I'd made my first recordings. I often sang in front of complete strangers, people from the industry, musicians who were curious to hear my voice, a whole audience of connoisseurs and professionals. And on two occasions, I was asked to do duets on other albums, one with Billy Newton-Davis, the other with Dan Hill.

Los Angeles can give a singer more visibility than anywhere. It was there that I'd very soon enter the world of international show business, the "big time," as René called it, by appearing on *The Tonight Show.* I'd sing at the Oscars before the most glamorous audience imaginable. And Prince, as he wished to be called then, would see me and would write a song for me called "With This Tear" that I would include on my second English-language album, *Celine Dion.*

In New York, I also felt at home right away. It's a harsh, in-your-face city that you can quickly grow attached to. Not at all cool like Los Angeles, but vibrant and energizing. Everybody talks to everybody, touches everybody, as if they've known each other forever.

Andy Goldmark, as well as the technicians and musicians he directed ("the best in the world," according to René), welcomed me as if I were one of them. No more and no less. We did the song "Unison" together, which is a song for the stage, very "danceable," powerful, and physically demanding.

Some artists can spend a whole career only through recordings, never performing onstage. But I like to do both. Recording an album for me is a little like preparing the supplies and "ammunition" that I can later take on tour. When we choose songs, we take into account their stage potential.

Andy was a firm, rigorous director. From the beginning, he knew the sound and rhythms he wanted. In Britain, Chris Neil did things a different way. Rather than imposing his vision on me, as Foster and Goldmark had done, he helped me find the sound and rhythms I wanted. This was a very new experience for me. At first, it threw me off balance. Knowing what you want isn't always so simple. Especially when you've spent years letting others choose for you. There's a great temptation to rely on them again. But Chris wanted to consult with me about everything. In the end, this taught me a lot about myself and my tastes.

He had wanted to meet with me several weeks before the recording session to prepare the orchestra tracks and the arrangements for "Where Does My Heart Beat Now?" He wanted to know what key I'd be singing in, but also how I wanted to work.

At the beginning, I didn't know how to answer. I tried to tell him that I worked best when all the people around me were involved and wanted to do a good job.

But he wanted to know more: "Tell me where, when, and how you like to work. Mornings? Evenings? At night? Do you want candle-light? Do you prefer to sing in a booth? Do you want a lot of people around you?"

René had told him that I didn't like to sing, or even talk, before noon. And that I wasn't completely myself until after three or four o'clock in the afternoon. So Chris scheduled studios and engineers for the evening.

I told him not to worry about the ambience. I've always loved recording studios and feel good in them. They put you outside the world, outside of time. Paris or Los Angeles, noon or midnight, it's all the same.

I have a good memory for songs. When I hear them two or three times, I know them by heart, words and music. I prepare them in my head, but it never takes long. When I enter the studio, I'm ready. The song has taken form.

The day of the recording, everything happened very quickly. I did a take, as a warm-up, while waiting for René and Vito, who were playing pool in the next room.

"That was perfect," said Chris.

And he ran to tell the pool players that we'd done it. We listened to the recording. Just to put our minds at rest, we did another take. But it was the first one that ended up on the album.

René and Vito were ecstatic. They dropped me off at the hotel and went to gamble at the casino. Not really to make any money, but to make sure that luck was really with us. René's famous theory of pat-terns . . . Later that night, when he returned to the hotel, he woke me up to tell me he'd won big and he was absolutely positive that the song would go very far. And so would we.

"You'll do *The Tonight Show* with that song," he kept repeating to me. "I'm telling you it's going to happen."

———ᘓ

After my mother's heart surgery, I'd bought a house in Quebec, at Sainte-Anne-des-Lacs, so that she could rest. It was a large house in which everything—walls, ceilings, floors, furniture—was white, and it had immense windows. So it had a lot of light, almost too much, especially in winter when the snow covered the lake and the forest. You needed to wear sunglasses almost the whole day. But my parents loved that house—and so did I. In the fall, after I'd finished recording *Unison,* I spent several weeks there.

For more than a year, I'd lived almost continually in hotels in the heart of very large cities, such as Los Angeles, New York, Paris, and London. Now I needed clean air and plenty of space. I wanted to reflect on what was happening to me.

When René and I were in Quebec, we had to pretend not to be together. When journalists asked me if I was in love, I kept answering that I didn't have the time or place in my heart, in my life or career, for a man.

These repeated lies, which I lived day by day, sometimes caused me a lot of pain. I was confused and torn.

I'd just recorded my first album in English. Twelve songs that all talked about love, about great passions. I was getting ready to shoot a video in New Orleans in which I'd appear as a very sexy, provocative young woman, looking like someone who'd had a lot of experience with love. For the press photos that were being shot for the launch of *Unison,* experts did my hair, my makeup, and dressed me to look even sexier. I was wearing tight jeans and a white camisole that showed my shoulders and stomach.

On the one hand, in real life, I was supposed to keep claiming that I was a young girl who knew nothing about love. On the other hand, on stage and screen and in my songs, I was supposed to behave like a mature, fulfilled, much-loved woman. It was just a game, of course, just show business and make-believe. But it was also an upside-down kind of world.

Strangely, it was in the world of show business, the world of illusion and fiction, in the songs, videos, photos, where every lie and disguise is allowed, that I was telling the truth. In real life, where I would like to have been frank, I had to force myself to lie every day, to claim that there was no love in my life. My greatest dream was for the whole world to know that René and I loved each other, that we made love together, that we wanted to have children someday, that we were going to spend our lives together. But René said no.

"It's too soon. Just wait."

However, more and more people knew very well what was going on. As Paul Burger, who had just become president of Sony Canada, recalled several years later: "As soon as I saw you, I knew that you were together. It was obvious. And I never understood why you took so long to say it."

"You'd better ask René that question."

Paul had come to see me, at Sainte-Anne-des-Lacs. As usual, the house was filled with people—my parents, my brothers and sisters, René, his children. We'd already become the center of attention for both our families.

Paul was American, but he'd lived in Israel, France, and England. He spoke several languages, including French with my mother and my sisters, who thought he was handsome and very charming. He was going to become a close, valued friend. And for years he'd play a very important role in my career.

He'd come to tell us, among other things, that he wasn't altogether satisfied with the songs we'd recorded for *Unison*.

"I think it's missing a couple more rhythmic songs that could really show off your voice. If you say it's okay, we'll go back to the studio, wherever you want, and with whomever you want."

I chose London, with Chris Neil.

René was thrilled. He was very satisfied with several of the recorded songs, but he too thought that the whole thing lacked something. But he'd been afraid that Sony would refuse to invest more in an album that had already cost so much to produce.

That day at Sainte-Anne-des-Lacs, Paul began to talk to me about my look, telling me he found it a little "old." This was his way of saying without really saying that he thought it was "out of it." He told me again that a singer has to have a look.

"I'm sure you're not dressing like you'd like to."

It was true. I had songs that were like me. But the clothes I was wearing weren't really saying anything. Quite often they had practically nothing to do with me. And this was true despite the fact that I had a full wardrobe—at least a hundred pairs of shoes, a hundred dresses, three or four fur coats, tons of underwear, and fine lingerie. In New York and Paris, I went around to all the shops. I followed fashion carefully. But all I was doing was following what other people were doing.

"That's not at all what you've got to do," said Paul. "You've got to *create* the fashion."

I wanted to do this. But I wasn't the type to provoke people by playing a character, like Madonna, who had already established a personal kind of theater and legend around herself.

I loved to experiment with different looks for myself, but what I loved above all was to sing, the physical pleasure of singing before a crowd. The bigger the crowd and the stage, the more pleasure I took in it.

I knew very well that my voice was what touched people, not any kind of look I might create. I knew this, but I also knew that what Paul was saying was also right.

I had the support of a very powerful multinational company. Close to me, an attentive and experienced, passionate manager, who was getting to know the ins and outs of American show business better and better every day.

No hope was beyond realizing. My life was truly beginning to resemble a fairy tale.

Shortly after the release of *Unison,* I accepted a role in a TV miniseries called *Des Fleurs sur la neige* (Flowers on the Snow). I played a young woman named Elisa, who'd been abandoned at an early age by her mother, beaten by her alcoholic father, raped by her father-in-law, abused by a wicked, brutal husband. . . . An unbearably real story.

For several weeks, then, I lived the opposite of my fairy-tale life, spending every day in the deepest regions of hell. No longer was I the singer preparing to conquer the American pop-music market; I was a poor, defeated, unfortunate girl, without money, without a future, without any other goal in life but to escape from a horrible environment.

Filming was difficult. First of all, it was frightening to assume the persona of such a pitiful, threatened, and wounded character. I had to learn to walk as if I were round-shouldered, keep my eyes lowered, talk in a low voice, act like a victim.

Especially at the beginning, I felt a certain animosity coming from the actors who'd studied theater and who saw me as an intruder. In a way, this helped me to get into the mind of Elisa, who was also rejected and scorned by her contemporaries. It helped me play it to the hilt, to really live her hell.

I played a lot of very violent scenes, on both a psychological and a physical level. When I was supposed to cry, I really cried; when I was supposed to suffer, I suffered. After a few days, black-and-blue marks covered my body and my heart felt crushed. I was afraid of everybody. It was terrible. But I loved the experience. And since then, I've dreamed of being in a movie. To play a character, enter her mind and really give her a soul, is a unique, marvelous experience.

One Friday evening, when I was on my way back to Sainte-Anne-des-Lacs after a long day of shooting, I saw René's nephew Martin's car on the highway. He was bringing Karine to spend the weekend at my place. The fresh Laurentide air would do her good. Her illness made her weaker and weaker, more and more pale and defeated. But she'd kept her smile, and was still fighting.

As I passed Martin's car, I gave him a big smile and waved to him. Then I lost control of my car, which skidded violently in a circle and went off the road backward.

I wasn't hurt, but the car was heavily damaged. I can't remember really being afraid. On the contrary, you could say that the shock woke me up, jarred me out of Elisa's character, and put me back in my own.

At the time, I believed that nothing bad could happen to me. I had too many plans in the works, too many hopes and dreams; in my mind, they had to be realized.

I would soon discover that nothing is that simple. Wishing and dreaming aren't always enough. This doesn't mean there aren't periods in your life when you feel invulnerable. And I was in one of those periods.

When René heard about the accident from my mother, he hurried from Las Vegas in a panic. He swore he'd never leave me again when I was working.

I knew that his promise would be impossible to keep. I knew that we'd always be different from other couples. He had his passions—Las Vegas, gambling, golf—his friends, his work, a whole network of contacts he was establishing in major American show-business circles. I believe, and always will believe that a woman can't prevent the person she loves from leading the life of his dreams or from having his own world. And vice versa. Otherwise, their union becomes a kind of slavery. Each person gets a little smaller and his portion of happiness, his stock of dreams, diminishes. And inevitably the couple diminishes too.

Of course, I was happy when he was with me. When he talked to me about our plans or when he told me about the fabulous adventures of the Beatles or of the King. But I also loved him for his passion for gambling, of every sort, for his need to be constantly surrounded by his friends. I loved him because he was free and unpredictable. I loved him even for his absences, his actual physical absences, when he left for Las Vegas or Los Angeles. Then I dreamed of him; we talked often and for a long time on the telephone and his voice continued to delight me.

I also loved him for those moments he spent lost in space, even when he was around me, deep in reverie, thinking about what we ought to do, what he'd say to the bosses at Sony or to a particular reporter. I knew he was working to build my career, putting all his talent into it, all his time and love. One of the things he loved about me was the confidence I had in him and my ability to be autonomous and independent. I didn't play the child-woman with him. I played a woman who was mature and strong. I'd become the kind of woman he liked. A free woman who trusted him and knew how to let him be free.

"I know that you're sincere," I'd tell him. "I believe you, but I won't hold it against you, I swear, if you don't keep your promises."

And I made my own promises to him.

"I am never going to stop you from traveling, playing blackjack or golf at the other end of the earth, with Marc, Jacques, Ben, Rosaire, and the others. I love you as you are. Don't change. We'll always tell each other everything."

I even accepted that he wanted to keep our love a secret. Especially when we were in the thick of things, as we were that summer, with a thousand things to do and our entire lives changing constantly. At times I was really very happy, fulfilled.

The day after the accident, he talked to me about the projects he'd been working on in Las Vegas. First he let me know that the album *Unison* wasn't taking off as fast as he'd hoped. It had been expressly conceived for the American market, but it had barely gotten out of Quebec. Despite the big publicity campaign I'd done in English-speaking Canada, none of the radio stations were playing my song in Toronto, Vancouver, or Halifax. And the bosses at Sony-USA had decided to wait to release it in the United States.

So much for the bad news. He probably never would have told me about it if he hadn't also had some good news, or rather, a solution to our problems.

In Las Vegas, he'd learned that Sony-International was holding its annual convention that summer at the Château Frontenac in Quebec. He'd rallied Paul Burger and the entire administrative staff of Sony-Canada into convincing the big executives to let me sing two small songs during the convention.

If anyone in the world knew René Angélil's charm, it was me. Nevertheless, I was fascinated and amazed by his talent for making connections, for building bridges.

I too like talking to people, but I don't have his sense of organization. I wouldn't ask people I met to come on board my boat, even if

I found them super-likable. He always did this. When he thought that someone could bring us something, he invited him or her on board.

When we began to put together *Unison* in Malibu, he quickly got to know a whole lot of people in show business. If we needed a trumpet player or a triangle player, he knew the best one and where to find him. So *Unison* was a high-quality, technically impeccable album.

"You know it's a great album, don't you, Celine?"

"Yes, I know it is."

"Now we have to get it listened to and get it on the market. To do that we need the support of Sony's big publicity machine. When they've seen you sing in Quebec, they'll pull out all the stops, you'll see."

In Quebec, I had to sing at nine-thirty in the morning, while the reps and journalists were having their breakfast. I don't think I'd ever sung before noon, even in Charlemagne, growing up in a house that was always full of music.

What's more, I knew a lot of the reps would only be half-awake. Most would have been partying the night before. Quebec is a big party town. They wouldn't really want to hear a girl singing along with some orchestra tracks.

I got up at dawn, so I could properly wake up, eat, and do my voice exercises and stretches. René had told me that all the big Sony bosses would be in attendance, along with the most important show-business reporters from America. Again, it was now or never—or we'd go back to square one.

René had had a powerful sound system installed in the ballroom of the chateau, powerful enough to shake nearby Cape Diamant and wake up the dead.

I sang "Where Does My Heart Beat Now?" for them. At nine-thirty in the morning, while they were having their second cup of coffee. For one long moment, they seemed frozen. So much so that I almost burst out laughing.

When my song was finished, I stood there, stock-still. I heard the crackling of amps, my eyes caught René's; he was at the very back of the room. It seemed to me that he too was wondering what had happened. Nothing, for several seconds. Then they exploded. They got up en masse and gave me a thunderous ovation, all the big bosses of Sony, the journalists from Hollywood and Broadway, and from Trois-Rivières, Val d'Or, and Sept-Îles in Quebec.

The next day the senior executive at Sony met with René. He'd decided to release *Unison* in the United States earlier than originally planned. He was going to organize a vast publicity campaign using the company's best strategists. We'd done it.

Two months later, the prediction that René had made to me in London, in front of Vito and Chris Neil, the day we recorded "Where Does My Heart Beat Now?" came true. I'd sing that same song on *The Tonight Show* with Jay Leno and *The Late Show with David Letterman* in front of I don't know how many tens of millions of people. Of all the songs I recorded, it was the first to really take off in the United States and later in other countries. It's also thanks to that song that James Horner and Will Jennings, the composer and lyricist of "My Heart Will Go On," from the movie *Titanic,* got to know me and wanted to work with me.

I'd often gone to Los Angeles, I'd already traveled a lot in America and Europe, even in Japan, and often went first class. But it was during this three- or four-day trip to Los Angeles that for the first time I had the impression of really belonging to the legendary "big time," as René had called it.

In the limousine that took us to our hotel in Beverly Hills, I heard one of my songs on American radio for the first time. The announcer pronounced my name "Celeeenn Dionn" (in French you don't pronounce the *n* in Dion) and said a couple of words about *Unison,* which would be available in a few days. René was jubilant. He asked the chauffeur if he knew the girl who had just sung.

"Don't have the slightest idea."

So René repeated my name for him two or three times.

In front of our hotel, he asked the chauffeur his name, which I think was Brian.

"Brian, meet Celeen Dionn."

I shook the hand Brian held out to me and I called René a big baby. But, like him, I was absolutely thrilled.

The next afternoon, still with Brian, we went to Sunset Boulevard to see the windows of the most well known record store in the world, Tower Records.

There were three giant displays, thousands of records by George Michael, New Kids on the Block, and Celine Dion. There was a big poster with my mug on it. Over it was a banner with the words: REMEMBER THE NAME, BECAUSE YOU WILL NEVER FORGET THE VOICE.

Immediately, I thought of that first TV show I'd done in France, Michel Drucker's *Champs-Élysées,* when I'd sung "D'Amour ou d'amitié." Later, at Guy and Dodo's, René never stopped repeating the words the host of the program had used to introduce me, when he'd said to the viewers: "You'll never forget the voice you're about to hear. So remember this name: Celine Dion."

That felt like an eternity ago, and at the same time it felt like yesterday.

The air felt very gentle in Los Angeles. René and I walked hand in hand for a long while without speaking. I'm sure we were thinking the same thing. We'd just come full circle. And we were on the verge of realizing our wildest dreams. The great gates of American show business had opened wide for us. In a few months, we could enter them with the show that we'd prepared and that we were going to break in across Quebec and English-speaking Canada. Everything seemed to have been written in the stars, like a beautiful score that we were going to perform in a state of elation.

But first I'd have to face one of the most terrible ordeals of my whole career. This time, the ante would be raised higher than ever, and it wouldn't be René or I who would raise it.

I had to begin the *Unison* tour by doing four shows in a row for my wonderful Quebecois audience. Two in Drummondville and two in Sherbrooke.

The tragedy happened on the third night.

My voice broke all of a sudden. It came apart like wet paper.

It was like entering a vacuum, total darkness. I felt as if I were blowing into a punctured balloon. At that moment I believed my voice would never return. Or that it would come back completely undone, changed, unrecognizable. During a guitar solo, I gave a signal to the stage manager that I could not go on. René went onstage to tell the audience what had happened and to assure them that I'd come back to the show later, in a few days or weeks, as soon as I could. Then people began to applaud. They stood up to show me their sympathy and support. After that, I dissolved into tears. I found Suzanne in the wings and she was crying too. And Mego. Everybody was crying or was silent.

René came into the room and took my head in his hands. In front of the musicians and technicians, but as if we were alone in the world, he kissed me, he took me into his arms very tenderly and rocked me. We were standing at the foot of the staircase that led to the stage. He wasn't crying.

He said to me: "Stop crying, stop crying. It'll be okay. You'll see."

He was right. Everything was going to be okay, but actually, that experience would turn my whole life around, change all my habits, my body, my mind. And as a consequence, it changed my voice. I'm not exaggerating. They say there is some good in all evil. In this particular case, it turned out to be more than true. I was going to learn a great deal from the accident that happened to me on that fall evening in Sherbrooke.

We came back to Montreal in the night, both of us silent, terrified, but at the same time, we were "together." The big premiere in Montreal was at least two weeks away. Now, just as we had gotten so close to our goal, everything seemed to have collapsed.

The next morning, René called the person everyone considers the best otolaryngologist in Quebec—Dr. Marcel Belzile. I'll never forget his name, his concern and kindness, and the things he taught me about my voice.

His office is in Longueuil, on the south bank of the St. Lawrence River. I spent the night at my place in Duvernay, in the northern suburbs of Montreal. This meant that René and I had to cross the entire city, in the middle of rush hour and across two bridges. After sitting in bumper-to-bumper traffic for a good half hour, it became clear that we'd be late unless we took the subway, something I'd done a few times with Maman or my sisters—or in Paris or Tokyo. But on this day, I really didn't want to be there. All the passageways and staircases down to the subway were being swept by violent gusts of wind. It was a strange, rather unusual kind of wind, a cold one badly mixed with a warm one, and there's nothing worse for your throat and lungs.

I was sad, anguished, and in a hurry. I certainly had no need to mingle with the crowd. And people were coming from all over. But I had no choice. If I wanted to finish my tour and make my comeback in Montreal, I had to see Dr. Belzile, and to get there, I had to take the subway.

I was wearing a coat with a hood, which I'd pulled around my face. People seemed intrigued by this, but nobody recognized me. In fact, nobody wanted to recognize me, out of respect for René, I think. He was as well known in Quebec as I was, and had been for a longer time; everybody must have recognized him. Consequently, they ought to have known who was with him hiding under the hood. But nobody bothered us in any way. I think everyone understood that something unusual or serious was happening.

Everyone must have seen by René's somber air that he wasn't in the mood for laughing or chatting.

It's one thing that I'll always like about people from Quebec, that politeness and kindness, that understanding that they have for each other. They respected the fact that we were riding the subway incognito. All that intuitive understanding they showed us really moved me.

That day I realized, as I looked around me, that I wasn't leading the life of Miss Everybody. I began to observe people discreetly. It was my world; these were the faces I saw each evening in the places where I sang. I watched them and listened to them. I told myself they were the people for whom I was working. They were the people who applauded, listened, loved me. They were the audience I'd be singing for in a few days at the Saint-Denis Theater.

We had to change trains, I think, at the Berri-de-Montigny station. René, who most probably hadn't ever taken the subway in his whole life, began asking passengers for directions. A young boy, a student, offered to show us the way, asking nothing in return, not even a hand-shake. He didn't try to see who was hiding under the hood. But he certainly knew I was there. When he left us, he said: "Good luck, Monsieur Angélil."

Five minutes later, we were at Dr. Belzile's office, which was right above the subway station. In my mind, I expected this whole thing to last a few minutes. He'd examine me, prescribe medicine for me, or give me a shot. He'd tell me to rest and drink plenty of fluids. And I'd be able to sing the next day.

That's pretty much what he did. But he also gave me a whole lecture that would force me to rethink my career from top to bottom. He gave me the scare of my life.

"Your vocal cords are fatigued and irritated, because you haven't taken good care of them. You've treated them badly. You can keep singing for a while, but sooner or later, you've got to give your voice a rest for several days, maybe weeks. If you don't, you'll need surgery. The operation might, probably will, change the timbre of your voice."

So I was at risk of becoming a kind of female Joe Cocker!

"Vocal cords are fragile little creatures that are surrounded with enemies," the doctor continued, "as much inside you as in the air you breathe."

Contrary to what I'd thought, drops in temperature or blasts of heat aren't the worst enemies of a voice. A voice in good condition can resist such attacks. Cigarette smoke, dust, and pollution are much more dangerous irritants. But worst of all are stress, fatigue, and ill use.

You can always banish smoke from your environment. Dust as well. You can keep away from people with the flu or a cold. But living without stress or fatigue when your dream is to sing in front of the largest audiences and throughout the world is a whole other ball game. I knew that, in my case, this was the problem. The problem was fatigue, overwork, pressure, and constant stress.

"And also, and of great importance, the way you've mistreated your vocal cords for too long a time," Dr. Belzile added.

He explained to us that the nodules or polyps that develop on vocal cords and finally rob them of a lot of flexibility and elasticity are rarely caused by an infection. Rather, they come from an error in technique. An inexperienced singer who forces her voice, by, for example, singing outside her natural register, or by pushing her voice beyond her limits, can dangerously harm her vocal cords. You have to know how to force, learn how to position, your voice.

"I can cure you for the time being. I can apply a mixture of cortisone and Zylocaine directly to your vocal cords. It will have short-term effects that will seem miraculous to you. Even if you've almost completely lost your voice at the time, you'll regain the better part of your voice in a few hours. But there are very grave risks. If you resort regularly to this kind of medication, you may provoke ruptures and tears. Then you could become incapable of singing for weeks or even months. You could also wreck your voice permanently. Then you'd have no recourse. Even an operation would be useless."

He looked me straight in the eye, very intensely. I could sense that his deepest desire was to heal me. I was touched by his compassion.

"You know, I'm really serious," he told me. "Once, maybe twice, you can use these kind of medicines. And on the condition that you don't force your voice too much. Then you've got to learn how to sing again."

I lapped up his words. I understood all of it, the dangers I'd been courting, the mistakes I'd made. Right then and there I made my resolutions. I'd get better, I'd change. I'd flee any smoky, dusty, or polluted environment. I'd avoid mingling with the crowd and end those group visits in my dressing room. I'd stop hugging everybody like I always did.

And I'd never let myself get overtired again. From then on, I'd make it my duty to sleep well and for a long time, to relax, to unwind as much as possible from all stress. I'd also eat well, not too much and only good things. I was also going to laugh a lot and be happy, because it's well known that laughter and happiness are good for the health and are enemies of stress.

First and foremost, I was going to rid myself of what the doctor had called my "singer's bad habits." I'd learn to sing again. Go back to square one, if I had to, start practicing the most elementary scales. I left Dr. Belzile's office with these resolutions stuck firmly in my head. I felt like a soldier who leaves for war. And I was certain of my recovery. I knew that it depended only on me. Dr. Belzile had said it and said it again.

"You can recover if you want to," he said. "It's up to you."

We were about to leave when he added, "I would feel better if you would consult Dr. William Gould in New York. He's the best ear, nose, and throat man in the world. He taught me everything I know. He could tell you if you needed an operation or whether you had other options."

We had been warned that at some point soon I might have to stop doing any concerts for at least a month. I knew I would benefit from seeing Dr. Gould. I just hoped it wasn't too late, and that he would teach me how to maintain and protect my voice.

After two days of silence, I went back to the tour. Before my shows, I did warm-ups, singing exercises. Between shows, I kept silent. I knew that my life as a singer had just taken an important turn.

I felt a little like those girls who, in the past, used to enter a convent. I imagined them in a state of exaltation, but also frightened by the prospect of living their whole lives, until the very end, in the presence of God, in silence and prayer, alone. For years my life was going to resemble theirs, a life of discipline and self-denial, of silence and meditation. And, of course, a life of intense joy.

But before diving into that new life, I had to finish the Quebec tour and do my show at the Saint-Denis Theater.

I don't think I've ever experienced such a highly charged premiere. Because of what had happened to me, the show had been postponed for a week. I'd rested and my voice was back in form. But for several reasons, I had not been able to avoid living this time under terrible stress.

At first, the rumor circulated that I was worn out. In the business and in the papers, they were saying that specialists had predicted that my voice was ruined, that the show at the Saint-Denis would be my last, my swan song, my definitive goodbye to show business. There were full-page articles on the subject in the tabloids, they were saying it on the radio, and a lot of people ended up believing it.

Of course, we knew it wasn't true. But René was worried that the Canadian and American producers would focus on these rumors and refuse to commit themselves any further to our projects. So that evening at the Saint-Denis, I had to offer stunning truth that my voice was in perfect condition. A tall order.

As if to add still more pressure, two days earlier I'd caused a scandal at the Adisq gala by refusing the Félix award for best English-speaking performer of the year.

Things had never been simple between English Canada and French-speaking Quebec. More so at that time than today, any Quebecois artist who wished to put on a show in English was getting him- or herself into a touchy, very delicate situation.

I'd learned this by sad experience two years earlier, when the French-speaking community of Toronto had invited me to sing at the Saint-Jean show being presented on an outdoor stage at the Harbour Front, facing Lake Ontario.

I was doing a few songs in English for the program, including that good old "What a Feeling," and some classics like "Over the Rainbow" and "Summertime." As soon as I began to sing in English, some people in the audience started booing me. Most of the Toronto French speakers use English at work and in the street. But the Saint-

Jean is a sacred moment when they reaffirm their sense of community. I wasn't used to being booed. I was really beginning to panic when a heavy rain hit the Harbour Front, and they had to stop the show. Phew! What a relief.

Later, shortly after the release of *Unison,* I did a show in English, for one night in Montreal and one night in Toronto. The newspapers in both cities wondered if the Quebecois public would accept me singing in English. In the business, people even went so far as to suggest that I was risking the destruction of my career in Quebec.

But nothing and no one could cause me to renounce my dream of singing in English. It was the only way for a singer to tour the world, whether she was from Quebec, France, Spain, or Japan. René and I were certain that the mainstream audiences of Quebec would accept this in good faith and would give me their blessings. It was the media that kept the useless controversy going.

Nevertheless, by refusing to accept the Félix for best English-speaking performer of the year, I wanted to set the record straight. I admit my speech was a little awkward.

"I'm not an Anglophone," I said, referring to the word for native English speakers. "Wherever in the world I go, I tell them I'm Quebecoise."

As a result, the English speakers of Montreal were now furious. My statement implied that they were not Quebecois, even though they lived in Quebec.

The issue is very complicated where we come from. So my premiere at the Saint-Denis was turning into a political event. We were worried about demonstrations and jeering.

And yet, for René and me, the evening was an absolute triumph. When René stepped into the house several minutes before the curtain rose, people applauded him loudly.

In Quebec, there was already a kind of aura around him, because of what he'd accomplished and because of all those contacts he'd established with them. And also because of his personal charm. Maybe also because people were touched by the story of our love. But René didn't want to hear about that; he didn't believe it could be true—not yet.

As soon as the show was finished, I went to New York to meet with Dr. Gould. He was adorable, very delicate and full of humor. On his waiting room walls were photos of him with his patients, among them John F. Kennedy, Frank Sinatra, Walter Cronkite, and many others he'd helped in his fifty years of practice.

He said all the things that Dr. Belzile had said about my vocal cords being in bad shape and that this was due to bad habits.

"You should probably have an operation," he said.

Tears rolled down my cheeks, and I was reminded that Dr. Belzile had told me my voice would probably change after such an operation. It might even change so much that it would be unrecognizable and gritty. In effect, it would no longer exist.

"There is, however, another solution," Dr. Gould said.

"I'll take it," I snapped back.

"If you are silent for three weeks, you could perhaps see some positive results without the risks and side effects of surgery."

I told him that my three weeks of silence had already just begun.

"When I speak of silence," he said, "I am talking about absolute silence. You can't even dream of speaking. No laughing—nothing. It's very hard, you know. Don't try to fool yourself. If you speak even one time, you have to start over again."

I stood up and gave him a wink.

When I left, he kissed me tenderly on the forehead.

I spent the holidays in the strangest way in my life. Almost every night, my brothers and sisters sang together, as we had been doing for as far back as I could remember. But now, for the first time, I couldn't join my voice with theirs. Instead, I played various percussion instruments. This made me feel very alone in my silence.

In January, when Dr. Gould examined me again, I could tell he was very proud.

"Honestly, I didn't think you could do it," he said.

He seemed very happy, as if I had given him a gift.

"You may now begin your training," he said.

His associate, Dr. William Riley, would be in charge of restoring my voice. It would demand a lot of hard work, work that was at once both terrible and marvelous.

Most often Dr. Riley had me work standing up. We talked a little, we did some warm-up exercises, then he literally threw himself on me—he pinned me with all his strength against the wall and had me sing scales. Or he placed me in really uncomfortable positions for a singer—my arms crossed, for example, and my head thrown back as far as possible. And I had to sing naturally during all this.

With him, as much as with Eddy Marnay in the past, I discovered the great pleasures of study, work, exercise, and effort. Eddy had changed my relationship to words. He had taught me how to give color, meaning, and weight to each of the words I sang. With Dr. Riley, I felt as if I were rediscovering Eddy's teaching, the same passion, the same intensity and pleasure.

One day as we were doing our exercises, there was a knock at the door. Dr. Gould entered with a very imposing-looking man. It was Luciano Pavarotti. After we were introduced, the doctor asked me to sing something for him.

"I just want Luciano to hear your voice," he said to me.

I was terribly intimidated, but I didn't dare refuse, so I asked him what I should sing.

"It doesn't matter. Whatever you like," he said.

I sang the first thing that came into my head, several verses of a song I hadn't thought of for a long time. It was called "You Bring Me Joy." Luciano Pavarotti complimented me, saying such things as, "You have a voice that could pierce the heart."

I didn't know how to respond. I was on the verge of tears. Dr. Gould looked at me. He seemed so proud and moved, as if I were his own child. Afterward, when I was onstage or in the studio, I have often thought of Signore Pavarotti. What a wonderful thing it is to have a "voice that could pierce the heart."

William Riley himself is a musician. He has a very attractive voice. He made me conscious for the first time of the infinite tones that you can give to words, to sounds, by changing the position of your tongue, lips, and cheeks. He taught me how to support my voice with my facial expression, how to "place" it in my head or exploit the resonating capabilities of my chest or face. He got sounds out of me that I had never heard in my life, ones I never thought I could produce. Thanks to him, I discovered a new musical universe that was vast and fascinating.

I was singing less with my nose than I'd done at the beginning, but there was always something nasal about my voice. To correct myself, I had developed some vocal techniques that the doctor considered ineffective. He would help me to get rid of them. In their place he suggested warm-up and loosening-up exercises that would last at least a half hour before each show. And we also spent long hours doing singing exercises.

The doctor was in the middle of giving me a demonstration of the kind of exercises I should do every day from then on when René interrupted us to ask how long it would take to see the results of such work.

"You won't notice much for three years. In five years, Celine will have a better voice."

René was dumbfounded. He kept his mouth shut for the rest of the session. While we were waiting for the elevator after leaving the office, he turned to me and said that he could easily understand it if I refused to go through such an ordeal.

"I can't ask you to waste your life for five years in order to achieve results that we're not even certain we'll see."

Once inside the elevator, he added: "If they'd given me a diet that would take five years to make me thinner, you can be sure I wouldn't be following it."

But I accepted the doctor's terms right away. I knew I'd never change my mind, never doubt my decision.

A few days later, I went back to Dr. Riley. He'd prepared a series of exercises for me to do every day. The only exceptions would be on the day before a show or recording, when I had to stay silent.

Then he made two recommendations. Since he himself was a good artist, first of all he advised me to forget all these techniques as soon as I went onstage.

"It should never show; if it does, that ruins the feeling. And also, don't do the exercises too much. Even if you train twelve hours a day, your training won't go any faster. You've got to give your voice time to undo the effects of these bad habits and respond to the new ones. Too much is worse than not enough."

Next to his office was the office of an otolaryngologist named Gwen Korovin, who was also going to be a great friend to me. I spent hours with her studying all the parts of the voice. She showed me pictures in books: the larynx with the vocal cords on each side, the trachea, the pharynx. She slid a tiny camera into my throat and I saw on a monitor the source of my voice, my fluttering vocal cords. She explained that the tension and movements I used to control these bodily parts could make sounds, noises that had very little shape to them. My mouth and my tongue would modulate this sound and create words and notes.

But all of it is like playing golf: at the beginning, you're paralyzed. When you first start taking lessons, you discover a million things to think of: how you hold your shoulders, your head, how you move your arms, and where to place your eyes. With Gwen, I discovered the extent to which singing, even talking, projecting a simple sound, even breathing—all were complex operations.

It was like starting from scratch, as if I were learning again not only to sing but also to speak, breathe, move, walk, stay in a sitting or standing position. For example, I learned not to lean on the back of my chair or put my elbows on the table or put my head in my hands. I no longer liked chairs that were too deep or too soft. I was hard: a real marine in training.

Fortunately, I was able to forget all these techniques when I stepped onto a stage. I sang for pleasure, without thinking about what I was learning about how the voice produces sound.

I followed my vocal regime with maniacal regularity, and I loved it. I found a genuine, almost sportsmanlike pleasure in it. And actually, it was very close to athletic training. I started with breathing and elongation exercises, neck stretches. Then I warmed up my voice; I sang a note and held it as long as possible, without forcing it, right to the end of my breath. I made my voice travel through my body, the head, the nose, the throat, and the belly.

I thought of textures and colors and tried to translate them into vocal qualities. I let out a crescendoing series of sounds, pushing harder and harder on each note, changing the rhythm and tone. And then I started over, and over, and over. That's mostly it: being able to start over again and again and put heart and passion into it each time.

It was a game, but it was also a kind of test. If something was wrong, if I was distracted or preoccupied, it showed right away; you could hear it. So I had to start over, calm down, get control of myself, until my voice rediscovered the desired vibration, color, and texture.

A voice has its idiosyncrasies and its whims. It too has cycles. Some days, when, for example, I was menstruating, it seemed drabber to me. There was nothing I could do about this. Sometimes, also, it was less obedient. I mean that it was harder for me to control. Then, it was as if we were having an argument, the two of us. It was as if my voice were sulking, keeping its distance from me.

But Dr. Riley's exercises always helped me to get it back again. My voice and I spent some great moments together in my dressing room or my bedroom.

At the beginning, being silent was the most difficult part, those deep-sea dives all alone to the very bottom of silence. Especially the first time. My grand trek across this desert lasted three weeks. I thought that it would never end.

During it, I began making little *film noir* movies in my head, real nightmares. One of them keeps coming back to me. I'd become permanently unable to speak. I was terrified and crushed. But even so, each time I kept the cameras running right to the end.

My mother would come into my room and find me in tears. I'd interrupt my mental filmmaking to signal by hand to her that it was just a game and that she shouldn't be worried. As soon as she left, I went back to my movie. I pushed on until the end, to a happy ending. I couldn't sing anymore, but I could still do interviews. My sister Manon would be there with me. Or Suzanne. They read my lips and translated my answers for the journalists. I had things to say and I was working. I'd become an accomplished pianist, I was writing lyrics and music for songs, novels, films, and videos. I was full of ideas. What was in my heart and used to pass through my voice now took another route—it was as simple as that. That consoled me and life went on.

Little by little, I began to get used to these periods of silence, when I was allowed to really tune out. It was like another world, a country like no other. I'll always go back to this place, just as I'll always go back to Quebec.

With my sister Manon, with Suzanne Gingue and a few others, I developed a sign language that was very efficient. Manon and Suzanne could also read my lips easily and rapidly. The women in my group are quite a bit better at that than the men. René needs a drawing or I have to call Manon to help him. A few times, because he thought it would be easier, he'd pretend he understood. But he's no good at pretending. I can tell. My brother Michel too. When I move my lips without speaking, the men I know start speaking louder and slower than usual. They articulate carefully, as if I were deaf or retarded. Women, on the other hand, do what I'm doing, they speak in a very low voice, most often without using their voice at all. And that creates an atmosphere of extreme peacefulness among us.

When my mother and I speak on the telephone, we have a code.

"Did you sleep well, my little girl?"

I tap my nail on the receiver once for yes.

"Did you get your a hair cut after all?"

Two taps mean no.

"Love from Dad . . . and from me too . . ."

A small series of fingernail taps means I'm sending them my love too.

Gradually, silence has become a kind of refuge for me. Certain days I feel as if I were invisible, as if other people weren't seeing or speaking to me. As if I had nothing to say to them. I observe the world without being seen.

It was during this period that I began to hear a little voice inside of me, a very soft little voice that came into my head singing tunes, melodies that sometimes delighted me. I'd work on them for several days, then forget them. I've tried storing them away so that one day I could turn them into real songs. Though I've never finished such projects, I hope that one day I will.

I always come out of my periods of silence stronger because of them—so much so that I don't think I could do without them. Today, even when I don't have to sing or protect my voice, I spend long hours without speaking. Nuns and cloistered monks have always done this. And they certainly had a reason for it. It gives one a different, clear, and distinct vision of the world.

I have a lot of respect for people who practice their religion seriously. I'm impressed by the discipline they impose upon themselves. There's wisdom in such a thing. Silence for me is a point of departure. It's very vast. Like being alone. Like music.

After two years of voice exercises and periods of silence, I hadn't seen the least results I was hoping for, but still I didn't give up. I never doubted. And each day I began to discover that singing was becoming a greater and greater pleasure.

René is always trying to create events. Every time he catches sight of a stage, he always wants me to climb up on it. Wherever a big crowd gets together, he wants me to sing and to have them listen and applaud. And he's always making it happen. One day he decided that my career had begun on June 19, 1981, the day I did the Michel Jasmin television show. So ten years later, to the exact day, he felt we should celebrate my decade in show business at the Montreal Forum.

I'd just finished my first truly big trans-Canadian tour, which had lasted all winter. That tour had taken off rather slowly. I did some small halls in west Canada—Edmonton, Calgary, and Vancouver. But then I won two Junos (for best singer and best album of the year) and "Where Does My Heart Beat Now?" had begun to climb almost to the top of the American charts. David Letterman invited me to appear on *The Late Show,* and from one day to the next, my name was becoming more and more familiar throughout the country. In next to no time, all the tickets for the tour were gone. I sang to sold-out audiences in all the big auditoriums of most of the Canadian cities.

I was afraid that the anniversary celebration at the Forum would seem too boastful, too self-important. But René wanted the concert to highlight the great moments of my career. In song, of course, but also in images projected on a giant screen. We spent two long evenings looking at TV broadcasts and shows that I'd appeared in over those ten years. At times, I couldn't believe what I was seeing.

Had I really worn that ridiculous dress? Had I actually gone on television with those teeth! With that hair! With such a nasal voice! But there were so many other moments that touched my heart and made me so very proud of what I had accomplished.

The June 19 show was, from start to finish, a total delight. I was accompanied by the Metropolitan Symphony Orchestra, which was made up of sixty-five musicians. And half the time, everyone in the audience knew my songs by heart. I talked a lot and was able to pay tribute to the writers and composers who had worked with me. Before singing "Ce n'était qu'un rêve," my first hit, I made a well-deserved tribute to my mother.

For the curtain call, I wore a Montreal Canadiens hockey team sweater and carried the Quebec flag. This was René's idea, at once kind of tongue-in-cheek and at the same time a way of reconciling independents and federalists, intellectuals and sports lovers. At that moment, I don't think I'd ever heard such a roar from a crowd. For several minutes, I couldn't speak. Then people began singing the very beautiful Gilles Vigneault song the Quebecois have adopted in place of "Happy Birthday":

> *Ma chère Celine, c'est à ton tour*
> *de te laisser parler d'amour.*
>
> *(It's your turn, Celine, my dove,*
> *to let yourself speak some words of love.)*

Earlier in the concert, I'd revived the medley of songs from the rock opera *Starmania*. Vito Luprano of CBS was so captivated by them that he suggested I do an album of songs by Luc Plamondon, who had cowritten the rock opera *Starmania*. I liked the idea because it was clearly a major challenge. In addition, Luc would write four new songs for me.

I was involved more than ever in that album. Earlier, I'd never come to the studio until everything was ready. The arrangements would already be complete and the orchestra tracks recorded; all I had to do was sing.

This time, I worked on the choice of songs and their production very closely with the arranger, the producer, the lyricist, and the composer. We recorded in the fall in French singer/composer Michel Berger's little studio on boulevard des Batignoles in Paris. It was a place where I experienced moments of great happiness.

One evening, after the recording of one of the four original songs for the album, René and I ended up alone in the small kitchen of the studio (yogurt for me, diet Coke for him). Then he confided to me, in a low voice, as if it were a secret: "You know, Dr. Riley was right. Your voice has never been so beautiful."

"But, darling, I haven't even been training with him for a year! He said it would take four or five to see the results."

"So imagine what these legendary results will be like when you can really see them!"

I hadn't spoken to anyone about it, but I too thought my voice had started to change. It was fuller and more subtle. Its tone was always clear and precise. And most of all, my choice of textures and colors was growing larger and larger, more velvety and crystalline. Singing was making me happier than it ever had before.

Every two months or so I went to see Dr. Riley in New York. Sometimes we had very intense workout sessions, and sometimes we just talked about voices, music, or sounds we liked. I always left his office feeling stimulated, energetic, and determined. Wherever I was—Montreal, Paris, or somewhere on tour—I did my voice exercises and followed my diet.

I loved discipline with a passion, the really strong, strict discipline I was imposing on myself at the time. I've faithfully performed it for more than ten years of my life. The hardest part is to never give in. Depriving myself of desserts, chips, or peanuts from time to time couldn't be easier. Depriving myself of them every day, at the same time as a lot of other little things, is a whole other ball game. It calls for constant, fanatical vigilance. You've got to turn yourself into a kind of machine who doesn't think about certain things, who, for example, forgets the taste of sticky toffee pudding, crème anglaise, and maple syrup. Bizarre as it may seem, all these little privations, taken together, create a kind of well-being, happiness. The kind that brings self-mastery, I think.

I organized my whole life around my voice. I satisfied its every requirement and whim. I felt as if it were a treasure I had to take care of.

In 1992, the Academy Awards took place on March 30, on my twenty-fourth birthday. That evening I experienced a great moment. Earlier I had recorded a duet with Peabo Bryson for the animated Disney film *Beauty and the Beast.* It was written by the team of Alan Menken and Howard Ashman, who had won two Oscars in 1990 for the music in Disney's *The Little Mermaid.* This duet, which was included on my second English-language album, *Celine Dion,* was already a huge hit and was being heard everywhere. Menken and Ashman would also win an Oscar for best song of the year a few minutes after Peabo and I finished our duet.

But just before we stepped out before the cameras, I had an unbelievable attack of stage fright. First of all, I kept remembering that I was going to sing on the greatest stage of my life, in front of the vastest audience ever assembled: a billion TV watchers throughout the world. What's more, I'd caught tonsillitis a few days before. And the doctor had prescribed some antibiotics that really dragged me down.

But what impressed me was the audience at the Dorothy Chandler Pavilion: Elizabeth Taylor and Paul Newman, Tom Cruise, Michael Douglas, Barbra Streisand, and Liza Minnelli. Here were all the idols I'd always dreamed of meeting. Now I was seeing them at my feet, and I was singing for them. Now they were watching and listening to me, just as I'd always watched and listened to them.

I felt very strong in front of all these people, but also a little like being at home and in a strange house at the same time. I wanted to thank them for letting me sing at this great event, but I could imagine René's reaction.

"You don't have to thank them. If they're applauding, it's because they think you're a real star, like them. All these people are impressed by you as much as you could be by them."

I didn't really believe it. I didn't yet completely see myself as a real star, equal to those around me. I wanted to go higher, farther. I felt I had a lot more traveling to do before being able to say that I had really passed through the looking glass.

René had a surprise for me. He'd invited my parents to Los Angeles and gotten them two seats in the Dorothy Chandler Pavilion, a nearly impossible feat on Oscar night. After the ceremony, René and I took a stroll among all these luminous stars. We too were as nervous and as impressed as everyone else who was there. And René, an inveterate stargazer, didn't stop naming the ones he saw. He was making me laugh. All his life he'd rubbed shoulders with celebrities, and here he was still marveling at them, like a little boy.

At a certain moment, my eyes met those of Barbra Streisand, and she gave me a small nod of her head, a smile. I almost fainted. I knew that from now on I was a visible, recognized person because I'd just sang onstage, in front of an audience of stars and TV cameras.

But I didn't have the time for such thoughts, time even for those personal little movies I'd been making in my head for so long. That same day, my *Celine Dion* album was released with great fanfare in the American and Canadian markets. The album that I did with Luc Plamondon, *Des Mots qui sonnent* (Words That Ring), had just been released in France. During the following months, I'd have to do two publicity campaigns simultaneously.

I headed off to Montreal two or three days after the Oscars. And for the first time, I admitted to a reporter from *La Presse* that I had a man in my life with whom I was madly in love. However, I said I didn't want to reveal his name.

"Is it who I think it is?" she asked. "Do I know him?"

I just laughed in response. This half admission was an enormous relief for me already. From now on, at least, people would know that I was part of the ranks of love, and didn't just sing about it. I lived it and did it too.

But this reporter must have known who it was, as did a lot of people in Montreal and Paris. Even in the scandal sheets they'd written that René and I were together. Despite that, he wanted to wait longer before saying it publicly.

A few days after that confession, I had to leave with René to do a promotional tour. First in the United States, then Japan, and finally Europe. About twenty big cities, dozens of interviews, TV shows, and galas. The nomad's life, that was what we lived. We were both very excited.

Until an unforeseen event changed our plans.

'*ve* already remarked that when really terrible things happen, you realize afterward that there were usually signs warning you about what was coming. When René had his heart attack in Los Angeles, I remembered that for several days I'd been feeling incredibly anxious. And recalling this made me feel guilty that I hadn't been more attentive to him. Perhaps I could have noticed his fatigue and possibly seen the attack coming.

We had checked in at the Four Seasons where we wanted to take a few days of rest. We had been working hard; René had had lots of meetings in New York, Los Angeles, Montreal, and Tokyo. And I'd just done *The Tonight Show,* where I'd become a regular, and I'd also been on *Good Morning America.* I'd given a lot of interviews recently, and in a few hours, we were leaving for New York to do even more. While we waited, we decided to soak up a little sun next to the swimming pool.

René went up to our room complaining about a pain in his back and about the heat. This worried me right away. Usually, René can never get enough sun and heat. In ten minutes, I called our room, and it took him a long time to answer. His voice sounded so weak that I didn't even wait for the elevator—I ran up the stairs to our room. He was lying on his back, disoriented and in pain. Within thirty seconds, I'd rounded up the entire hotel staff. Then I found a wheelchair and some help. When the ambulance arrived, I already had René, along with the hotel nurse, downstairs in the hotel lobby. I'd already told the emergency room at Cedars-Sinai that we were waiting for the emergency team. I'd done all of this, without even thinking, it seemed.

René thought he was going to die. He was crying as he talked to me about his children and his mother.

"You, Celine, you've got to keep going. Whatever happens, even if I'm not there, you have to keep going on."

And he named all the people he trusted and with whom I should work when he was gone. I begged him to keep quiet, I swore to him that he wouldn't die, that I had far less interest in my career than I did in him.

At the hospital, I again moved heaven and earth to get someone to attend to him as quickly as possible. Then I stayed close to him until he was safely in intensive care and all we could do was wait for his condition to stabilize.

As I spoke with the doctors who examined him, I realized I was still wearing my bathing suit, and now I was in an air-conditioned place, where I risked getting a chill that would harm my voice. For once, I'd completely forgotten all caution and discipline. But of course, my voice was the least of my worries. Even though René was now out of danger, I was gripped by fear and grief. I don't think I've ever felt so alone and helpless.

As soon as I could, I called his mother, Tété. The following day, they were all there, surrounding René with their affection: Tété and the children, Patrick, Jean-Pierre, and Anne-Marie; and his friends Marc Verreault, Pierre Lacroix, and Paul Sara.

Someone—Pierre or Marc—brought René a copy of *The Wall Street Journal,* which said, among other nice things about me, that I'd proved that a French Canadian can forge an international career without abandoning her culture or renouncing her roots. René read and reread the article until he knew it by heart. I think the recognition we received in that article made him happier than any other praise we'd gotten since the beginning of my career.

"You see, even people who don't belong to our industry, who have nothing to do with show business, recognize our success."

I was ready to call it quits. I could have canceled everything. No more publicity, TV shows, nothing, until my love was completely out of danger. But he wouldn't hear of it. He didn't want me to stop.

"Even if I died, I'd want you to go on. If I died and you had stopped like that, just when you were going full speed ahead, I would have died a second time."

I understood that he was very serious, and understood that in a way my career was his masterpiece, his song, his symphony. The idea of it remaining unfinished would have hurt him terribly. I understood that if he ever disappeared, I had to continue without him—*for* him.

But for me all my success would lose its meaning if René were no longer there to see and know it, to tell me about it from day to day. I needed his commentaries, his voice, his glance, his admiration, and his love. More than ever and more than anything in the world, at the very moment when all the doors were swinging open for me, I needed him at my side.

Sooner or later, you risk losing the ones you love. I'd thought about it often. I was surrounded by people who were all more or less twice my age. And sometimes I told myself that I was going to lose them one by one. I'd end up completely alone. In a way, when I let myself dwell on such thoughts, I was already all alone. And I'd begin to film somber little movies in my head, with almost no action, just simple tableaux.

I imagined myself as a very old woman sitting in front of a window with a shawl on my shoulders, and I was looking at a very beautiful garden full of birds and flowers, where a light rain was falling. I wasn't really sad, but I was very much alone. Who could I talk to about this? Certainly not to the people I was so afraid of losing, such as René, my parents. Although René recuperated quickly, it would never be the same. Something, a feeling of being carefree, perhaps, had been taken from us.

The doctors told him he had to lose weight and exercise regularly; he'd have to eat better and less. In short, he had to change his life. And to begin with, he needed to avoid stress. That was asking a lot.

Like me, René thrives on stress, and the profession we'd both chosen is full of it. For us, something that doesn't cause stress and demand risk brings little pleasure and probably isn't worth the trouble. At any rate, that's what we believed at the time. The higher the prize, the higher he was tempted to reach in order to win it. After my car accident, René was with me constantly, as he'd promised he would. But now, before I went back to my publicity tour, I insisted that he break that promise. I wanted him to rest and to follow his diet. This time, the first time in our lives, he listened to me.

Passing through Montreal, I continued to reveal the truth about our relationship. A reporter asked me if I'd been afraid of losing René.

"More afraid than ever in my life," I answered.

"You would have lost your second father."

"I have only one father, Adhemar Dion, whom I love and who loves me. René isn't my father, he never has been and never will be. René's the man who makes my heart pound, he's the man of my life."

Then I added that I didn't want to talk about certain things in my life, in *our* life. Until then, we'd always avoided these questions, pretending not to be together. I'd been hiding the truth when I'd said I didn't love anyone. As a result, reporters seemed to give less and less credence to my words.

But the statement I'd just made changed all that. Quite blatantly, I'd said we were in love, but that we didn't want to talk about it, that the subject was off-limits. We too had a real life, our own "secret garden."

Soon after, I left for Europe with Suzanne Gingue. Our first stop was at the World Music Awards in Monaco, where I received a prize. My two albums *Celine Dion* and *Des Mots qui sonnent* were selling millions of copies. This was great, but the more an album sells and the more awards an artist wins, the more she has to work.

Near the end of the tour, I'd often wake up in the morning wondering what city I was in. All the hotel rooms looked alike. It was the same marble, bronze, ceramic, and porcelain in the bathroom, the same mirrors everywhere, the same soft carpets, and the same half-light.

To help me fall asleep when I was home, I had a nightgown that belonged to my mother. It was cotton-candy pink and so worn-out that the fabric had an almost unearthly softness to it. I never wore it, but like Linus's blanket, it provided me with a feeling of security to have something from home. I'd sleep every night with my face buried in my mother's nightgown. But I was afraid I'd lose it if I took it abroad, so I left it behind. And sometimes I felt very lonely when I was too far from home.

Whenever I had a chance to return home, the hurricane that had swept me away would begin to calm. For a few days, there was a brief lull. I often stayed at my parents' house so that I could spend a little time with my mother. Each time I came home, I had the impression of being farther and farther away from my brothers and sisters. They were still just as warm, just as kind, and they were extremely happy about my success. But I was no longer the little girl they'd taught to dream big dreams. Several of them also had all the talent and desire necessary to succeed, but I was the one who'd gotten a real chance at it.

During the European publicity tour, I spoke to René five, six, ten times a day. We both knew where each other was and, more or less, what we were doing, hour by hour. René promised me he was resting, that he was exercising, that he was playing golf with Marc, Jacques, or Rosaire, and that he wasn't eating much and was sleeping a lot.

When I returned to Montreal, I'd discovered that he hadn't been resting at all. He'd put together our next year, planned it all out day by day, in a highly regimented fashion. We left together for Seville, in Spain, where Expo '92 was taking place. I was supposed to sing in the Canadian Pavilion on July 1, which is Canada Day.

On board the plane, René told me the story of my future adventures in the marvelous world of show business.

First a tour in the United States, opening for Michael Bolton, then a tour in Quebec later in the fall, and next a tour of Canada. And interspersed with that, some big outdoor shows and two or three videos. By next fall and winter, we'd begin recording my third album in English. He'd already made an initial selection of songs. He had some demos for me to hear, including one with words and music by David Foster that delighted him, called "The Colour of My Love."

"Everyone wanted that song," he told me. "Whitney Houston, Barbra Streisand, and Natalie Cole. But David wanted to give it to you—actually, to both of us—because it's truly a love song and he knows we're in love."

"And why does he know it when my neighbors in Montreal don't?"

I was certain of René's love, but I understood less and less his continued insistence upon denying the obvious. Nobody, anywhere, was fooled at this point; not in Paris, not in Montreal. I was reproaching him more and more often about refusing to let me tell the world he loved me. Each time, he brought up our age difference and his fear that I'd be unhappy in ten, fifteen, twenty years. He also worried that people would laugh or say he'd abused his power and had exploited me.

"It could ruin your career."

"Could the lie that we've been telling for four years be any less destructive? Luckily, people don't believe us anymore. How could a woman who's supposed to live without love and has never known it in her whole life sing songs like all the ones I sing?"

For me, none of his arguments held any water. For more than ten years, we'd shared the same experiences. Everything he had learned before me, he'd taught me. He'd told me everything, given me everything. We'd been partners for more than ten years, lovers for more than four. And soon I'd be twenty-five. I didn't see why I had to hide my love life. Every time I brought up the subject, he told me to wait a little while longer.

"I'm warning you," I told him that day on the plane to Seville. "The first time I sing 'The Colour of My Love' in public, I'm going to sing it for real. I'm going to announce the colors of my life and give my love a name."

He knew I meant what I said. He also knew I loved him deeply. But above all, he trusted me. And he loved me too.

At the time, nothing infuriated him more than to hear or read that he had absolute power over me. Or that he told me what to think, say, or do. Especially in Quebec, a lot of people believed or wanted to believe that. I knew this, but it really didn't interest me.

There was, of course, some truth behind it: at the beginning of our relationship, René *had* completely guided me; he had formed me. I can't deny it and I thank heaven for it every day. But little by little, he let me fly with my own wings.

"Be yourself. Say what you think, say what you have to say."

I realize today the moment when he encouraged and pushed me to become a free and independent woman. I know and have always known that he wouldn't have loved me as much if I'd obeyed his every command. He doesn't like weak people who have no opinion on anything.

Sometimes during interviews or onstage between songs, I would make an outrageous remark. Often these made him laugh. In Seville, however, he winced a bit. Because this time what I said was beyond outrageous. During the press conference before the show at the Canadian Pavilion, a journalist from Montreal asked what I thought of the "separatist" movement in Quebec.

I spontaneously said I was against boundaries.

The Canadian media tried to make this into a huge story, claiming that I considered the possible secession of Quebec from the rest of Canada to be a horrible nightmare for Quebec. I had stepped on dangerous ground and should have said that politics were outside the realm of my knowledge. René thought that to ask a singer to talk politics was a kind of dirty trick.

"Did that writer ever think of asking the prime minister to sing in front of twenty million people like you do? All he was trying to do was to embarrass you."

Even more troubling, I received a congratulatory message from the Canadian prime minister, who'd always been on very bad terms with the Quebecois nationalists who were campaigning for separation. Thus I found myself in the middle of a controversy that had been going on for generations and for which there was really no solution in sight. In my innocent way, I'd thrown oil on the fire. But René told me again that I'd been right in saying what I thought.

"You can even change your mind, if your heart tells you to. Don't listen to others. Say what you think. If you have no thoughts about something, say it. People like you because you're real."

But I was very upset about my statement at Seville. I felt I'd really hurt and disappointed the people I loved the most in the world. I tried to explain myself to other Canadian journalists. I told them that I actually believed that there was nothing to win by separating and that if it were up to me, there wouldn't be any borders anywhere. I know that such statements show a naïveté about politics, history, and public affairs, but I have never pretended to be knowledgeable and informed about such things. All I really wanted was for the Quebecois to know I had a special love for them.

I was beginning to realize the frightening power the public grants too easily to stars, even when it comes to subjects in which they have absolutely no expertise. I've done ads for, among others, Coca-Cola and Chrysler. I'd always been spokesperson and sponsor for the Quebec Cystic Fibrosis Association. I know that being visible, listened to, and imitated is part of a star's life, that what you say or do can carry a lot of weight and have enormous consequences. But in Seville, for the first time, that power seemed stifling. Thus, everything that I did from then on, everything I said, would be repeated, analyzed, and commented upon, even if it had nothing to do with my career as a singer.

"It's because you're not only a singer," René told me. "Now you're a star in Quebec. The biggest one they've ever had. And one day, not far off, you'll be a star in France and the United States too, everywhere in the world."

To me, that also seemed like an outrageous remark. I would never have dared to say such a thing. But René had no qualms about it, not only in private, between ourselves, but in public. I knew some people thought he was an egomaniac who'd tell anyone that one day I'd be known as the greatest singer in the world. In Quebec, it had become something of a national joke.

But that was how René did things. He never worried about counting his chickens before they hatched. He saw himself as a millionaire and acted like one long before he became rich; he saw me as a gigantic star, even though in the United States I was still only a small, rising star who could disappear in a twinkle.

Opening for Michael Bolton was exhausting, particularly because we had to change cities every day. But we were finally doing what we had always dreamed of doing: working in the country that created the "big time." In the beginning, I sang for very restless, impatient audiences who were waiting to hear Michael Bolton and weren't interested in me. I had a defective sound system and very little space because the stage was taken up by the mixers and instruments for the main act. What's more, the concerts were held outdoors, and it was still daylight when I went onstage.

But I put my whole soul into it. Little by little, a rumor started to circulate that my show was definitely worth getting to the theater early to see. Eventually René was able to convince the producers to begin my show a half hour later. By the end of the tour, I had good lighting and a better sound system.

During this time, keeping quiet about our love was madness, especially because the papers were having a field day with the rumors. At the end of the summer, when I returned to Quebec, the press was waiting for me.

"Well, Celine, what about your love life?"

They could have asked me a thousand questions about my career, about the U.S. tour, about my next album, about René's health, or about the six pounds I'd lost while touring. But nothing interested them more than my love life. And I still refused to talk about it.

Ahead of time, René had agreed to let me do a one-hour interview, one-on-one, with Lise Payette, the queen of TV confession. He certainly knew she had the means to make me admit everything. And I knew it too.

Up to then, interviews had never made me nervous. I always saw them as an occasion to tell the whole truth. That morning, I accused René of wanting to keep our relationship secret because he believed it couldn't last.

"If you don't want me to talk about it, it's because you're not sure you love me."

I'd often presented him with that argument. This time, however, I must have found words and gestures that hit home, because he was really rattled. He told me I was right, that it couldn't go on like this. He really liked Lise Payette, and he thought that this would be a good opportunity to tell her our secret rather than let the scandal sheets get hold of it first.

But on the way to Télé-Métropole, he changed his mind. He convinced me to wait.

"We've got to prepare."

"For what?"

"We've got to do it all in a big way. I've got a better idea. You'll see."

I reminded him of the deadline I'd set, that when I sang "The Colour of My Love" I'd say his name.

"Thinking of that was exactly what gave me my idea."

When we arrived at the studio, he immediately went to the control room. The makeup person and the hairdresser must have found me cold and distant. I was distracted. I was thinking of this whole senseless story. Of René and how he always won. And always had a better idea! I was also thinking of myself, and how I always gave in.

Lise Payette had me talk about my family, my tour, my next album, about René's heart attack. I began telling her what had happened, how he'd felt sick when we were at the pool, how I'd alerted everybody, and how I'd ended up at the hospital in a bathing suit.

She interrupted me and asked if I was in love with René. After all, I spoke about him so much.

This threw me off balance. I began to splutter that I did love a man, but that I couldn't divulge his name because it would compromise my career. The lie made me feel even more off balance and upset. No one would understand. I burst into tears. When she handed me a box of Kleenex, I burst out laughing through my tears. All in all, I think the two of us came off as very real people.

But I'd let a good occasion for my "coming out" pass me by. I had to live even more months with these lies. I convinced myself that it would be better if René and I made the revelation together.

He too was very shaken up by the interview. For a moment, he wished I'd admitted everything.

"Oh, really? And what would we have done with your better idea?"

"It's not my idea, Celine. It's yours."

On March 30, 1993, the day of my twenty-fifth birthday, I woke up with a burning throat. Three days later, I was supposed to do an important show at the Montreal Forum.

I was tired. For six months I'd been living in hell. The anxiety following René's heart attack, the stress and constant effort required by the American tour, that intolerable waiting, the publicity, the trips, and the recording sessions. Just a few months earlier, I'd even sung at President Bill Clinton's inaugural ceremonies. Everything had built up to a level that overwhelmed me at times.

I kept having the same nightmare. I was on the roof of a very high building—probably in an American city like New York or Chicago. There were a lot of people on the ground watching me and shouting at me not to jump. I wanted them to know I had absolutely no intention of jumping. But either they didn't hear me or they weren't listening. They seemed panic-stricken and were running left and right.

Then I saw that thousands of people were entering the building, like ants, taking the elevator up to the roof in order to stop or save me. I didn't really know anymore. They got to the roof. They ran toward me, shouting nonstop. They told me to be careful. But this time, I was the one who wasn't listening. I jumped into empty space to escape them. And I fell for a long time, very slowly. I could see the deserted, empty, dark city. No one was left to watch me fall. I tried to cry, but no sound emerged from my mouth.

I woke up just before hitting the ground. I wanted to find Maman's nightgown under my pillow, and would have buried my face in it. But I stayed awake for a long time, until I remembered what city I was in.

During the next two or three weeks, I did publicity in Europe. With a raging cold, I hosted the Junos in Toronto. Then I sang at the Grammies in Los Angeles, where Peabo Bryson and I received an award as best pop duet for "Beauty and the Beast."

When I reached the podium, I said a few words in English and then spoke to the Quebecois in French with my native accent, the accent of my childhood. I knew they were watching me from the other side of the continent and that they were proud of me. I also knew they were the only ones who could understand what I was saying. It was as if I was speaking directly into their ears. At the same time, it was a way of telling the American public that I came from somewhere else. And that I stayed in touch with my roots.

I'm not sure how, but at the banquet following the ceremony, I found myself seated in front of Michael Jackson and Brooke Shields. We laughed quite a bit, particularly Brooke and I. Michael seemed rather timid to me. He spoke so softly that I had to lean closer and ask him to repeat himself. With Brooke, I spoke about clothes and hair. She told me she would love to sing: I told her I would love to make movies. I'm not sure if she was serious, but I know I was. I love making videos. But I don't have time for movies, not even for the little features that run through my head all the time.

I worked day and night putting together my new show, working on the direction, the spoken transitions, the scenery, lighting, sound. I even designed my stage costume: a red satin blouse with a ruffly jabot at the neck and tight black leather pants.

I was beginning to feel that I'd gone too far, too fast. I had to realize that somewhere inside of me, there was a tired and puzzled little girl I hadn't been paying attention to or listening to for quite a while. Now she was making signs to me, reminding me of her needs.

This little girl had no need for applause and ovations, no desire to give the biggest concert in the world. She just wanted a little peace and a little rest.

Around this time, I went with Suzanne Gingue to meet with Dr. Riley and Dr. Korovin in New York. They listened to me, scolded me, and reassured me. Then they recommended two days of silence.

When we returned to Montreal, René was waiting at the airport. In the limousine, I told him I wouldn't be speaking for two days. He'd always respected my silent periods, but that evening, he asked me to wait a few hours before plunging into one.

"Why? What's going on?"

"Nothing. Wait, you'll see."

He'd reserved a luxurious suite in a downtown hotel. He'd ordered dinner for two, with candles and Baroque music.

During the meal, he pulled a small box out of his pocket and put it on the table between us. He was nervous, intimidated too—it was very touching to see.

"I love you, Celine," he told me. "I love you like I've never loved anyone. I want to live with you."

His voice and eyes were velvet.

I opened the box and saw the engagement ring. I knew this meant that our love could finally be revealed.

6

wish I had better memories of the first of my three shows at the Montreal Forum that spring. As usual, the audience was unendingly generous with me, but from beginning to end, I felt that I was kind of out of it.

I still felt very tired, and now that I knew how fragile my voice was, I continued to worry that it would be damaged. Perhaps I was also focused on the happiness René had given me, and for all these reasons, I had trouble projecting myself into my songs and really living them.

Occasionally, I nearly gave way to my worst enemy, to what I call "my singing robot." She does everything mechanically. She has my body and voice but not my soul.

On my finger was the engagement ring René had given me a few days before, but still I felt uninvolved and incapable of connecting with the audience.

I must admit that singing certain songs night after night, for months, for years, can be extremely difficult. When a song has been repeated too many times, it begins to seem empty of meaning and emotion. Somehow I have to find meaning and emotion deep inside myself, and with each passing day this demands more and more effort.

Of course, I'm lucky to have a vast repertoire. And I can dip into an entire French and English repertoire from the last ten, twenty, fifty years. This supplies me with thousands and thousands of songs that I love, such as "Calling You," "All by Myself," or "Quand on n'a que l'amour" (When You've Got Nothing but Love), "The Power of Love," and "All the Way." I literally fell in love with those songs, and wanted to reinterpret them, even if they'd already been performed by others, often masterfully.

This is why I can change the content of my shows regularly; I always have songs that are new and striking. But I also know that I can't just perform what I like. I have to take into account what my audience wants to hear.

For example, we knew from the audience's initial reaction to "The Power of Love" that this was a song the world would adore for a long time. But some evenings, singing this song felt like an incredible chore. I'd already sung it so many times that I thought the "singing robot" would get hold of it.

I always go through a honeymoon period with songs. The first encounters are inspiring and deeply affecting. I remember, as a mother must remember about the birth of her children, the first contact I have with a song. I even remember where I was—a hotel room, a studio, a plane, a limousine. I recall the clothes I was wearing, the lighting, what the weather was like, who I was with.

But the chemistry doesn't last. It's a little like love. Sometimes you have to fight against habit so it keeps feeling like the first time. You have to reinvent the song just as you have to reinvent love, finding something new in it each time.

That notorious night at the Forum, I worked like a maniac from beginning to end, but with bad results, I thought.

René didn't run through the details of my show as he usually did. He seemed overwhelmed himself.

"You're tired, it's my fault. I've pushed you too hard. You need to rest. You'll take the time you need," he said.

But the second night was the complete opposite; it was one of the best shows of my career, even if I'd imagined the worst when I started.

An hour before the curtain rose, I was visited by my niece Karine with two nurses and a doctor from Sainte-Justine, where she'd been hospitalized for several weeks. When I saw her, my heart leaped. She was so pale, so defeated, so tiny and shriveled in her wheelchair with oxygen tanks attached to the back. Her lungs had become weak and congested and she couldn't breathe by herself.

For the first time, I could tell from her smile that she was ready to stop fighting. I told myself that she'd come to say goodbye.

As close as I'd been to Karine since she was a baby, I couldn't manage to make contact with her that evening. I no longer knew what to say or even how to look at her. And she noticed it. So she came to get me, speaking to me, as if nothing was the matter. She talked to me about my songs, my last album, my stage costume as well as asking plenty of questions about Paris and Hollywood. She wanted to hear about all the great cities of the world where I'd sung. She was especially interested in Princess Diana, with whom I'd dined a few weeks earlier in Ottawa.

With a pale smile she told me: "I found out that you are now in love. I'm happy for you."

I couldn't prevent myself from thinking of everything I had, of all the happiness I could expect from life. All the things that would never come to her. Those thoughts broke my heart and took away all my desire to go onstage and sing my love songs.

We were sitting off by ourselves, and little by little, I was able to talk to her, like a very close friend, about many things, including my good fortune to be loving a man and having him in my life. I was no longer afraid of hurting her.

She listened to me and kept saying: "I'm happy for you, Celine."

I was very touched, and also disconcerted. When I went onstage, I felt the singing robot at my heels. But I knew that Karine would be in one of the boxes René had reserved for family and friends. In thinking of her, I was overwhelmed by a great peace and by strength, Karine's strength. From that moment on, I sang every song for her. I felt her supporting me and knew she'd always be there near me, that she wouldn't die.

I almost wanted to tell the audience at the Forum, and especially her: "You won't die, Karine, you won't die."

I didn't see her after the show. Her doctor and the nurses thought she was too tired to join the crowd. The next afternoon, she called to tell me how much she loved my show. I told her I'd really liked it too. It had been a good show because I'd done it with my whole heart. I'd performed all the songs, even the oldest, as if it were the first time.

A few days later, I left for Europe, and when I returned on May 3, I knew that Karine's condition was worsening. As soon as I got off the plane, René and I rushed to see her at the hospital. Liette was at her bedside and I could tell she'd been crying a lot. I sat down on the bed and the three of us stayed like that for a long time without saying anything. There was a lot of tenderness and serenity among us.

René remained standing at the foot of the bed. I remember how touching and helpless he seemed. He always knows what to do, but this time he didn't. During such rare moments, he acts like a little boy, which I find very moving.

The doctors had given Karine morphine, but still she was having a lot of trouble breathing. I asked if I could do something for her.

"I'd like to have a new pair of pajamas."

It was Sunday. René found a way of getting hold of the owner of a sleepware store who agreed to let him in. He bought a pair of pajamas and a nightgown. He told me he wept as he chose them. We knew that Karine was resigned to dying, that we were dressing her for her last voyage. It was like a ritual, a ceremony.

I helped my sister change and wash her daughter and comb her hair. Both of us were holding back our tears. Karine chose the red-and-white pajamas. Her mother and I took turns rocking her in our arms. I sang her "Les Oiseaux du bonheur" (The Birds of Happiness). Liette spoke softly to her as she smoothed her hair.

Karine began to list the things she'd loved the most in life. Things without any connection to each other, but very, very specific: the salmon pâté my mother made, two or three of my songs, the river at Repentigny, the dresses she'd most loved wearing. It was a kind of inventory or testament; she was packing her bags with memories for the voyage she was about to begin, as if she wanted only to take with her the few beautiful things she had known. And to forget the rest.

She died just after midnight. She was sixteen years old.

Karine, that cheerful little spirit who was always there in some nook or cranny of my memory, had affected me deeply. She was the first child I was close with and with whom I'd established a genuinely mutual understanding. Now, this was no child like the others. Although illness had prevented her from growing in body, she'd matured rapidly. And there was a strong and powerful light in her. Life is not fair, but people like Karine—the broken, the disadvantaged, the sick—aren't here for nothing. They bring something to us.

During the weeks and months after her death, I couldn't think of her without feeling—aside from a great hurt—a terrible confusion and a sense of rebellion, feelings that I don't like. Karine had left without having known love, after a sad life spent constantly trying to catch her breath. She was always crushed by fatigue and had to submit to constant diets and dreadful treatments.

There's nothing you can do against death or the injustices of nature and life. Even love isn't enough. It would be too beautiful, actually, and too easy, if loving were enough to solve all the problems in the world, if loving were enough to make everyone we love happy.

You've got to face reality. You've got to act, fight. Perhaps give in someday, like Karine did. But give in to what? I really don't know. I hope and I believe there is another life. I even believe that the emotion that comes from songs comes in large part from that other life. And it's the artist's role to bring that feeling into our lives.

Each evening, in our house in Florida, I light candles in every room of the house, dozens and dozens of little flames. I love the soft glow they create. Before going to bed, when I blow out the last little flame, I almost always think of Karine. And of death. And I always feel a twinge of fear.

Karine made me discover and explore an entire world of emotion I would never have known without her. For me she isn't dead, and she never will be. I always feel her very near, helping me, inspiring me, lighting up my life. And when I feel the singing robot coming near, all I have to do is think of Karine and it goes away.

I don't really have a mind for figures and dates. But November 8, 1993, will always be etched in my memory as one of the best days of my life. This was the day my third English album, *The Colour of My Love,* was released in the United States. I had a completely new look; for the first time, I had very short hair. But that isn't the reason this day was so memorable. It's because it marked the moment when I told the whole world that René Angélil and I were going to be married.

I announced it to a supercharged audience at the Metropolis and in front of the cameras of all the Montreal television stations, both French and English. On the back of the album cover, I'd written several lines addressed directly to René, reminding him that I'd kept the secret of our great love inside for too long and that now I wanted it to break out into the light of day. I finished by saying: "René, you're the color of my love. L.V."

We've never told anyone what *L.V.* means. Is it Las Vegas? No. Love and Victory? Not really. The number 55 in Roman numerals? Absolutely not.

It's our secret, a symbol. When I salute René during a show or when I go on television, I always make our sign for him, by making an *L* with my index finger and thumb and the classic *V* for victory and peace.

A lot of people have almost firsthand experience of our intimacy. Especially since that day, November 8, I've been speaking very freely to the media—René has as well—about our love, our misgivings, our joys and sorrows, our feelings, and even about our arguments. Almost everything that we do somehow ends up known, in one way or another. We believe that the best way to avoid being harassed by the paparazzi is to be faster than they are and beat them to the punch. She who serves herself is best served. So, in a way, we are our own paparazzi.

The media assumes that the public is fascinated by stars. I'm sure that's true, but the media also wants us to believe that the public is curious to know what celebrities own. How many bathrooms and houses they have and how much money they earn. In this way, I think the media is deceived, and deceives people, by creating a false relationship between the stars and the public. I'm convinced that people are more interested in the smaller details of life.

During my shows, between songs, I've always talked about what's happening in my life. Every time I bring up the subject of shopping, for example, and talk about the pleasure I get from trying on new dresses or shoes or discovering a new beauty cream, all the women in the house laugh and applaud. Each time that I talk about the pleasure a woman feels in making a meal for her husband, there's the same reaction. The simplest and most common things of life—that's what people like to hear about.

When they come to see me after a show or in the letters they write to me, people tell me their dreams. And it's never been about taking the Concorde, nights at the Beverly Hills Hotel, or evenings with Barbra Streisand or Prince Charles. They dream about being happy in love and about having confidence in themselves. Basically, we are all the same.

Some artists want to change the world. That's all well and good, but I'm not like that. I'm not trying to change the world. I just want to sing to the world. It's as simple as that. I have no anger or dissatisfaction raging in me. I'm not a tortured soul.

Nonetheless, I need my little intimate, secret garden, which only the man I love can enter. Without that, a couple couldn't exist. We need space and words, and signals, like our special *L.V.*

On the evening of my new album's release, I did several of its songs for the audience at the Metropolis. During the applause that followed "The Colour of My Love," René came onstage and took me in his arms. I slid my hand behind his head, drew it toward me, and drank a tear that was running down his cheek. Then I kissed him on the mouth, in front of two thousand people and all the television cameras.

There were shouts and applause. On the giant screen, out of the corner of my eyes, I saw a close-up of our kiss.

The next day, as I saw the unanimous reaction of the media, I shouted for joy. For once, René Angélil had been wrong. For years he'd been afraid people would think we were wrong for each other and would accuse him of manipulating me. But just the opposite happened. There was an immensely sympathetic reaction, and not just for the moment. The public never doubted that we truly loved each other.

René has always had a tremendous affection for the Quebecois public. Wherever we are in the world, he makes sure to let them know everything that is happening to us. On the day after our kiss, I think, his respect for the Quebecois climbed a notch.

We were going to discover quickly that the response was just as warm elsewhere. The public and the media were fascinated by us as a couple. After years of living our love secretly, we now began talking about it openly. Our love would become the central theme of my whole life, of all my shows, my trademark and my banner. Finally, I could sing about that life experience without pretending I wasn't living it.

After the launch of my new album, I went on a promotional tour across North America. To the great disappointment of the people of Sony, I hardly spoke about my new album, or about the show I was preparing. Instead, I talked about René and our happiness. I told Arsenio Hall, Jay Leno, and Oprah Winfrey that he was my inspiration. I told the story of our first night together in Dublin and of the years we lived our love in secret. I told everyone that soon we'd be married.

"When?" they'd ask.

"One day when we have the time."

The summer before, we'd bought a large house in Rosemere, Quebec, and several months before our public announcement, we had begun living together as man and wife. On the wall at the top of the staircase leading to our room, René had hung a gigantic photo of us together. In the photo, it's clear that we're aware of the crowd around us, but we're facing each other, lost in each other's eyes, both of us beaming.

René often stopped in front of that photo.

"Everyone had to have known already," he would tell me, laughing. "Just by seeing our expressions."

"That's what I was always telling you, darling. Love can't be hidden. It's like light."

Never had the whirlwind of our life been as powerful as it was in the months leading up to our marriage. I was in Osaka, Japan, with the Tokyo Symphony Orchestra. Onstage with Michael Jackson at the MGM Grand in Las Vegas. Doing publicity in London. Filming a video in Prague, recording new songs in New York. Dashing up to Montreal for a quick visit. Spending three days in Paris. Then returning to Tokyo . . .

Never before had I really understood the expression "not to have a minute to oneself." We couldn't stop, nor did we even consider it. I even think we were incredibly happy being carried along this way. We made some short stops, most often in Florida, where we finally bought a house in Palm Beach, right on a golf course. Then, for a few days, we'd see other couples: usually Murielle and Marc Verreault or Coco and Pierre Lacroix, who were René's golf partners. I'd sit in the sun, relax, check out the shops on Worth Avenue, walk a little. Sometimes, but rarely, I'd golf, but I didn't get any particular pleasure out of it yet.

I definitely wasn't getting into the spirit of the sport. I never played, not even once. I also didn't really like the atmosphere of golf courses. But primarily I wasn't comfortable being idle or on vacation. As soon as I stopped working, I felt fragile and anxious. It was never long before I started looking for something to occupy my time and my mind.

One day, in the gardens at The Breakers, a very well-known, spectacular old hotel on Palm Beach, we began to talk about our wedding with Pierre and Coco Lacroix. René wanted it to be simple and rather conventional. For example, he wanted to find a priest who'd marry us in a small chapel. I suppose the idea was rather romantic, but to my mind, it lacked pizzazz.

I wanted a fabulous, unforgettable wedding. A real princess's marriage, with a lot of ceremony, not a little. I wanted to be the "big time."

"There's no way I'm getting married 'small time,' darling," I told René.

At bottom, I'm more extroverted than he, infinitely more eccentric and exhibitionistic. I wanted to create a unique and very spectacular event. I wanted my marriage to be a declaration of love and a vow of fidelity that the whole world could witness.

My friend Coco understood perfectly what I was trying to create. And from the beginning, she got involved in the entire project.

At first I'd thought about a cruise in the Caribbean. We'd rent an ocean liner, bring our whole world on board. We'd get married on the high seas, on a night with a full moon.

"We can't really expect two or three hundred people to attend a wedding that lasts several days," said René.

"You mean five or six hundred."

He was laughing. Everything I suggested seemed completely excessive and extremely expensive. And that's finally what captivated him about my project: the excessiveness, the risk, and the extravagance.

Later, he admitted that he didn't think we had the money to pay for such a luxurious wedding. We were already selling millions of records and were rich, but what I was planning with Coco was going to cost a *lot.* This was before my *Falling into You* and *D'Eux* (Them) albums and tours, which would bring in millions of dollars. Nevertheless, René let me take charge of this event.

"All I'm asking is that it should take place in Quebec," he said.

I fully agreed with him. That's where our roots are and where most of our friends and family live. And that's where my first audience is found. So we were getting married in front of God and man, with the most spectacular ceremony ever seen.

Because of my concert schedule, we had to postpone the date of the big day from month to month. While waiting, I used all the crumbs of time that I could collect, all the hours I spent in a plane, for example, and my periods of silence and solitude, to prepare the event, to make a small change in the decor, and to design wedding dresses. I pored over hundreds of them in fashion magazines.

First I did a rapid inventory of the dresses I loved the most. Then I tried to make a selection. I was attracted first to costumes from olden times, dresses worn by marquises and princesses, very elaborate and heavily decorated stuff, all white and very spectacular, full of pearls, sequins, and embroidery, with very narrow waists, lots of veils, taffeta, and flounces, and of course a long train. A white mink bolero on my shoulders. For my head, a diadem or tiara full of jewels.

I was discovering that my tastes were rather retro and nostalgic. I didn't resist this tendency. I wanted my wedding gown to be dreamlike. For me, of course, but also for the public. As far as I'm concerned, very contemporary dresses, which are often very beautiful, don't provoke as many dreams as those of earlier times.

But there was quite a distance between my dream and reality, a thousand and one details that eluded me. I sent Mia all sorts of drawings and sketches that I'd scrawled on paper. Dozens of magazine clips as well. Little by little, the image of my fabulous wedding dress grew more precise.

During the summer, in New York, Los Angeles, London, and Paris, I tried on countless dresses. I saw and wore the most beautiful gowns in the world. We also made the rounds of all the great bootmakers, corsetières, jewelers, and furriers.

Mia came over one day with the cassettes of two films, *Dangerous Liaisons* and *The Age of Innocence.* In these films, Glenn Close and Michele Pfeiffer wear dresses very similar to the one I was looking for. The look was beautiful, emotional, and elegant. But I wanted more taffeta, pearls, and sequins.

So we went further in that direction.

At the end of summer, when we officially announced the date and place of our wedding—December 17, 1994, at Notre Dame Cathedral in Montreal—I had a good idea of what my wedding dress would look like.

However, we needed to settle on precise details; first we had to have this dress drawn on paper, then actually made. But no one could find an available couturier who could quickly assemble a team of seamstresses, pearl and sequin experts, embroiderers, and lacemakers to create a masterwork of this type in a few weeks.

Surprisingly enough, it was Pierre Lacroix, general manager of the hockey team the Colorado Avalanche, inveterate practical-joker, and a cuddly lovable bearcub of a man, who found what we were looking for. He knew—I don't know how—a couturiere in Montreal named Mirella Gentile who made magnificent clothes. Mia and I went to meet her in her Saint-Leónard studio in the eastern part of town. And both of us were really impressed by her expertise.

For hours we talked to her about the dress we referred to as "the Age of Innocence." We showed her our designs and our clips from magazines. I even think Mia had her watch the film.

In September, when I left for Paris to give a series of concerts at the Olympia, a mannequin with my exact measurements was standing in the middle of Mirella's studio. Already several seamstresses were bustling around it. The fabric, pearls, buttons, sequins, jewels, and taffeta had all been chosen and ordered. The dream was under construction.

I was there to sing for the Paris audiences, but also to meet with writer-composer Jean-Jacques Goldman, who wanted to write an album for me. The idea pleased us a lot. Goldman is a remarkable composer who knew how to bring me into a musical universe that was different from the one I'd explored with American composers.

In France, he was a kind of "antistar." Millions of young people had made a veritable cult of him, but he systematically refused to be talked about in magazines like *People* or to participate in showbiz events. In other words, he was the exact opposite of me.

We met for the first time in a tiny restaurant near the Place de l'Opéra. It was a lovely, warm September afternoon. He was there before us, in blue jeans and T-shirt, a helmet, and motorcycle boots.

I don't really know how we ended up talking about our families and about our childhoods. Jean-Jacques made us laugh a lot when he launched into a very detailed summary of my life. He knew about our house in Charlemagne, my brothers and sisters, most of whose first names he knew, and all of the great moments of my career in chronological order. Sony had sent him boxes of documents and press clippings.

Finally, we spoke a tiny bit about our album project. René liked him right away because he spoke "about real matters," meaning family, life, and happiness.

We met again a few days before my premiere at the Olympia. This time, Jean-Jacques seemed nervous and distracted. We were halfway through the meal when he pulled out some big sheets of paper with the words to his songs written by hand. He held them out to me, then changed his mind.

"I'm going to keep them until tomorrow. You'll come to the studio. I'll have you hear the music at the same time as the words."

The next day, he was confident and relaxed. Like musicians at the studio. He sat down at the piano, a guitar on his knees. We were sitting quite close to him. He gave us the sheets of paper from the day before. And he began to sing "Pour que tu m'aimes encore" (So You'll Still Love Me).

Three-quarters of the way through, René and I were holding hands and were both crying. Jean-Jacques wasn't looking at us. He'd gone on to "J'attendais" (I Was Waiting). And then to "Je sais pas" (Don't Know). Then he stopped and turned toward us. He was very disconcerted when he saw that we had been crying. He gave us a smile that was full of such pleasure that we began crying again and laughing at the same time. For a long time, no one said a word. Then he snatched the pile of papers from my hands and told me there was a song that he wanted to rework.

He seemed devastated when René told him we had only two weeks, until the beginning of November, for the recording. Before that, I had to be in Washington for a special broadcast in honor of Bill and Hillary Clinton. I also had another show at the Forum in Montreal, ten days of promotional work in Japan, and an appearance on *The Tonight Show.* And none of this took into account the fittings for "the Age of Innocence" dress.

Jean-Jacques wanted to work with me for a few days before going to the studio. He found certain effects, certain vocal tics I'd developed irritating. For example, he thought that I added too much ornamentation to songs. He didn't like the way I rolled my *r*'s or put too much palate into the dental consonants. He told me quite frankly what he liked and didn't like. And he wanted me to take the time to correct what he thought were some bad habits.

"She really understands what you want," René explained to him. "You don't need to work with her for days. I know her. You can trust her."

René was right. I had understood because Jean-Jacques had explained what he wanted in a way that was authoritarian and warm at the same time. His music demanded a more low-key, controlled voice.

When we left, he seemed worried, but he promised us that the tapes would be ready. When I came to the studio in November, after my concerts at the Olympia, all I'd have to do was add my voice to his music.

And my voice had never felt so flexible and powerful. I'd never gotten so much pleasure out of it. It was my companion, my sister, my best friend, my confidante. That voice, which I love, is the surest and the shortest route between what's inside me and others.

Dr. Riley had seen it clearly. He'd said I'd need five years of training to develop that voice. It was definitely worth it.

The day of my premiere at the Olympia, as I was walked onstage to do the sound tests, I noticed my brother Michel. For some time, he'd been a part of our team when we toured; he was, as he himself said, the shepherd of musicians. He took care of scheduling all their trips, hotel and restaurant reservations, the transporting of their instruments, and their stage costumes.

Standing behind my mike, he reverently looked at the rows of seats and, at the very back, the shadow, that big void that is always so terrifying and so enticing. I saw him lean forward, a hand on his heart, as if he were bowing to the audience.

Then he came toward me and said he'd just realized an old dream. It wasn't as he'd believed it would be, but even so, he'd actually stood on the stage of the Olympia in Paris. A few hours before me, his little sister, his goddaughter, his ex-fan, was going to triumph there.

"Today I decided to stop dreaming. I've finally accepted that I won't have a career in show business."

"But it's been years since you sang," I said to him.

"But every day I dreamed of beginning again. And it's been ruining my life. Today, finally, I decided that it's over. Everybody doesn't get the chance you've had to realize his dreams. When you don't, it's better to put them aside and to make another life."

I was at the absolute summit of my dreams. I was singing in one of the most prestigious venues in Paris. I was selling millions of records, and in a few weeks, I was going to marry the man of my life.

The day following my last show at the Olympia, Jean-Jacques Goldman sent me the demo of a song called "Vole" (Fly). As I listened to it, I understood why he hadn't wanted me to hear it a few hours before going onstage at the Olympia. He knew I'd be too moved. In a way, "Vole" is the sequel to the song "Melanie," which Eddy Marnay had written for me a few years earlier. "Melanie" was a song I'd sung for little Karine.

"Vole" revived the painful memory of Karine's death. And in some way, I feel as if my niece is the patron saint of this album. It's as if she were the one who inspired it from beginning to end.

I've always considered *D'Eux* to be my most successful album, the most fully realized from every point of view. With Goldman, I rediscovered the pleasure of singing in French. For some reason, in English, I almost always sing spontaneously in a higher key, and I load the singing with my own inventions, a lot of ornamentation and volume. Not only because of the structure of the songs but also because of the texture of the sounds, and of course, because of the tastes of the producers and the public. Americans are very fond of ornamentation and vocal arabesques. In France, singing is much more contained, restrained, and personal. The words take on a much greater importance.

D'Eux is basically the story of René and me. "Pour que tu m'aimes encore," the first song I heard and the first one I recorded, immediately made me think of "L'Hymne à l'amour" (The Hymn to Love), a famous song by Edith Piaf. It's the same theme, same structure, and same woman, one who is consumed by love. It's a hymn to passionate, possessed, possessive, and absolute love—like my love. In recording it, we knew it would forever be a part of my life.

"I have a feeling you'll be singing that song for a very long time," René told me. "And singing it everywhere in the world."

I actually have sung it everywhere I've gone in the world, from Seoul to Stockholm, while passing through Memphis, Dublin, Munich, and Edmonton. And I still love it as much as I always have.

When we came back to Montreal to get married, we had *D'Eux* on cassette, a unique treasure that we kept for ourselves, that we listened to at the house or in René's car, alone and quite selfishly. I told friends, reporters, and fellow musicians, "You know, René and I have this treasure, this fabulous album."

But Sony had decided not to release *D'Eux* for several months so it wouldn't interfere with the still lucrative market for my previous albums. René and I had agreed not to let anyone hear it. But it was inside us, in our hearts. We could feel its vibrations, and it made us happy.

Two days before our marriage, we spent a few hours in Mont Carmel, a cloister in Montreal, where we met with the priest who would marry us. Then I went to sleep at my parents' house. I spent the following day in a spa with Maman and my eight sisters, who would be my live-in companions. An army of masseuses, manicurists, waxing specialists, and polishers of every type busied themselves with us.

I know it's not very popular to think this way, but I believe that sometimes you have to suffer to be beautiful. When I started wearing my sisters' high heels, my calves, heels, knees, and back killed me.

"Too bad," said my mother. "You can wear high heels all you want. But don't come complaining to me. It's your choice. Take responsibility for it."

The day of my wedding, I definitely had several good reasons to complain, but I was too excited to do so. I got up at dawn with my mother and my sisters. It was snowing; Montreal was gray and icy. I did my makeup myself. Then little hands were fluttering all around me, dressing me and doing my hair. My hairdresser had to rack his brains and even add a fake chignon so that he could attach the pearl tiara that Mirella Gentile had created.

"It's too heavy. It'll hurt your head," he said.

"I don't give a damn. Even if you have to stick pins in my scalp, I want to wear that tiara. I'll deal with it."

I knew I wouldn't really be satisfied with this celebration unless I gave the best of myself. For me to be happy and satisfied, I've got to put a lot of energy into what I do. That's how I am. I truly believe that you get nothing from nothing.

Our wedding was spectacular—like nothing ever before seen in Quebec. A very elegant, romantic dream.

Thousands were massed along the route of the convoy of limousines that left the Hotel Westin to go to the Cathedral of Notre Dame; it was accompanied by a police escort on motorcycles. A blue carpet bearing our intertwined initials ran up the street and across the church square and the nave, right up to the altar, where René was waiting for me surrounded by his best men. I entered on my father's arm, my eight sisters carrying my train. It was magnificent, gorgeous, and thrilling.

And I thought, as I moved toward the altar where I would be married, the sound of the great organ in the background, of the path I'd taken since the birth of that love. I'd always known that I'd stick with it to the very end, for better or for worse.

For the reception, parts of the hotel had been transformed to give the guests the feeling of a dream. You walked on carpets made of flower petals. You entered a gallery whose walls, floor, and ceiling were pure white. Also immaculately white were the large cages filled with fluttering, cooing doves. You passed through a salon that reminded you of Aladdin and *A Thousand and One Nights* and then through a Parisian bistro, a sushi bar, a Wild West saloon, and a Spanish tapas bar. There wasa flood of champagne and flowers everywhere. Magicians, musicians, a string quartet in one room, a rock band in another. And of course a casino, with blackjack and roulette tables. And everyone we loved was there.

When the guests entered the banquet hall, bouquets of flowers fell slowly from a starry heaven to gently rest at the center of each table. My thirteen brothers and sisters surrounded me and sang "Qu'elle est belle la vie" (How Beautiful Life Is) for me.

In Quebec, this event was talked about a lot, before, during, and after—and in every tone of voice. Certain people said I put too much into it, that I was making a display of my wealth, and that it seemed like a vulgar marketing event.

But I'd been a little girl from Charlemagne who'd been kept from smiling at the world by two overlong teeth. I'd come a long way and gone far, carried by my voice, by the love of my family, by René, and by the Quebecois public. To show it and share it with others isn't publicity, it's gratitude.

René and I were supposed to take two, maybe three months off, but by that time we knew that we were stress and pressure junkies. So by mid-January, I was in London to do publicity. Despite the enormous pleasure I took in being alone with my husband, I couldn't ignore the request of Paul Burger, who was now the head of Sony-U.K.

The album *The Colour of My Love,* which had been a sensation for more than a year, even in Japan and Korea, simply wasn't taking off in Britain.

Paul had told René he could get me on the biggest variety show on British television, *Top of the Pops.* If I would sing "Think Twice" or "The Power of Love," the album might start climbing in the charts.

René had refused, but he very cleverly told me about it. We were, at the time, in the kitchen making supper.

"Paul called . . . I told him that it couldn't have happened at a worse time because we'd promised to take real vacations . . ."

I thought for a moment, then told René to call him back. I could tell from his eyes and his smile that this was what he'd expected me to say. That man, René Angélil, does what he wants with me. And my fondest wish is that it will always be that way. Because I know that more than anything he wants me to be happy. I've never doubted that.

But I realized, a few weeks after my wedding, that I had become as ambitious as he, if not more. I had no real desire to stop working. Both of us wanted to go farther, higher. It was a fascinating journey. The road was beautiful and the scenery magnificent.

Even when we finally took a honeymoon trip to the Fiji islands, nearly six months after our marriage, with Pierre and Coco Lacroix, my principal activity, in one of the most beautiful vacation spots on earth, was to sneeze, wipe my nose, cough, and clear my throat. I could have and should have taken it easy, but I was incapable of it. It was as if, for some inexplicable reason, rest and relaxation filled me with anxiety.

They say there are two kinds of people: those who look back, who always focus on the past, who are always very reflective, who ask themselves about the meaning of life, who think about death, about the passage of time. And there are those who look ahead and keep moving. By nature, I've always been one who looks ahead and not behind me.

On the way back from the Fiji islands, I stopped at Calgary, in the middle of an immensely popular fair called Stampede. It was dusty, nasty, irritating, and very lively. All of a sudden my cold was gone. I rediscovered my energy. I liked the party atmosphere that dominated Stampede, and I'd just had some very stimulating encounters.

Mego, my orchestra leader, had put together a new band that would accompany me on tour. The guitarist André Coutu, who'd already been with us for two years, was joined by drummer Dominique Messier, bassist Marc Langis, and percussionist Paul Picard. Since music is my profession, my relationships with musicians have always been very memorable. In Calgary, this was even more true than usual.

Even though we'd never played together, we immediately developed a chemistry. After a few minutes of rehearsal, at eight in the morning, on an open-air stage, in the midst of the chaos of Stampede, we found our rhythm, our beat, and had a lot of fun as well. All six of us knew we'd do great things together.

David Foster, who'd watched our meeting and our first rehearsal, came onstage to ask the musicians if they wanted to come to the studio the following week; I was going to record Eric Carmen's hit "All by Myself."

It was at the Record Plant, in Los Angeles. The day before, David told me he'd changed the orchestrations in the last part of the song. I'd have to sing a little higher, actually up to an F, which is almost at the limit of my range. But even worse, he wanted me to hold that note for several measures. In all honesty, I was dying from fear. I knew I couldn't do more than two takes without jeopardizing my voice. David saw my fear.

"If you can't manage to do it, it's no big deal," David told me. "We'll just go back to the original arrangement."

All right; now that was an insult. On the day of the recording, René and I had an argument. About nothing. We always squabble over insignificant things and then can't remember what they were. Even so, I sometimes sulk for a few hours, sometimes for a few days. René, more rarely. He doesn't like to be cold to me. And he always tries to cheer me up, to make me laugh.

That day, he wanted to sulk seriously and didn't go with me to the studio. So I left all alone, "all by myself," for the Record Plant, where I found David Foster cold, condescending, and almost contemptuous; and he didn't even ask me why René wasn't with me.

I'd tried each key already and had done my voice and warm-up exercises. While the technicians finished putting in the orchestra tracks, I paced around the studio. I think David purposely delayed starting, as if he wanted to unsettle me even more. At one point the brute came near me and said, half in earnest and half in jest: "I can tell you're worried; but don't worry about that fuss over the F. If you can't handle it, I told you, we'll find a solution. I can always ask Whitney to do it."

Whitney Houston was recording that day in the adjoining studio.

"I know she can reach that F and hold it as long as necessary," David made a point of adding.

I didn't say a word. I knew it was a kind of game. And I decided to play it all the way. I went back into the studio. I sang "All by Myself" with all my strength, all my soul, and all my rage. When it came time to climb to that famous F, I pushed my voice to the maximum, to the point of hurting it, and held the note for a very long time. When I recovered from this, the musicians on the other side of the bay window got up to applaud me.

I left without saying goodbye to David Foster. Without even asking the technicians if everything was okay and whether or not we needed to do another take. I knew I'd pulled it off perfectly. The evening was very mild and I was no longer angry and thinking of René. I was trying to remember why we had our argument.

When I got into the limousine, I knew that David was probably already on the telephone with him. And I could imagine exactly what they were saying.

"It's done, René. That was a good idea of yours not to come. She was enraged. When she held the note, her voice took on a texture you've never heard. It's better than anything we could have hoped for. I'm sending you a cassette."

When I arrived at the hotel, René was waiting for me in the lobby, smiling and nervous. A messenger had already brought him a cassette by motorcycle and he'd already listened to it. I threw myself into his arms.

Once more, he'd understood how to raise the ante a little higher, how to give me a new challenge and force me to transcend myself.

From then on, I too became more and more demanding. For example, I wasn't satisfied with the first version we did several days later of the song "Falling into You." It's filled with nuances and muted colors. I thought the arrangements were too harsh, my voice not flowing enough. Everyone else, however—the technicians, the writers, even David and René—seemed satisfied. I didn't say anything. But René sensed that I wasn't happy. We were at the hotel. He was watching his golf on TV and I was doing my nails, when he asked me what was wrong.

I explained to him. He seemed surprised. So I hummed "Falling into You" while describing the arrangement I imagined for each measure. He rapidly agreed with me. He seemed amazed, as if he'd just made a discovery.

"You're right," he said. "You're totally right. You should have said something!"

"I didn't dare. I figured that it would mean redoing all the arrangements and rerecording all the orchestra tracks."

He took me in his arms. I laughingly pushed him away because my nails were still wet.

"You've got to learn to dare, darling. You've got to learn to say what you think."

He was proud of me because I'd made that decision, because I'd changed his ideas for the first time in our professional life. I'd also had a truly good, truly artistic idea.

I was proud too. I called the producer and arranger myself, to explain how I saw the song. They agreed and were happy about it. We went back into the studio and redid "Falling into You." It never became a great stage song, because it's too soft and subtle to work up a crowd. But I think it's one of the most touching songs on the *Falling into You* album. And I love the words.

That song was a step toward my emancipation as an artist. From then on, I took a much more active part in artistic decision making. René was still in control and still decided when to up the ante, but he listened to me more and more. David did as well. And so did the people at Sony. I was becoming a mature and autonomous artist.

A few days later, we returned to Quebec to break in my new show. Then I left very quickly for Europe without René, who was returning to Los Angeles to spend several weeks in the studio with David Foster, putting the finishing touches on the new album.

We spoke on the telephone every day. He would play my newly mixed songs, and he listened to my first shows on the telephone. He criticized them severely, suggested or insisted on changes in the order of songs or in the transition texts.

Everywhere in Europe, the songs on the albums *D'Eux* and *The Colour of My Love* were topping all the charts. For this reason, Sony put off the release of *Falling into You*, although they considered it the best album I'd ever made in English.

It was at this precise moment that we came into real money—as you come into a country where everything suddenly becomes possible and within your reach. One day, when a reporter asked the traditional question "What kind of dresses do you like?" I spontaneously responded, "Expensive ones."

I was actually teasing, because normally, I dress very simply. But there was some truth to my answer. Very quickly, I had developed a taste for beautiful things, which more often than not are expensive. And I also developed a passion for real extravagances. I wanted to build the house of my dreams, a house that resembled René and me. I'd call it "La Maison du Bonheur" (The House of Happiness).

René didn't like the idea at all. He was perfectly happy with our house in Palm Beach. He wanted me to take up golf rather than throw myself into a project that would devour the little free time that I had.

"Why move? It's fine here."

But I was already off and running. As soon as the idea of a new house had been planted in my mind, it just kept growing and growing. And finally it occupied a very large place, one much larger than I would have believed.

During that European tour, I began collecting pictures from architecture magazines and taking a good look at the palaces and hotels where I stayed. I observed everything: the furniture, the doors, the molding, the table linens, the cutlery, and the windows. I added things that I thought would please René. I know his tastes. Or rather, the places that he likes, like Caesars Palace in Las Vegas. I wanted him to have the ambience of that hotel in our future house. I filed my objects away according to categories: plumbing fixtures, tiles, floors, drapes, door handles, bedspreads, and chandeliers.

I was happy and in good shape. I loved my new, all-consuming passion. I loved my show, which had been so well structured and mounted. Soon I was meeting René in Paris to prepare a televised version of the show I'd be doing at the Zenith, a theater I adored.

And yet, the first night at the Zenith, without feeling any sign, without any pain as a warning, my voice gave out and completely fell apart. A total vacuum. I was crying. The entire team would be walking a tightrope because of me. Two evenings later, our smallest mistake could put everything in jeopardy.

When I'd lost my voice a few years earlier, I'd chalked it all up to inexperience and inadequate vocal techniques. Since then, I'd trained my vocal cords like an athlete trains his muscles. Very seriously and very regularly. Even when I was silent for a day or two, I thought of my vocal cords, taking care of them and pampering them. I regularly saw specialists and trainers. I followed their advice to the letter.

But this incident showed that even this wasn't doing enough. Outside factors could cause problems. It hadn't rained in Paris for several weeks, and the air was very dry and any wind, no matter how weak, caused clouds of dust to rise up from the streets. Absolutely nothing is worse for vocal cords. I should have known this. Actually, I did know. I shouldn't have gone out to every shop in the city. This is what was bothering me. It was my fault, and I was being punished.

No one panicked. In the end, everything went well—by some miracle—doubtlessly because my vocal cords were in good health. My voice came back quickly. I prayed and gave thanks. And I swore to myself that it would never happen again.

But I was going to have to live more than ever as a recluse, far from the world, often very alone. It didn't frighten me at all because I had René, my house project, and my music.

At the beginning of summer in 1997, I did my tour of the great stages of Europe, eight shows in seven cities:

Dublin, two shows in London, then Amsterdam, Copenhagen, Brussels, Berlin, and Zurich. This was actually the last segment of the *Falling into You* tour, which had begun in early 1996.

This journey, which at the start was supposed to last six months, was reorganized and extended several times. Finally, it was ending in Zurich, more than a year and a half after its premiere at the other end of the world, in Australia.

This very long tour, which from beginning to end had been full of unforeseen occurrences, was among my happiest memories. We lived through highs and lows, we endured several heavy dramas, but also and more extraordinary than anything else, there were unforgettable moments. Everyone on that tour learned a lot and grew a lot.

For me, the tour was also the story of a healing. It was about certain important discoveries too, which would change my life. At the beginning, in Australia, in the eastern United States, and in western Canada, I sang in arenas that held fifteen to twenty thousand people. I also performed to audiences of twenty to forty thousand in those large open-air amphitheaters that you now see just about everywhere in the south, the midwest, and the west. Finally, there were the offers to bring the tour to the great stages of Europe, which hold forty to sixty thousand spectators. Somehow, it just got bigger and bigger. The troupe that went with me numbered about forty people when we began—musicians, technicians, public relations people—but we expanded to more than a hundred when we arrived at the grand finale in the summer of 1997 in Europe.

On the road, we had to keep adapting the stage, sound, lighting, and all the technical equipment. And to a certain extent, the show itself had to evolve. During this time, I had to prepare special events, such as the song I sang at the opening ceremony of the Olympics in Atlanta, and performances at the Oscars, the Grammies, the French pop-music awards show, the Adisq gala in Canada, and the World

Music Awards. While all this was going on, I was preparing another album in English, three or four videos, appearances on TV specials, promotional work everywhere, and interviews without end, some private shows in Las Vegas and Atlantic City, a show for the Sultan of Brunei, and the annual fund-raiser for the Cystic Fibrosis Association, held in Montreal just before the holidays.

Until the Olympic Games in Atlanta, everything went along smoothly. But that day, we were all excessively nervous. As usual, I'd chosen to ignore, deny, and hide my fear from everybody—especially myself. If I had let it show, it could have crushed me.

I overheard René tell his friends on the phone that I was in great shape, that I wasn't afraid of anything. This wasn't really true. I was actually terribly afraid of going onstage in a gigantic stadium in front of hundreds of television cameras from around the world. It's like a leap into the unknown. And the more people and eyes and cameras there are, the greater and more terrifying this unknown becomes.

The stadium was full to bursting with eighty-five thousand people, even during the rehearsal and the sound test. On the telephone, my mother said she didn't want to come because she felt too much stage fright and would watch me on television. That certainly didn't dispel my fears or lessen the pressure.

There was a lot of music in Atlanta and some magnificent voices. The chorus that was accompanying me was one of the most beautiful I'd ever heard. Georgia is gospel-music country, the country of Martin Luther King Jr. and his famous "I Have a Dream" speech. So it was not by chance that the song David Foster wrote for the occasion took up this same theme in its very title—"The Power of the Dream."

When I performed it, early on in the evening, during the opening

ceremonies, I knew I was singing to the largest audience ever assembled. I'd been told that four billion people were watching throughout the world.

As soon as I began to sing, my stage fright went away, and I felt
good. For several days, I lived in the euphoric aftermath of that
incredible experience. But I also felt enormous fatigue and moments
when I felt I couldn't catch my breath. I was punchy, like a boxer,
even when he wins a hard fight.

Two or three weeks after the Olympics performance, I began to
feel the first symptoms of an illness that would take over my body
and mind for several months. I'd thought it would go away after a
few days. I hadn't spoken about it to anyone. But one evening in Las
Vegas, I began to really get worried.

At Caesars Palace, I was singing a very beautiful song by Jacques
Brel, "Quand on n'a que l'amour" (When Love's All You Have).
Radio Canada was planning to include this song in a spectacular a
few days later at the Molson Center of Montreal on behalf of the victims of Saguenay. A few weeks earlier, at the exact moment when I
was singing "The Power of the Dream" in Atlanta, that entire region
of Quebec was literally drowned in a downpour. The rivers and lakes
had overflowed, dams had burst, bridges, roads, entire streets of
houses had been carried away. Quebec and Canada had mobilized to
come to the aid of the victims.

I'd prepared a short speech to read after my song at the Molson
Center and to the TV viewers of Radio Canada. But as I sang, I felt an
enormous weight, like an iron hand pressing on my heart. My voice
began to quaver. I managed to finish my song, but I had to cut short
my speech, out of fear that I'd burst into tears.

I was moved, of course, but most of all, I was exhausted. I realized
that the bad feeling I'd been experiencing for some time, only at
night, had come to harass me onstage, in full daylight. I told myself
that it would probably be here for a good while.

The following week, in Denver, it was worse than in Las Vegas. Standing, I was constantly in a fog, and I was practically incapable of swallowing anything. I stayed away from restaurants. The slightest odor of cooking nauseated me. As soon as I lay down, I had gastric reflux and nausea. If I managed to sleep, I had horrible nightmares. I'm one of those people who have recurrent dreams, seeing the same sequence over and over.

Almost every night, I dreamed I'd swallowed a big, hard, cold apple that had gotten stuck at the back of my throat. I'd wake up terrified. Sometimes I'd go for hours without sleeping because of the sensation of that apple in my throat. I don't think I'd ever felt so vulnerable and so helpless. I wasn't eating anything except crackers and sugar water. Soon I knew I wouldn't have the energy to give a good show.

One morning, in San Francisco, things suddenly got worse. Suzanne and Manon called René, who was then in a clinic somewhere in Arizona trying to cure his bad eating habits. He immediately canceled and postponed the three or four shows I was supposed to give in the next few days on the West Coast. And I went into a hospital.

The three doctors who saw me didn't need much time to discover what the trouble was: overwork and stress. They said the medicine they prescribed would have no effect if I didn't get some rest.

So what does a girl do when she feels done in and when she really needs to rest? Well, this one calls her mama.

"Maman, Maman, your little girl needs you."

My mother came to Florida to take care of me. She wasn't worried, but she was determined. For about a month she was going to watch over me like a she-wolf. I found out later that she was inflexible. No one could bother me when I was resting, an event that lasted between twelve and fifteen hours a day. Even René didn't have the right to talk about work with me during this time. Not a word about the interrupted tour, the postponed projects, the French and English albums that were in the works.

Maman tucked me in at night, took me walking after my afternoon nap, and made me broths, herbal teas, and fruit salads.

The two of us were alone for hours and for days. Even Papa went out with his friends so we could be alone. Then she'd talk to me about her childhood, which I didn't know much about. And she'd tell me about mine, stories I'd heard a hundred times, but that I loved to hear again and again. I guess all children are like that.

I'm not the type to dwell on old memories, but I've always enjoyed hearing the story of my birth and my childhood. I like my mother to describe the anger she felt at my father when she discovered she was pregnant. How she then fell head over heels in love with me the moment the nurse put me in her arms.

She'd had a completely different life than mine. She was born on March 20, 1927, in a little fishing village situated on the north coast of the Gaspé peninsula. Her father was the sacristan and the choir director at the church. He managed to get permission to settle on some land deep in government territory, a full day's walk from the sea. With his sons, he carved out a road, and built a log cabin, a cowshed, and a woodshed. During the first snows of the year, he came to get the rest of the family.

In a horse-drawn carriage they tied down bundles of clothes, curtains, blankets, and sheets, some furniture, barrels of dried fish, salt pork, molasses, flour, and tea. Six chickens in a cage. A cow followed along behind.

My mother was a little girl; she sat under the furs with her sisters Jeanne, Annette, and Jacqueline. And she was filled with wonder.

"I was five. It was the most beautiful trip of my life."

To hear her speak about her childhood, about the forest and sky of the Gaspé peninsula, about the very peaceful life the people lead there, of the music her father and her brothers made, of her first violin—all this soothed and relaxed me, made me forget my trouble. She had had a happy childhood and youth, which proves that it isn't material comfort and riches that create happiness, but what comes from inside you.

By the end of September, when I left for Europe, I was already much better. I still felt that bruise inside, but I was stronger. My appetite had come back. Little by little the pain began to leave me, and no longer came to torment me when I was singing. Anytime I was onstage or at a television studio, I felt perfectly fine. But as soon as I walked offstage, it was there waiting for me. Still, the pain wasn't too bad, and I was able to forget it for long periods.

I spoke to my mother every day, then I passed her to Manon, Suzanne, and René, who, under her orders, pampered me, prepared me herbal teas and broth, vegetable salads and fruit salads, and made me rest whenever I needed to.

And then one day, on a plane that was flying us across the sky from Europe, I suddenly turned toward Suzanne and Manon, extremely excited, and signaled to them (it was one of my days of silence) that the pain had left, without a trace. I'd even stopped thinking about it altogether for several days, perhaps even a week. I slept well, ate well, sang well.

I was healed. I had forgotten my trouble and it had left me. I thought about what my father used to say when I was little and I went to show him a boo-boo that I'd gotten: "Don't think about it anymore, my little girl, and it won't hurt anymore."

When I was young, I thought that was how hurts went away. But now I know you forget your hurt when it causes itself to be forgotten. Not before. When it's in us, we think of it nonstop, whether we want to or not. The reason we stop thinking about it is simply because it's gone.

A few days later, in Stockholm, I willingly put myself through the great test. I, who drink practically no alcohol, partied with the musicians, ate rich, spicy food, then we went to a bar and drank a lot of tequila. I didn't feel sick that evening, or even the following morning. I took this as a sign that I was cured and happy.

The tour went like a house on fire, we returned to America, then took off for Asia in the winter before returning to Europe. It was June, and it was cold and raining in sheets almost every day from one end of the continent to the other. But wherever we went, two hours before the show, the rain stopped. The sun came out to dry and warm things up. Because of that, and doubtlessly for all sorts of other reasons, we were all in a state of euphoria and great excitement.

Held back by some business in Quebec and the United States, René didn't go with us to Australia, Japan, Korea, or Brunei. But he joined us for the tour of the European stages. I don't think we'd ever been so happy. I'm not speaking only about him and me, but about our entire entourage—the musicians, the technicians, and the hundred or so people who then constituted our wandering tribe. The atmosphere was fantastic.

We knew that we were at the end of that long tour, that soon we'd be going home to see familiar faces and places. Despite the rain and the cold, the long trip ended beautifully. The stadiums were filled with wonderful, warm, happy audiences. Everywhere it felt like a party.

René told a French journalist who'd come to meet us in Amsterdam that the dream he and I had created had surpassed us for the first time and was now moving faster than we were. It was more extravagant than us, and more marvelous than anything we'd imagined. No longer did we need to struggle for our dream; now we were being carried along by it.

He hadn't envisioned that tour of the European stages in his wildest fantasies. And neither had I, obviously. Some young producers from Belgium and Holland had urged René to add this final leg to the tour. And according to him, it marked a turning point in our life, in my career.

In the past, I'd seen Madonna, Whitney Houston, or Tina Turner perform on the great stages throughout the world. I had envied them for being so big. And now here I was in the same place. In that very select club that the media have now dubbed the "divas of pop." I was traveling in a private plane. I lived in the most magnificent luxury hotels. We were at the top.

"What will we do now? Where will we go?"

I no longer had the slightest idea. I merely had a premonition that one day I would really need to stop. To take it all in. To cast an eye on the road we had traveled. To finally get the house of my dreams built. But while waiting for that time, I was exhilarated by the speed and the enormous audiences.

René has always loved a life of constant celebration, and I do too; it runs in my family. But I love playing the clown more than he does, even when we're alone together. If someone from my family is there—Michel, Dada, Ghislaine, Manon, or Claudette—we can spend hours improvising completely absurd sketches. René doesn't really join in, but he's a good audience.

Before a big show, when everybody is dying of stage fright, Manon and I often find a trick that will set off torrents of laughter. In Atlanta, a few minutes before I went onstage, I was reminded of the show I did ten years earlier in Quebec when the mayflies flew into my mouth and slid up my skirt. At any other time, we probably wouldn't have thought that this was very funny. But everyone was so tense in the dressing room that just imagining me spitting out mayfly wings sent both of us into wild laughter that lasted right up to the moment when they came to tell us: "Miss Dion, two minutes."

Every day, we need to take a dose of laughter. And on tour, René manages to find moments here and there when we can all be together. He believes that socializing is necessary and fun. It's a bond that strengthens us.

On days before one of my silent days, he organizes parties for us, either in a restaurant or hotel suite, or such places as a mountain chalet near Zurich or a barge that he rents for the fifteen or so people who constitute what we call our entourage. And we spend the evening on the Seine, in the harbor at Amsterdam, or in the bay in Hong Kong.

Everyone will be there: Suzanne, my tour director; my sister Manon, my confidante and hairdresser; my bodyguard Eric; René's four or five "right arms"; people responsible for organizing the tour; some friends from the press; sometimes people from Sony, our record company, or people from the local production company.

Apart from shopping, I have few diversions when I'm touring. On my days of silence, I sometimes spend hours looking at fashion magazines. I'd tear out pages and fax them to Annie Horth, my stylist, who is sometimes inspired by them to make costumes for my shows.

For me, fashion has become a world almost as vast and exciting as music. Every one of us sings his own little song of fashion every day. Some of us are off-key and others have perfect pitch, but like it or not, fashion leaves its mark on us all.

For four or five years, Annie Horth has been my mentor, my partner, and my companion in this domain. She sees all the shows, all the collections, and she knows everyone. She has access to all the great couturiers of Europe and America, and always knows what they'll be showing tomorrow and the day after. Most of all, she knows what I like and what suits me. From time to time, she gets in touch with me. And she comes to Amsterdam, Los Angeles, or Chicago with a ton of clothes she's pulled from the latest collections of a half dozen of the great couturiers. We spend hours together looking at them, trying them on, and discussing them.

Often, especially during the last two big tours, friends from Quebec have come to spend a few days with us. Among them, of course, are René's golf partners—Marc, Paul, and Guy. And sometimes, especially in Paris, New York, Florida, and Las Vegas, my parents join us. We also love seeing Anne-Marie, René's darling daughter. And Jean-Pierre too, who stays with us for a few days, and sees his father, his sister, and his elder brother Patrick, who works with us as a production assistant. We make a happy tribe, and René, the Grand Organizer, is responsible for entertaining and feeding us.

For René, a meal is a ceremony, a way of getting everybody together amd creating links among all of us. He likes to eat. Everything. And much too much—to the point that sometimes it becomes dangerous for his health. But it's just like his gambling. Once he's started, he finds it very difficult to stop, even if he knows that later he'll regret it.

After his heart attack in Los Angeles, I got into the habit of keeping an eye on him. Now it's become a game between us. He's the mouse and I'm the cat. I watch him try all kinds of ways to escape my watch, and I see him looking for other big eaters to hang out with.

It's not surprising that he and Luciano Pavarotti became fast friends. A few days after the recording he and I did together—"I Love You, Then I Hate You"—for my *Let's Talk About Love* album, Luciano invited us to dinner at his New York apartment. He had prepared the antipasto, the pasta, and the veal dish. Between him and

René, it was a veritable banquet. They discussed eating for hours. Pavarotti travels with his olive oil, his cheeses, and his wines. Whether he's in New York, in Modena, or in Rome, he does his own shopping, choosing the wines and fruits. René was impressed.

I remember how surprised Pavarotti was when René told him, after a glass or two of wine, that he preferred to drink Coke. René doesn't like wine, beer—alcohol of any kind.

His doctor recommended that he drink a glass of red wine from time to time. He does this, but in the afternoon rather than at night. He drinks his wine as if it were medicine. Then, whether he's in a Chinese restaurant, a French bistro, or a New York deli, he orders a diet Coke. Or two. With a lot of ice.

My relationship with René on the subject of his overeating is very ambiguous. I find him a bit on the plump side, but handsome. He carries his girth well. I do think he eats too much, but I am touched by the pleasure he takes in doing it. I always find it very difficult to deprive the man I love of this pleasure. Just as I don't like tearing him away from the gambling tables.

Personally, I never eat too much. It's not difficult for me: Once I'm no longer hungry, eating gives me no more pleasure.

Articles about me have often claimed that I'm anorexic and that I nourish myself on dead leaves, tofu, grains, and seeds. Sometimes this really irritates me. Who wants to hear themselves described as "a manic-depressive, psychotic woman" as I have been described in certain media.

I've never understood the pathological need that some media outfits have to invent unbelievable stories about stars of show business, sports, and politics. It seems to me that a person's real story is infinitely more interesting than unfounded rumors or obvious lies. I don't think that anorexia is a shameful illness, but I detest being surrounded by false rumors. What's more, even if I don't claim to be a beauty queen, I have been and always will be proud of my body.

My work requires me to be in great physical shape. I wouldn't have been able to give up to a hundred shows a year and travel ceaselessly from one end of the world to the other if I had eaten too much or not enough, or if, as certain magazines have claimed, I made myself throw up after each meal. Sometimes I've had to eat enough for two people, especially near the end of the *Falling into You* tour. As fragile as I had felt at the beginning, that's how sturdy and in shape I felt at the end.

I handed over all the photos and articles I'd pulled out of architecture and decorating magazines to Paul Sara's wife, Johanne Dastou, my advisor and guru on decorating. She spent most of the winter sorting through them and collating the notes I'd made on them.

"I love this chair, but not the lion heads on the armrests," or, "I like the light in this living room, but definitely not the curtains," or, "I'd like to have statues like this in my garden, but without the stupid look on their faces."

Little by little, Johanne brought furniture and various objects she had found, and we spent hours examining and touching them. I learned to identify period styles, to distinguish the real from the fake, the beautiful from the banal. I was in school, and I loved it.

Through this work, I got to know myself and my tastes a little better. I love very romantic decor, rococo, the style of Louis XV. I need a cozy atmosphere, warm colors, and old furniture. I think you have to respect your tastes; I want to live in houses that resemble me.

Sometimes I ask Johanne what she thinks of my choices. Her response may sound funny, but I know what she means. She reminds me that I like sugary desserts. In other words, my taste leans toward busy decor that is very heavy and enveloping, yet also soft.

"You're the cocoon type," she told me. "Not very modern."

Modern—I'll get there one day, but not in a house where I'm going to live. If I had an apartment in New York—someplace where I spend only a few days while I'm recording an album, shooting a video, or just shopping—I'd make it as modern as I could. But for my real home, this look creates a cold and not very comfortable environment.

I also don't like having functional objects sitting out where everyone can see them. At my place, the televisions are always hidden in cabinets, behind panels or a painting. I know the kitchen is a workplace, but I don't want pots and pans and utensils hanging everywhere. No refrigerators with transparent doors that let you see everything that's inside.

I have to say that my house project seemed to annoy René to no end. He liked our home in Palm Beach and could have stayed there contentedly for our entire life. What is more, the preceding fall, he'd bought an immense golf course, the Mirage, in the Basse-Laurentides, a half hour from downtown Montreal. He'd already begun some major renovations of it. He was talking about building a house there to live in during our old age. But unlike me, he didn't get seriously involved in these projects.

When it came to show business, René was always in control and wanted to check out everything. But nothing interested him less than a construction site. He didn't understand why I wanted to involve myself in such craziness.

But despite René's lack of interest, we bought a large lot in Jupiter, north of Palm Beach, along a canal that flowed into the ocean. There was nothing there but grasses and scrub. On either side of it there was a large house, and behind it was a dock where a sixty-foot yacht was moored.

Johanne assembled a team of architects and draftsmen who began drawing up plans based on the documents I'd collected. And at the beginning of summer, when we returned to Montreal, I realized that my work was finished. Johanne and her architects were just starting theirs. All I had to do was wait. To keep my mind off the house, I began taking golf lessons.

After my next tour, I started playing golf quite seriously, I'd say almost excessively, whether the weather was good or bad.

René considered this a personal victory. For years, he'd been trying to get me to take up golf, which for him was practically a religion.

"Golf was made for you. You have everything it takes. You're tall and flexible, you have great powers of concentration, a lot of discipline. What's more, it's a clean sport. You spend your time on well-maintained lawns, there's sun, water, and everything you like."

It's important to René that someone he likes, likes what he likes. He's always trying to turn his close friends on to Lebanese cuisine, gambling, golf, Elvis, Sinatra, Piaf . . . and, of course, to Celine Dion!

Having been with him for so long, I was marked by the spirit of golf long before I ever picked up a club. I entered that world as if I were returning home after a very long absence. Even so, I never thought it would become a grand passion and change my life.

Golf is more than a sport. It's a way of living, a discipline requiring determination and rigor. It's a constant search for perfection, balance, and a kind of meditation on happiness. Above all, it's a study of the self. It's very much like singing, music, like all art or all activities that are practiced with seriousness and passion.

I like the fact that the game has a strict order and a very powerful ritual, a body of rules that each player must respect. . . . I know next to nothing about religions, but golf feels very close to what I know about Zen. It is first of all a way of meditation and concentration as well as a study of beauty. The beauty of places, but also the beauty and harmony of its movements and the state of mind it requires.

All of us must learn to master and control our emotions, gestures, and strength. That's what games are about. You have to learn to reach a compromise with the wind, the variations of the ground, and the sun. But you must also come to terms with your own moods and worries, and make something harmonious out of them.

By autumn, when I left for New York and Los Angeles to record the songs for my *Let's Talk About Love* album, I had turned into a golf fanatic. René had scheduled the recording sessions so that we could spend at least one day out of two on the golf course. But after just a week of work, music again gained the upper hand. The singer chased away the golfer, promising her we'd see each other again soon. I stayed at the hotel alone to avoid the heat and cold and the pollen-laden air. Above all, I had to do my voice exercises, keep silent, rehearse, and learn my songs one by one.

I love the atmosphere of the studios, this time more than ever because I was going to have some fascinating encounters. Carole King gave me a song; Sir George Martin, the man who created the sound of the Beatles, was serving as director for the song "The Reason." The Bee Gees came to sing "Immortality" with me. As I said earlier, I sang a duet with Luciano Pavarotti.

I'd always dreamed of singing with Barbra Streisand, but I'd also always been afraid to. She'd been one of my idols, and it's dangerous to get too close to your idols. It takes practically nothing to destroy your image of them. And just as little to crush you.

The idea of our collaboration began the year before, during the Oscars. I'd sung "I Finally Found Someone." This was a song Barbra had recorded, along with Brian Adams, for a film she'd directed, produced, and starred in, *The Mirror Has Two Faces*.

Actually, Natalie Cole was supposed to perform the song for the show, but a bad cold had kept her in Montreal. Twenty-four hours before the show, I'd been asked to replace her. I sang Barbra's song in addition to my own—"Because You Loved Me," from the film *Up Close and Personal.* No one had ever performed two of the nominated songs at the awards before.

René was thrilled. Nothing is more exciting, especially in show business, than doing what no one else ever has. But preparing a new song in twenty-four hours, singing twice at the Oscars, and doing it in front of Barbra Streisand was terrifying.

It turned out, however, that Streisand wasn't in the auditorium when I sang her song. During a commercial break, she'd gone to the ladies' room and had found that the doors were locked when she attempted to return to her seat; no one's allowed to enter the auditorium while the show is in progress. René was really disappointed. I was upset, of course, but not to the point of ruining the great pleasure I'd just experienced.

The media tried to make a story out of Barbra snubbing me for singing her song. But it absolutely wasn't true.

Two days later, I received an enormous bouquet of flowers with a note in Barbra's hand. She said that she'd seen the recording of the show, and thought I'd sung "beautifully," that I was an "incredible singer," and that she was sorry she wasn't in the room. "Next time, let's do one together," she wrote.

René kept her note in his wallet for months. Every time he had a chance, he read it to friends and journalists. He quickly contacted Marty Erlichman, Barbra's agent, and asked David Foster to write a song for us. Then he waited for a sign from Streisand or her agent.

David Foster was the one who finally created the link between the two of us by proposing a song he'd written called "Tell Him," about an older woman giving romantic advice to a younger one.

Barbra sang her part in Los Angeles, and a few days later in New York, I added my voice to hers. One evening, after the arrangers and technicians had mixed the song, we listened to it together, Barbra at the Record Plant in Los Angeles, and I at the Hit Factory in New York. When it was over, silence fell over the studio. We all were watching the telephone, which took an eternity to ring. David answered it.

"It's for you, Celine."

It was Barbra calling to say how much she liked my interpretation.

"You've succeeded in doing marvelous things with your voice. How did you manage to blend so well with the music and with my voice?"

I didn't dare tell her I'd sung with her hundreds and hundreds of times before in my bedroom on the rue Notre-Dame in Charlemagne. I just said I'd been working hard and I trained like an athlete.

"You'll have to teach me," she said.

"Teach you what?"

"To have discipline."

"But there's nothing I can teach you, you're the greatest singer in the world."

"We can all learn from each other. But you learn more quickly than all of us because you have a fantastic voice and a great spirit. I'm really proud of you."

I was paralyzed. She was so self-assured, she said such lovely things to me and so simply. I wish I'd been able to tell her how important she'd been in my life, and how thrilling it had felt to blend my voice with hers. It was as if our voices, after having sought each other for such a long time, had finally found each other. But I told myself that Barbra must have known she was a role model for me and that I'd learned a lot from her. You can hear it in my voice.

When I couldn't speak on the phone, I began to cry.

René, who was also very moved, took the telephone.

"For Celine, you've always been a role model and an idol. She's very touched by what you just told her."

"I know," said Barbra. "I felt the same thing the first time I sang with Judy Garland."

She insisted on talking to me again.

"I want to know you better. Come see me in Malibu as soon as you can. Tomorrow, if you want."

But the next day I was recording "I Love You, Then I Hate You" with Luciano Pavarotti.

I asked her if I could come on Tuesday.

"Tuesday's fine. I'll show you my rose garden. We'll take a walk on the beach."

To be invited to dine with your idol and to be embraced by her is a great moment of happiness. However, actually getting to know your idol can be nerve-racking. But the day I spent with Barbra couldn't have been more wonderful. I still felt very shy around her, but she couldn't have been more lovely and generous. I hope we will always know each another.

Working with Pavarotti was like entering a completely different world for me. He too is imposing. And he likes to make his presence felt. But I found nothing intimidating about him. Our sessions were very relaxed even though we had to grope around for a long time to find the right tone.

Pavarotti sang his part, and then I did mine. The result was correct but not very surprising, so we switched it around. I sang and he added his voice to mine. Same thing. It was good, but not great.

Finally, I said what I'd been thinking all along: "I'd like to try it together."

"I was thinking that too," Luciano said.

He took me by the hand; we went into the big studio and sang while looking into each other's eyes. This changed everything and we had something special.

I adore duets because they are very intimate and disconcerting. It's a very serious game, like the one played by actors in love scenes.

In April, the composer James Horner had come to Las Vegas to propose something that excited René to the nth degree.

"I'm writing the music for a film *Titanic*. The director, James Cameron, has access to the highest budget ever seen in Hollywood. It's a great love story."

He'd written a song with Will Jennings that he wanted to put at the end of the film.

"It's one of the most beautiful that we've done together."

René didn't quite trust any of this. Recently, the megafilms with staggering budgets had been real disasters. But Horner insisted that *Titanic* would make movie history.

"For the moment, Cameron has no interest in a song," he said. "But I'm sure I can change his mind if Celine agrees to sing the one that I've written with Will."

A few years before, we'd had a sad experience with Horner and Jennings, the writer-composer team that had won about ten Academy Awards for music and songs for film. This was soon after my first album in English, and I was still unknown in the United States. They'd asked me to sing the theme song for the animated film *An American Tail (Fievel Goes West)*, produced by Steven Spielberg. I loved their song, "Dreams to Dream," which still comes into my head quite often. But due to complications and disputes between record companies it fell apart. René was very injured by it. With *Titanic*, he hoped we could put all that behind us and settle the differences between the record companies.

"First we have to convince Cameron," said Horner.

"First you have to convince Celine," René corrected. "And convince me."

We met in a suite at Caesars Palace. Horner sat at the piano to play his song. He is perhaps one of the most brilliant melody writers I know, but his voice is dull, dreary, and dry. It didn't really go over well.

In back of him I was sending René signals that I didn't want this song. I loved the words, but the melody seemed flat.

We hadn't reached the middle of the song when René was already pretending not to understand me. When Horner turned toward us, René told him: "In a month we'll be in New York at the Hit Factory, where Celine is recording her next album. If you give us an orchestra track, she can do a demo that Cameron can listen to. I think that's the best way to convince him."

Horner hadn't expected this much, so he was in heaven. I, on the other hand, was furious. I started trying to figure out how to tell René off as soon as we were alone. But in the end, this was another moment when René taught me a lesson.

"You were stuck on Horner's voice, but you didn't really listen to the song. The melody is fabulous and you can turn it into one of your biggest hits."

A month later, James Horner was at the Hit Factory in New York with his orchestra track. Before I added my voice to it, he took me aside and told me the story of the film in great detail. I was very moved by it. I listened to the orchestra track and knew right away that René was right: it was an extraordinary melody.

I composed myself for a few minutes and sang "My Heart Will Go On" effortlessly and without affection. That day I was starting to come down with a flu, and my voice sounded unsteady to me. It had a kind of fragility, which to me gave the song a very romantic feeling. I let the words come from deep within me. The big bosses at Sony— Tommy Mottola, John Doelp, and Vito Luprano—were there, and they all said from the first take that we had a big hit.

A few days later, Horner called to tell us that James Cameron had listened to the song and was taken with it. He even wanted to show us the film before its release when he came to New York. Everyone was so pleased with the demo we'd recorded at the Hit Factory that we never went back to the studio to rerecord the song. That demo would go out around the world and would become what I've been told is the bestselling song in the entire history of records. At Christmas, when the film *Titanic* was released on thousands of screens across the world, my new album, *Let's Talk About Love,* was already at the top of the charts.

One thing I discovered when I became famous was that people start appearing from nowhere offering their services. If I say on TV that I want to build a dream house, hordes of architects, decorators, and contractors try to reach us. When it was (falsely) rumored that I'd gone to a fertility clinic, twenty doctors or charlatans let me know they had the solution to my problem. Others wanted to dress me, do my hair and makeup, tell my fortune, write songs for me and write my biography and my memoirs.

We quickly got into the habit of saying no to everything. But a number of charities, more discreetly and delicately, reminded us that we had the power to help. This was hard to ignore.

"It's a part of our life now," said René. "We've been given a lot. Too much, if you want my opinion. Now we have to learn to give."

For him it wasn't at all a matter of image or marketing. He really believed you had to give back in return. This reminded me of my mother's belief that you get nothing for nothing and "what you get too easily, you don't get much advantage from."

René is by nature profoundly generous. As much as he likes to play hardball, he also takes pleasure in giving. He felt this way even when we weren't rich. Now he began to consider the requests we received from foundations and charities.

At the top of our list will always be the Quebec Cystic Fibrosis Association, with which we were already connected. For years, we'd brought Christmas baskets to poor families in Charlemagne. The people recognized us, but they were sometimes very ill at ease.

With my brothers and sisters, the gifts I've given them have always raised a sensitive issue. Some of them have needed money, but others will never ask me for anything. It was René who said to me one day: "For the holidays, you should give a hundred thousand dollars to each of your brothers and sisters."

It was a great idea. During the holidays, we all gathered in a suite in the Montreal hotel where we'd celebrated our marriage. I gave each of them the same little envelope. We laughed and cried. I knew I was bringing them happiness, of course, but at the same time I felt I was creating a certain embarrassment and distance between us. I was afraid they'd feel they owed me something. I hated this because it was they who had taught me everything. The dream René and I have realized is in large part due to them. And that's what I wanted to say to them that evening, if only I'd been able to find the words. But we were all too moved for me to come up with anything at the moment.

Finally, we all sang together, like in the good old days, forming choruses and rounds.

At five minutes after midnight, July 28, 1998, we inaugurated our house in Jupiter. "Twenty-eight, that's two plus eight, which makes ten. And ten divided by two, because we're two, makes five. It'll work."

There is a gate and a guardhouse at the entrance to Admiral's Cove, the community where our house is located. We were arriving about ten minutes too early. René asked the chauffeur to wait a bit, then we drove very slowly toward the house. For more than two years, I'd followed all the stages of construction and decoration of that house, even when I was at the other end of the world. I had come to see the construction site form time to time. But I'd stopped myself from coming for the last few months. Now I was incredibly nervous about seeing the finished product.

As we approached, the iron gate was open. At five after midnight, we knocked five times on the main door. To our left was a flowering gardenia, which they say has a perfume that changes the nature of our dreams.

The first thing that touched me was the light from hundreds of candles that lit up each of the rooms. Then we heard violins. And the crystal sound of a harp, up above. I thought: Just like in the first stanza of "Ce n'était qu'un rêve."

> To a magic garden I did stray
> And woke up one enchanted day
> To hear a harp and violins play.

Both of us began to weep. Two mimes were so perfectly immobile that we could hardly distinguish them from the marble statues that filled the large inner courtyard. A waitress dressed exactly like one from Caesars Palace brought René a can of diet Coke.

He couldn't get over it. Even though he'd never really been interested in that house, he was finding familiar objects there that reminded him of Las Vegas or our former homes. And of course, for this TV fanatic, there were thirty-three televisions, as well as a large movie theater.

Almost all the rooms of the house, the nine bedrooms, the dining rooms, the kitchens, the living rooms, even the dressmaking studio I'd had installed for my mother and my aunt Jeanne faced out on the patio. It was a sort of immense living room open to the sky, with a lot of nooks, an English alcove, a Chinese one, little gardens, a large swimming pool at the bottom of which you could see our inter-twined initials . . . a dream house. The house of happiness. And of love.

Until dawn, I walked from one room to the next as if in a dream, finding familiar objects everywhere that I'd seen only in photos. For me, this was really a conquest. I had really accomplished something. I was finally going to be at home, in a house that resembled me. I was going to learn to manage that space, to bring it to life.

I was thinking of the child that I would perhaps raise there one day. My gynecologist had warned me that I'd have difficulty having a child as long as I was on tour. The pressure, the stress, the jet lag, that great whirlwind, as well as frequent physical separations would make it difficult. But I knew that one day, we'd settle down for a year, maybe two, in that house. And then I could perhaps realize that other dream, the most beautiful of all, of having a child.

For about two months, my sister Linda had been living near us. I was counting on her experience to help me take care of our child. Alain, her husband, would have a lot to keep him busy.

The evening of our arrival, he'd prepared the meal. The next day, he made us smoked-salmon crêpes and omelettes. When he asked us what we wanted that evening, René said offhandedly: "How about an osso buco?"

It was excellent, and a few days later, we offered Alain a job as our chef. In this way our life got organized, with Linda, Alain, and three maids. All that was left was for me—someone who'd lived for years from hotel to hotel—to learn how to keep house.

But beforehand, I had to go back on the road. Around the end of that summer of 1998, I was starting a new tour for the *Let's Talk About Love* album and the new Jean-Jacques Goldman record. I was very proud of both of these albums, but for the first time in my life, I was heading out on tour almost reluctantly.

he premiere of *Let's Talk About Love* at the Fleet Center in Boston was preceded by one of the worst nightmares of my life as an artist. I guess I should have expected it; everything seemed to indicate that we were moving toward a total fiasco.

We'd been preparing this show for months. The main stage, which was shaped like a heart, was built in Montreal. Above it, on four sides, were giant screens that would project close-up images of the show. At times, it would show film clips of the Bee Gees and Barbra Streisand that I would sing along with.

My stylist, Annie Horth, had asked several couturiers to design costumes for me, the background singers, and the musicians and chorus. I'd even added extensions to my hair. Five minutes before the show began, I was enclosed in a box that the technicians then rolled under the stage, where the wings were located. The musicians were perched on what looked like lozenges that were moved by hydraulic systems. It all seemed horribly fragile to me. I knew the musicians and I would have a great rapport on stage, even if we'd never done these songs in public. But the rest—the hypersophisticated lighting, the luminous stage, the screens—could all go wrong.

For several hours before curtain, we all felt we were part of something that was out of control. The machine was too enormous. The day before, René had gotten everybody together in a room of the Fleet Center, and told us: "At this time, thirty-two hours before the premiere, we have no show. We have the plan for a show, we have a dream about a show, a show under construction, as big as the Empire State Building. But we haven't gone beyond the seventh floor."

My eyes met Mego's for a moment, and we were thinking the same thing. We'd heard that sentence "we have no show" before. It was in Vancouver, the evening of a premiere. We weren't well prepared. We arrived in Vancouver the evening of the show with a wicked case of stage fright.

The show got off to a bad start. The musicians played well, but we were never really together. Between songs, I tried to speak to the audience, but nothing I said either moved them or made them laugh.

René never reads me reviews (except when they're good), but the next day I wanted to know. What I read certainly hadn't been written by a visual person or a music lover. There was nothing about missed cues, lighting, or mistakes. The guy was interested solely in the song lyrics, which he brought down in flames. Actually, he could have written the review without seeing the show.

"Exactly," René told us, "there wasn't any show. That was our mistake. We weren't prepared. It's my fault. If the show had been good, he probably wouldn't have written that. He would have talked about the show, not the song lyrics. But how could he talk about the show if there wasn't one."

There was that line—"we have no show"—and now it was starting all over again at the Fleet Center in Boston.

After René's talk, the technicians, engineers, and electricians spent the whole night at the Fleet Center in Boston. They worked on the visual appearance of each song. In the afternoon, everybody seemed paralyzed by stage fright. It was very hot. I was wearing pounds of very curly hair that I was beginning to regret putting on. I wasn't at all sure of my look, which I found alternately fabulous and ridiculous. I was no longer sure of anything, actually.

In the end, everything went well. Despite a few technical blunders, I think we gave a pretty good show. This time the critics didn't have to settle for my words or even my look. They spoke about the aural and visual beauty of the show. But that premiere remains in my memory as a nightmare and, I believe, the end of a chapter.

That evening, I told René I never wanted to live through such a nightmare again.

"You know, I just don't have any more desire to. There are other things in life."

That decision too was a kind of discovery for me. Five years before, it never would have occurred to me that I could have any kind of life outside of show business.

René understood perfectly. I even think that he was even happy I'd finally discovered this. I think he's also had his overdose of pressure and stage fright. That's when we swore to each other that we'd take a long sabbatical after the end of this tour. We'd been thinking about it for several months already but kept putting it off, probably because we weren't yet at the point of really needing it. Now the ambition that had always carried me had changed course.

I wanted peace and rest. I began making up little movies: almost no action and only two characters, René and me. Usually they took place on a deserted beach or at the golf course near our house. A hundred thousand times I restaged my evenings: we were alone in the house; I'd prepared pasta or a barbecue for him while he watched a golf tournament on TV. I'd set the table on the terrace. It was just the two of us. We talked about everything and nothing, like yesterday and the day before.

The *Let's Talk About Love* show was even more physically demanding than all my other shows. I had to fill up that immense stage for about two hours, sometimes more. I left it highly charged, in a sweat, always with the euphoria you get from an intense workout. And then the next day, I'd have to find a way of building up my momentum to do it again that evening.

The tour was scheduled to run through the next year and maybe longer. Once that great machine has been launched, it's not easy to stop. You don't produce a show like that for a little tour of a few months. I had the feeling of climbing up a very high mountain. But I kept asking myself how much higher could it go?

Every chance I got, I tried to spend a few days in our house in Jupiter. I'd started collecting images again, this time for a house in Montreal. I saw it as a gray stone house, very solid and heavy, with wood paneling, rugs, furs, big fireplaces, very warm colors, an immense greenhouse where I'd go every day to take care of my plants. And unlike our house in Jupiter, which is a cocoon, this one would be wide open to the outside. I imagined fields of snow all around.

I really love the hot weather of the south, even the extreme heat in Florida in June and July. I don't really like the cold, but I adore winter—the whiteness and the fresh snow crunching under your feet.

We bought an island with several acres on the Mille-Îles River. It's about twenty minutes from downtown Montreal and the Dorval airport and ten minutes from the golf courses at Terrebonne. There are rabbits, deer, a lot of green, and tranquil water all around. I've always needed to be surrounded by water.

"We're going to stop for good on New Year's Day, 2000," René told me one day.

Everywhere in the world, they were organizing megashows to celebrate the millennium. René was already considering several proposals, but I was certain that only one place interested him: Montreal.

This great event—which would be followed by our long-needed rest period—seemed a long time away. But just knowing that it was coming, and that I could look forward to it, renewed the fervor and pleasure I got from singing. Knowing that the whirlwind would be calming down somehow sped me forward.

Our plan for the beginning was a long stay in Quebec, a full month in summer. We would play golf and start building our house. But then something happened—the worst thing we've ever encountered—that would force us to put off this project.

7

On the plane between Minneapolis and Dallas, where we were going to be based for about ten days, I noticed that René kept touching his neck with his hand. I'd noticed that he seemed preoccupied all day, and I asked him what was the matter, even if I knew the answer I'd get.

"Nothing."

"Let me see."

My hand grazed his neck. I felt a mass on the right side, in the hollow under his ear. It felt hard and fat like an egg.

"How long have you had that?"

"It's nothing," he told me. "It'll go away."

I was furious with him.

"Why haven't you seen a doctor?"

"I haven't had the time. It just happened in the last few hours."

"Does it hurt?"

"No, not at all."

Immediately, I thought it was serious. A bump that forms in several hours and doesn't hurt is something to be concerned about. During the whole plane ride, I tried not to think the worst, but it was impossible. I still felt the nasty sensation of that hard little mass under my fingers.

The next morning, very early, René went to be examined in a Dallas clinic. He didn't want me with him.

"You sleep," he told me. "You have a show tonight. You've got to be in shape."

He kissed me on the cheek and left with Martin Lacroix, the son of our friends Coco and Pierre, who were handling the logistics of the tour. No matter how much I told myself that I ought to rest, I couldn't seem to sleep. At the end of the afternoon, I went to the hospital, where I found René, who was visibly worried.

"They might have to operate," he told me.

Never in my life will I forget that terrible moment when a young doctor came to meet with us in René's room. He told us he'd first have to take a biopsy. I felt I was in a dream, and I'd already heard that terrible word no one wants to hear—the one René and I had been thinking since the day before. The doctor didn't say it right away. He used technical terms, saying that perhaps the tumor was "malignant." I remember exactly how he said that word, in English. I insisted that he tell us exactly what he meant so there wouldn't be any doubt.

I held René's hand and asked: "Is it or isn't it, Doctor?"

"The biopsy will tell us," he said.

He wasn't reassuring, but he didn't alarm us either.

"If it's cancerous, it will be necessary to operate."

The biopsy would be done by the end of the day. We'd know the results before night. René got in touch with a friend of his in West Palm Beach, a Dr. Sid Neimark, who promised to find the very best surgeon.

I got on a plane without René and headed for Kansas City for a scheduled appearance. I didn't talk to anyone about what had happened. I simply said to the musicians, to Manon, and to Suzanne that René had some business to take care of. I wasn't trying to keep a secret; I just knew I couldn't talk about it.

I phoned the hospital just before going onstage, and René told me they'd done the biopsy. We'd have the results before the following morning.

"*In Allah Rad,*" he said, which meant, "by the grace of God."

Suddenly everything seemed frightening and terrible. I was alone in that dressing room with my pain. Suddenly I was so exhausted my ears started ringing and I had difficulty articulating correctly. That evening, I had to turn my stage over to my worst enemy, the singing robot. My mind was elsewhere.

Maybe I should have told the audience what had happened. But I would have broken down crying. Instead, I let that detestable robot have as much space as she wanted. I remained outside of my songs and listened to her, I watched her do her song, my song. My heart and mind were elsewhere. Right until it was time for me to sing, "The First Time Ever I Saw Your Face." The words put me right into the heart of that song. My performance was very good, I think, even if my eyes were drowning in tears.

I was on my way back to Dallas a little after midnight, and went directly to the hospital. As I pushed open the door to the room, I noticed in the darkness two beds very close to each other. René was in one, and his friend Pierre Lacroix was in the other. René was sleeping. Pierre got up and led me into the corridor. He reassured me, told me to go to sleep, that Coco was waiting for me at the hotel. Then he gave me a moment with René. I didn't want to wake him up because he seemed so peaceful. I could see the bandage on his neck, where they'd done the biopsy.

My night was short and troubled. I'd barely fallen asleep when there were loud knocks on my door. A major pipe in the hotel had burst and my bathroom was flooded. I looked down and saw my slippers floating away. Workers came to mop it up, close the valves, and reconnect the pipes. They were very polite and spoke in very low voices.

I went back to sleep. Around nine, I woke up to find Coco sitting on my bed, bending toward me. She had taken my face between her two hands and was looking me straight in the eyes.

"Celine, my darling, your husband needs you."

I understood immediately what had happened. A half hour later, I was at the hospital with Coco.

René was sitting on his bed and was trembling. Pierre was near him.

"I have cancer, Celine. The doctor told me. I've got cancer."

Pierre, Coco, and I gathered around him. We spoke to him as if to a child. We stayed like that for a very long time, all four of us with our arms around each other.

The date was March 30, 1999, the day of my thirty-first birthday.

René didn't cry, except when I came toward him and took him in my arms.

"Our happiness has been destroyed," he told me.

He was wrong, and today he knows that.

But at that time, I was crushed by the fear and the pain of that terrible news. I tried to catch my breath and find my words. But as always in these situations, I soon found myself on automatic pilot.

I decided not to cry. The man I loved needed me too much. I couldn't crumble. I had to be strong. I had to be his strength, his health, and his healing. That's what I told myself right away.

I also thought about how much I wished this had happened to me and not him. I'm strong, and I have a lot of stamina. No matter how much René told me what he was feeling, I couldn't experience it the way he did.

Dr. Bob Steckler, whom Dr. Niemark had put us in touch with, came to meet with us. He'd seen René the day before and had been present at the biopsy and studied the results. Earlier that morning, he'd told René his cancer was serious and that he was going to operate on him in a few hours.

Bob is a very warm and cheerful man. Without lying to us, he reassured us a lot. He even made us laugh. He made us feel we were leaving in a group for a pleasure trip. René's son Patrick, who is part of the team when I tour, was also with us.

For my birthday, René had invited my parents and some friends, as usual, who arrived from Montreal at the end of the afternoon and came directly to the hospital: Papa, Maman, Paul and Johanne, Marc and Murielle. Dr. Steckler had put his office at our disposal. His very sweet, very beautiful wife, Debbie, came to meet us and brought coffee and cake. Jean-Pierre and Anne-Marie also rushed to be with their father.

René had already figured out that I wanted to cancel my upcoming shows. A few minutes before leaving for the operating room, already feeling the effects of the sedatives, he told me I had to continue.

"It's especially important that you don't stop," he said. "It won't change anything, as you well know."

I remembered what he'd said to me when he'd had his heart attack.

"If you stopped, I'd die two times."

He convinced me to continue. Anne-Marie was on the other side of the bed, large tears running down her cheeks.

"I'm here," she told me. "I'm going to take care of Papa."

And she stopped crying immediately. There's no better way to channel your emotions than to have a duty, a mission.

Nurses came to get René. We were all around him, the whole tribe, a dozen people, and we followed him into the corridor right to the operating table.

We came back to Dr. Steckler's office in silence.

He would call us two or three times from the operating room to tell us that all was going well. Bob Steckler is an optimist. He always sees the bright side of things.

After the operation, he told me he was certain he'd removed all the cancer. And that it was necessary to have faith and to look to the brighter side of things.

"René's recovery has just begun."

He told us that René was sleeping, so we all went back to the hotel. He'd had the dining room of our suite decorated and a birthday meal prepared for me, with a big cake with five candles.

But for the first time we'd be without our great organizer of everything.

We really did try to follow Dr. Steckler's recommendations, and were happy about the results. But no one felt like a banquet. Even so, we ate my birthday cake, because it brings happiness and luck, and we felt we all really needed it.

We took group photos, as we always did, but something horrible flashed through my mind. For the first time in many years, René wasn't in them. I also thought, despite all that Dr. Steckler had told us, that René could actually die, that maybe he wouldn't ever be there anymore.

I was seated at the end of the table, between my mother and my father, and I nearly collapsed, almost literally fell to the ground between them.

The next day Johanne, my decorator, came to see us with her bags bursting with sketches, plans, and a half ton of samples of stones and tiles destined for our future house on the Mille-Îles River.

To put our mind on other things, we opened her bags. We placed the stones on the rug and looked at them one by one.

The following night, I was to sing in Houston, and René refused to cancel the concert. "Show business as usual," he said. That evening, once again, the singing robot tried to take over, but I could also feel a great calmness in that arena. It was almost as if the crowd understood what I was living through even though no news had yet been released about René's illness.

I felt my voice tremble as I sang "All the Way," our good-luck song. I could have summoned the singing robot, but instead I let my voice tremble and allowed my feelings to flood me.

Right before the show, in my dressing room, I got together my musicians, Mego, André, Marc, Yves, Paul, and Dominique; the members of the chorus; Daniel and Denis, the sound people; and Lapin, the lighting person. I felt I needed to tell them what was happening.

I didn't want to "soft-pedal" the news because we had a show to do. But when I saw their eyes mist up, I couldn't hold back my tears. We all cried. Then each of them embraced me one by one. Perhaps we had never been so together, so attentive to one another as we were that evening. They gathered around me and enveloped me in their music, which was sweeter and more caressing than ever. After the show, Mego told me he felt that the evening's music was like a prayer we'd made together. I don't think any of us will forget those moments we experienced.

On board the plane that took me back to Dallas, I decided to cancel all scheduled shows, all recording sessions, TV appearances, and interviews. Until René was completely out of danger, I wanted to concentrate on him.

Predictably, he felt the same way about this as he'd felt the day before.

"What will that change?" he said.

This time I was determined to stand up to him. I wanted to share this ordeal with him; I couldn't continue to tour and work knowing he was alone with his illness and fear. I did offer some concessions. I gave four of five shows that were coming up so soon that it would have been unreasonable to cancel them. But the final segments of the Canadian and American tours were postponed until the fall.

We wanted to be alone. René admitted now that he rested better when I was with him. I lay down beside him, and we stayed for hours in the darkness of his hospital room, without speaking.

One day, about a week after his operation, while we were sleeping, the door of the room opened without anyone knocking. It was Dr. Steckler.

"Hello, lovers, how are you?"

He always called us "lovers." He spoke very quickly, with a strong New York accent that he loved to exaggerate. He brusquely sat down on the bed. René still had a thick bandage on his neck with a drain or catheter coming from it. For a week he'd hardly moved or spoken.

"What are you doing this evening?" said the doctor.

René smiled feebly without answering.

"Well, I'm going to see your wife sing. I can get you a ticket, if you want!" Dr. Stickler said.

This time René gave a real laugh, and said: "I'd love to go with you, but what about this bandage and this drain . . ."

"Oh, well if that's all it is . . ."

And in one stroke the doctor tore it off.

"If you don't come to see your wife sing this evening, I'll end up thinking you're not a good husband."

He then told us about the radiation treatments René needed to have.

"We'll begin them as soon as you're rested. There will be a few disagreeable side effects but nothing serious. You'll recuperate very quickly, you'll see."

I could see that night, more than ever, how much everyone on our team loved René. They all came to greet him.

"We're with you, champ, take care of yourself."

And our champ was at my show that evening. He had always been my critic, my audience, and my most intimidating fan. For more than fifteen years, every evening, when he was in the house, I knew he was judging me, taking a lot of notes, and detecting my smallest error. I needed him to be there. At the same time, having him there always added to the pressure I already felt in front of the audience. If my eyes ever crossed his, I'd imagine saying to him: "Let go, stop looking . . . it will ruin your concentration."

But that evening in Dallas, I sought his eyes and sang only for him. His health and our happiness counted more than my performance. We were both at a turning point in our lives.

A few days later, back in Jupiter, in our big beautiful peaceful house, René began his convalescence. He had to be in good shape to face the radiation treatments. They had scheduled thirty-eight sessions, five per week.

Laughingly, he said that at least his illness caused something good: he'd lose a little weight. But the doctors wanted him to eat as much as he wanted, because the treatments would deplete him of a lot of energy. In any case, he would surely lose weight as well as his appetite and strength.

After his operation, perhaps for two weeks, he couldn't swallow anything that wasn't pureed. But eventually his appetite returned. For the first time in years, he could eat without feeling he was doing something wrong. And for a while he did so with a lot of pleasure.

His friends continued to arrive from Montreal: his old buddies, Marc Verreault, Paul Sara, Jacques Des Marais, Ben Kaye, Rosaire Archambault, Guy Cloutier, Pierre Lacroix. They came to spend two, three days, a week with us. Pierre and Coco Lacroix were also around a lot during this time. They all surrounded René with their affection and humor, and stayed near him like bodyguards.

It was May 1999, and René had started playing golf with his

friends. He wore a scarf and a hat to keep from getting too much sun. René has always loved the sun and heat, so it pained me a little to see that he had to protect himself like that. When anyone acted surprised to see him going outside in the sun like that, he'd say, "You're forgetting I'm an Arab."

I spent hours on the patio or around the swimming pool, with my sisters Manon and Linda. I continued to comb through fashion and architecture magazines. The guys left early in the morning for golf and returned in the afternoon to watch hockey, golf, or baseball on TV.

René had a whole world I almost never entered: the world of his buddies. He had strong, close bonds with them. He knew their birthdays by heart and always phoned them. They often got together in Las Vegas, which they called "the House." Among them, he was called "champ," or "chief," or "doctor." They had a special handshake, secrets, their own language. They traveled across Canada or the United States to see important baseball and hockey games. And they loved show business and big cities.

Every morning, five days a week, Alain drove us to the hospital for René's treatments. They always used the same car, always took the same route, and always left at exactly the same time, ten minutes to nine. Every day, during his treatment, René thought of a friend, often a couple. Alain asked them to think about René during the fifteen minutes that the treatment lasted. Often, as Alain's Explorer drove down I-95, the designated person would call René to remind him that he'd be thinking of him. This was also a way of reminding René that he'd come through this.

One morning, when I came out of the room, Alain and René tried to leave without me.

"We didn't want to wake you," René told me.

This made me angry. I knew very well that he wanted me to rest.

But it made me feel that he lacked confidence in me. Or as if he didn't take seriously the most important vow of both our lives.

"Have you forgotten, René Angélil, that on the day of your marriage, I promised to live with you for better and for worse?"

Afterward, he came to wake me in the morning.

He never complained. Not to me, or his children, or his friends. I pestered him. I wanted him to tell me everything, every doubt that he had, any fears or worries. But he never said anything. He seemed so far from me at certain moments, living things I couldn't share. And that saddened me deeply because we had always shared everything.

When his doctor saw that he reacted well to the radiation treatments, he proposed something else.

"To put all the bets on our side, we should do a little chemo. Just a few sessions. It could be quite difficult. This time there will be heavy, uncomfortable side effects. But it will make it surer. You have to decide."

That day René's three children were at the house, and he asked them what they thought. Each had the same answer: "The doctor's right. You've got to put all the bets on your side. We're here. We'll help you."

I knew they'd do anything to help him. They're good children, generous and loving. But in the struggle that he was about to begin, René would be alone. You can't really share suffering and fear, not at its deepest.

Once more, as I extinguished the last candle in our room, I thought of Karine and of death. I was afraid. That night, we stayed awake a long time.

"I wish so much that this had happened to me instead of you," I said.

"I knew you'd say that to me. You'd be strong, you'd fight right to the end without complaining. I know. That's what helps me the most. In a deep way, you *are* in my place. You're with me. I know it. I feel your strength with me."

Among the side effects the doctor described was the danger that René would become sterile for a period of time, and that we would no longer be able to have a child.

Of course, there was a good solution, even if it wasn't the most romantic. Several days after René began his treatments, we went together to a sperm bank. This way our dream would be waiting, frozen in a test tube.

I had been so open in the media about the child I wanted that sometimes I had the impression that the newspaper and TV reporters were really sharing this part of my life with me. In every press conference or interview I gave, I was always asked for news about the child.

Rumors about the subject were rampant. They said we'd taken steps to adopt a child, in Russia or China—even when René's illness was at its worst. In truth, we never even thought of that, yet the media began talking about it. If I were to have a child, I'd want it to be René's and mine, the incarnation of our love.

I've never thought that my life would fall apart if I didn't have a child. I never said that. I wouldn't "sink into eternal sorrow," as certain members of the press like to repeat. But even so, I was waiting for it, looking for it, and making it part of my plans.

During tours, I stop ovulating completely for months. Each time I am late, I make up little movies where I'm experiencing spells of nausea, where I take a pregnancy test, and where I can see close-ups of René's face as he learns I'm pregnant and takes me in his arms.

For a long time I've thought I would have a girl. I created some very precise images of her. And I quickly wrote her some small roles. I always have her with me in my dressing room and on board the plane. She's very jovial. During the sound test, she comes onstage near me. All the musicians and technicians are crazy about her.

For some time as well, I saw a boy. Unlike my daughter, he was very reserved, almost timid. He didn't come to see me onstage. He waited for me very quietly in the wings. He was dressed like a little European boy, with golf shoes and short pants. I took him to the shops with me and bought him clothes. He was very independent, very secretive. Every time that he became distant, my heart broke. But I loved him for that also, for his coldness, his indifference.

*L*ittle by little, after the first chemo treatment, everything René ate began to taste like sludge, chalk, or iron, and he lost the desire to eat. He had periods of nausea, moments of great fatigue, and deep sadness. He'd stopped playing golf. The only time he went out was for his treatments.

Anne-Marie, Linda, Alain, and I watched over him day and night. He was sometimes irritated, I think. But we forced him to take a nap, then to do a little exercise, and to eat even if he wasn't at all hungry.

Alain prepared light and varied meals that were less spicy than he usually cooked. René made a big effort, but soon he could only swallow purées. At the end, any odor turned his stomach. For days, he only ate sorbets or ice cream—"nothing," Alain said—or drank a very weak tea.

The doctors told him that sooner or later he'd feel a great fatigue. Whenever that fatigue hit him, even if he was expecting it, he found it horribly heavy and crushing.

What we were living then completely changed my vision of things, my needs, and my plans. I no longer played golf and I didn't miss it. A game of golf is like a trip inside yourself. With René sick and incapable of taking this voyage, I no longer had any desire for it. You have to be in shape to find peace, beauty, strength, and rest in yourself. When you're sick, you've got none of that. Or a lot less of it.

All René's friends had now left, and my parents as well. For days, neither Alain, nor Linda, nor the maids came. We were living on an island, isolated from the world. Sometimes we even spent whole days without any news from the outside world. When René's illness became public knowledge, we decided not to read the papers, for fear they'd contain rumors about what was happening to us.

From time to time, our Montreal office sent bundles of faxes and cards with get-well wishes that I read to René when we took tea under our five-trunked palm.

We were together and closer than ever. His illness had become *our* illness, *our* cancer, and *our* battle. We would fight it together, right to the end.

Like all players, René is a believer.

"I've chosen to heal. The doctor told me that good humor is good for the health. I decided to be in good humor."

He saw life, health, and salvation like a bet. He had chosen to look first and foremost on the brighter side of things. According to him, what had happened to him was only justice, the good Lord knew what it was.

He told his friends: "I've had a wonderful life. I have to pay back, I have to pay for my happiness. It's only just."

We believed in healing. We prayed and wept. Even at the most difficult stage of that ordeal, we had moments of profound happiness because we were together.

I am, in life and death, the woman of only one man. I've never had any other love, never any other lover, only a few little insignificant flirtations when I was fifteen or sixteen years old. I remember vaguely having been attracted to a professional hockey player, who probably never knew anything about it. I'm not even sure if I remember his name.

Men never really court me. I don't miss it and it doesn't hurt me at all. I'm not the type of woman who makes men come on to her. In truth, I very rarely find myself alone with a man, except for René. It should also be said that I've proclaimed my love for René enough times to all the men who approach me that they know I'm a satisfied women who isn't looking for adventure. Some might make innuendos or wink at me, but nothing comes of it.

It's obvious that I'm not the kind of woman who arouses passion in men. There's no tease in me. Or else I don't perceive it in myself. That could be it. All my feminine charm, all the sex appeal I have for men I invested in my conquest of René Angélil.

A lot of women my age already have had a number of lovers. I don't envy them, nor do I judge them. I choose to live another way. It's not a question of principles or of morality. It's just that René and I love each other because of who he is and who I am. That's the greatest, strongest, and most beautiful love of my life.

I know that it sounds naive, but I just can't understand how people who are really in love can one day choose not to live together. It must be that they don't really love each other, or that one of them has loved the other badly. When two people are in love, it has to be forever. That's what I believe.

I was brought up in respect and love, in the certainty that love is stronger than everything. You're powerless before it, you can't resist it, but still it makes you strong, solid, and invincible. René and I believe in that remedy. More than the chemotherapy and radiation and all the treatments the most learned doctors could give him, it was that love that we share.

René never agreed, even during his most difficult periods, to postpone my European tour that began in mid-June.

"When you leave," he said, "I'll have finished my treatments. I'll be cured."

His confidence had come back, and the nausea was gone. Alain was making him purées that were more and more substantial and which he was able to swallow. He'd rediscovered smells and flavors.

When I left for Europe, he was still weak, but I saw in his eyes and voice the signs of recovery.

From March 30 until I left, we were always together, night and day. Even when he was at the hospital for his chemotherapy treatments, I slept next to him. For most of the time we'd known each other, we'd regularly been apart for days and sometimes weeks. He had his business to take care of and people to see, and I had my shows and publicity to do. Never during the eighteen years we'd known each other had we spent so much time together. And this time had brought us both a lot of happiness. So by leaving, I was breaking a kind of spell.

René told me it would be a rest for me. For two and a half months, I had taken care of him. I saw that he ate well, took his medicine, rested, and exercised. Above all, I made sure he kept up his morale.

We had installed a satellite dish that would offer a direct hookup with all my shows in Europe. And we'd be able to talk to each other and see each other while I was in the wings or under the stage. This way I could feel his presence that was so precious to me.

Some people never say they love each other. We're the opposite. Every day, René told me he loved me, and that he'd love me forever.

The time I was the most touched was at the Stade de France, in front of ninety thousand people. I think I had the most beautiful show of my career there. The atmosphere was as warm and intimate as in a very small auditorium. After having sung "Pour que tu m'aimes encore," I received a standing ovation.

I bowed to the audience, which surrounded the stage. People waved posters that said: "We love René." I knew my husband could see and hear all that. He'd asked Daniel, the sound person, to hook him up to my earphones. And suddenly I heard his voice in the hollow of my ear, his velvety voice.

"I love you, Celine, forever and ever."

I wanted so much to cry, to cry out of fear, pain, and joy all mixed together. But I couldn't. I didn't want to. If I did, my voice would be ruined. All I could really do was answer that I too would love him forever and ever. We had agreed on a sign.

"When you see me touch the end of my nose, it means that I love you."

My hand holding the mike trembled.

When Jean-Jacques Goldman, who had written the songs on my *D'Eux* album and who was also a big rock star in Europe, came onstage a few minutes later, there was such thunderous applause that for a long time neither of us could say anything or do anything.

Jean-Jacques doesn't speak much in life or onstage. He walked toward me as they applauded. Then he put the mike to his mouth and spoke very softly to me. The clamor died down immediately, as if people wanted to hear what he was saying to me.

He thanked me for being there, as if he were speaking in the name of France. We both looked at the audience standing there, their arms outstretched toward us, while here and there, I could see placards of well wishes for René.

As if he had read my thoughts, Jean-Jacques told me: "All that I can add, Celine, is . . ."

And he began to sing a cappella the first lines of "S'il suffisait qu'on s'aime" (If Love Were Enough).

This time, even more, it took all my strength to hold back my tears. I touched the end of my nose again. I had about twenty seconds to get control of myself before joining Jean-Jacques in the song. I held myself back a little, out of the light, and took some slow, deep breaths. When it was time to sing, I'd regained my control and moved toward the light.

*W*hen I came back to Jupiter at the beginning of July, René was already much better.

We had developed a taste for being alone. I sometimes asked Linda and Alain as well as the servants to take some time off. We made our meals together. I can still see myself in the kitchen on certain evenings, with René peeling, crushing, and slicing vegetables. Sometimes he came near me and took me in his arms. We danced, without any music but our own, alone in the kitchen. Happy.

Then one day, he asked for pasta again. I knew that meant he was on the road to recovery. In a few days, he'd fully recover his appetite.

Then we spent the day, the first for more than six months, without thinking of his illness, of *our* illness . . .

The only anxiety-provoking subject was the return to Montreal, to public life. René had changed, gotten thinner. His voice was hoarser and more muffled than ever. Often he choked when he spoke. He needed to have a bottle of water in his hand all the time. I'd never seen him as tense and nervous as he was during this time. It was a few days before a show I was giving at the Molson Center.

He knew all eyes would be glued to him. They'd ask him a lot of questions about that cursed illness, about his voice, about the treatments he'd undergone, and about those he still had to undergo. All of that made him incredibly nervous. Me too. He was still very tired at that time. He was afraid of choking or of starting to cry, or of not knowing how to answer the questions he would certainly be asked.

We knew that the best thing was to hold a press conference and set the record straight. As soon as he found himself in front of the cameras and a mike, René began to speak.

"Everything is going well. Celine and I have gone through a difficult ordeal. We're closer, more in love than ever. And not to hide
anything from you: We're happy."

The reporters applauded. For an hour we spoke about the show
that we were preparing for December 31 and of the sabbatical that
we were going to take. And, of course, of the child we dreamed of
having.

A few days later, we were at the Quebec Coliseum, where
I hadn't sung for four or five years. I knew I probably
wouldn't be back there for several years. The producers had organized
a large press conference. But this time, René was calm and very confident. It was one of those days when everything is lovely and good,
and everything goes well, even if you don't know why.

During the course of that press conference, René said some things
that moved everyone. Starting with me. A very young journalist
asked what he was proudest of in his life. He answered that his greatest pride was that I'd remained a woman capable of being happy,
attentive to others, strong and independent. Obviously, that touched
me a lot. He also said that our greatest success, as far as he was concerned, was that we'd always been capable of being happy together.

"As a manager, it's my greatest success," he added. "Colonel
Parker may have created one of the greatest artists of the century,
Elvis Presley, but he failed the essential, I think. He didn't make
Elvis happy. The challenge for a manager who has been able to take
his artist to the top is to keep him there. But an even greater challenge is to keep him happy, to make sure that he doesn't fall apart,
that he also doesn't become an unsavory monster."

It's not really my place to say that I'm a good girl who is generous
and attentive to others. But I don't think I'm an unsavory monster. I

don't have the tantrums of a diva and if I demand something, there's always a good reason.

One evening, for example, in Montreal, the day before an important concert, I went into my hotel room and could tell immediately that I'd have a hard night. The mattress was very hard, and I never sleep as well as I do on a soft mattress that I can sink into a bit.

"If I spend the night on this, I won't sleep well, I won't get any real rest, my voice is going to suffer tomorrow evening, I won't be in my best shape."

I had to spend more than a month in that hotel. And I had approximately ten shows to perform—in Montreal, Quebec, Ottawa, Boston, among others.

René immediately understood and had my mattress and the linen sheets I liked brought from Rosemere.

While they were installing my bed in my room, I began to think of that princess who could feel a pea under ten mattresses. When I was little, my sisters used to say she was only a stuck-up, capricious, and spoiled little thing. And you'd probably have to cook her peas and swallow them for her. I never liked her very much either. And yet here I was having the mattress changed because it was too hard.

I didn't have a choice. I needed to sleep well so that my voice would be at the top of its form the next day. And for that I was ready to come off as a stuck-up, capricious, and spoiled little thing. And even to be taken for a diva.

But in normal times, when I don't have to worry about my voice being threatened, I adapt to everything, eat anything, and talk to everybody.

I'm perfectly capable, thanks to the man I love, of being a happy woman. And because of that, I know that my husband is the most extraordinary manager an artist can have.

To win the highest honors of show business has nothing to do with succeeding in your life. What counts, despite the success, despite the tens of millions of dollars and fans, and despite the constant pressure, is to remain a balanced individual, capable of feeling wonder, surprise, and passion.

Of course, René is more than my manager, he is my lover, my husband, and that changes the rules of the game completely. But even at the beginning, he didn't think only of my career. He's always taken into account first and foremost my well-being and my happiness. He's always wanted me to lead the life that I wanted, to have my mother, father, brothers, and sisters near me often and for a long time. Life must, and always must, be beautiful. It's our greatest and only priority. Today more than ever.

That day in Quebec, while listening to René speak about happiness right at the press conference, I told myself that the only failure would be to no longer feel happiness. But when it comes to that, I have had a successful life. Thanks to the man I love, I became a singer and a happy woman. I was able to stay happy, and that's not always so simple to achieve.

I knew René was on the right track the day he started playing golf and blackjack. In October, while I was finishing the last segment of my American tour for *Let's Talk About Love,* he played nine holes in Denver, with Pierre Lacroix, Marc, and Rosaire. Then we spent a few days in Las Vegas. I never knew if he'd won or lost a game, which wasn't very important. All that counted was that he had regained some pleasure.

Today I believe that in every misfortune there is good. René's illness brought us closer together. It changed our priorities and our dreams. I don't know what might have become of us if René hadn't gotten sick, but I think that it's definitely helped us gain depth and maturity in our relationship

One day in spring, we were getting ready to leave for golf. René came into the kitchen where I was having coffee with Linda and Alain. He went into ecstasy about the play of light and shadow from the sun rising against the wall. Never before had he been sensitive to that kind of thing. Never before did he stop, as he now does more and more often, to smell a flower.

One day, a long time ago, when I was still a teenager, we were flying over the Atlantic on the way back from Europe when we saw a comet streaming toward the south. I went to get René so he could see it. He bent toward the porthole and said: "Oh, good!" Then he sat down and went back to his magazine. Today, I'm sure he'd watch that comet, that he'd want to know how long it would remain in the sky, where it came from, and where it was going

On the night of January 1, 2000, immediately after the show at the Molson Center, we left for Las Vegas with my parents, my musicians, and a few friends.

On board the plane, we were all strangely calm and silent. The show we'd just given had been so charged with emotion that we were completely empty, punchy like boxers after a fight.

I knew my voice had been off a few times. The crowd was shouting from every direction and I was so overwhelmed that a lot of times I couldn't hear my voice or the music.

"No one except you could have noticed it," the musicians told me. "Even us, we couldn't hear you any longer."

In normal times, being off would have plunged me into a deep despair. But that night was magic. It was the big shift into the year 2000, of course, but also it was my last show. It was the last time I'd be in front of my original audience, all my people, my family, my country, and my loves. Now the circle was complete.

Each of the songs I did that night took on a new dimension. We were living the end of a dream, the end of the century. It was both heartrending and marvelous. At the stroke of midnight, René had come onstage and the two of us kissed for a very long time. I'd just sung "L'amour existe encore" (There's Still Love). All around me twenty-five thousand people were embracing.

It wasn't only on the way to Las Vegas, but on the way to a new life. Before plunging into it altogether, I was going to give a big party. For our parents and friends, René and I were going to get married again. And renew our vows before God and man.

As soon as he knew my intentions, Arthur Goldberg, owner of a dozen casinos in Las Vegas, one of which is Caesars Palace, contacted us and demanded he take everything in hand. In the end, he offered us that party, "as a wedding gift," he said. Mia and Johanne worked with Anna Dimartino from Caesars Palace to conceive and install the decor and organize the ceremony and the banquet.

I wanted the decor, the music, the songs, the religious ceremony, and the reception to reflect René's Lebanese and Syrian origins. The star and the crescent, symbols of the culture of the Middle East, were present everywhere in the decoration. The music, dances, costumes, and games recalled the different Arabic cultures. There were even two camels and two exotic birds. René was a resounding success in the role of the Grand Vizier or Caliph; I was Scheherazade.

To decorate the chapel where the religious ceremony was to take place, we were inspired by the architecture and atmosphere of an Arab mosque. And in the main ballroom of Caesars Palace, we re-created an immense Oriental garden with six Berber tents.

The guests were seated in Oriental fashion on cushions. They were served a meal of five courses prepared by Lebanese, Syrian, and Moroccan chefs. All the men were in black; the women wore long dresses in the colors of precious stones—emerald, sapphire, ruby, and diamond. René was in white; I was wearing a gilded dress by Givenchy.

A lot of people again said we were making a display of our wealth. Perhaps we were, and what's so wrong with that? Wealth doesn't hide itself. And I wanted that event to be first and foremost a public proclamation of our love. I wanted the whole world to hear the most important thing I had to say: "René, I love you." That was the purpose of the affair. There was nothing discreet about it.

A few days later we were in Jupiter, where we would spend the most beautiful winter of our lives, often just the two of us alone, or surrounded by dear friends.

Sometimes I went out to do errands with René. In order not to be recognized, I wore dark glasses and a hat. I cut my hair very short. Quite often, René was the one recognized first. From then on he was part of my image. And that really made me happy. We were more than one. People saw me and thought of him; they saw him, they thought of me. We were together for life.

For the first time in years, we watched the Grammies and Oscars on TV, alone in our living room. And I realized how painful and exhausting these bullfights could be. I'd never said it, not to René, and not even to myself, but I really don't like galas, the false joy that reigns, the invisible daggers that the women point at each other, all the while with fake smiles. Everybody wants to flatten everybody else. Every woman wants to have the most beautiful gown. Or maybe the one that's most talked about.

René never liked to hear me say anything at all negative about anything, especially not about another singer or someone in show business. Except when we were alone, of course. And even then! For him, talking bad about other people is vulgar.

And yet after we had begun our vacation, as if the roles had been reversed, it was me especially who talked and recounted to him what we had lived, just as he had recounted each of my shows to me in the past. Every evening, after supper, we sat down in the main living room, we watched TV a little, and I began to talk about certain events that had happened when we were touring or about an encounter that we'd had two or three years ago, during the period when we were caught up in that great whirlwind.

I told René that I'd loved a certain city and not another, that I didn't like a certain producer very much, that I thought another was adorable. And he laughed a lot, because, in truth, he'd known all that. But at the time, in the jaws of the beast, we didn't really speak, not in that way. We didn't have the time—or very little of it.

And then little by little, in the spring, we stopped talking about the past and analyzing it. And we turned toward the future. A great happiness came into being and we took it as a sign. That child was waiting for us, had always been waiting. And more than anything, it will come to enrich and change our lives.

On August 24, we learned that we will be having a boy, and René and I are so happy. I imagine he will have René's smile, his eyes. I know I will be crazy about him.

In a few months, I'll sing him a lullaby. Everyday I say a little prayer for him to be good and happy. He is already an important part of my story.